KV-052-571

Maintaining Universal Primary Education

Lessons from Commonwealth Africa

Council for Education in the Commonwealth Project Team
Edited on their behalf by Lalage Bown

Commonwealth Secretariat
Marlborough House
Pall Mall
London SW1Y 5HX
United Kingdom

© Commonwealth Secretariat 2009

All rights reserved. No part of this publication may be reproduced, stored in a retrieval system, or transmitted in any form or by any means, electronic or mechanical, including photocopying, recording or otherwise without the permission of the publisher.

Published by the Commonwealth Secretariat
Edited and designed by The Pen and Ink Book Company Ltd
Cover design by The Pen and Ink Book Company Ltd
Printed by Hobbs the Printers Ltd, Totton, UK

Views and opinions expressed in this publication are the responsibility of the authors and should in no way be attributed to the institutions to which they are affiliated or to the Commonwealth Secretariat.

Wherever possible, the Commonwealth Secretariat uses paper sourced from sustainable forests or from sources that minimise a destructive impact on the environment.

Cover photo credit: Rebecca Nduku

Copies of this publication may be obtained from

The Publications Section
Commonwealth Secretariat
Marlborough House
Pall Mall
London SW1Y 5HX
United Kingdom
Tel: +44 (0)20 7747 6534
Fax: +44 (0)20 7839 9081
Email: publications@commonwealth.int
Web: www.thecommonwealth.org/publications

A catalogue record for this publication is available from the British Library.

ISBN: 978–0–85092–827–3 (paperback)
      978–1–84859–045–8 (downloadable e-book)

Maintaining Universal Primary Education

Lessons from Commonwealth Africa

A research project carried out by the Council for Education in the Commonwealth commissioned and funded by the Commonwealth Secretariat, with additional support from the CREATE Project of the University of Sussex.

Main researchers
> Francis K. Amedahe
> Felicity Binns
> Balasubramanyam Chandramohan
> Alba de Souza
> Fidelis Haambote
> Pai Obanya
> John Oxenham
> Gituro Wainaina
> Peter Williams

Project coordinator
> Lalage Bown

List of persons consulted
> Brendan Carmody
> Trevor Coombe
> Michael Kelly
> Alison Kennedy
> Keith Lewin
> Kalifunja Osaki
> T.C.I. Ryan
> Tony Somerset

Advisers from Commonwealth Secretariat Social Transformation Division
> Ann Keeling

> **Education section**
> Henry Kaluba
> Fatimah Kelleher
> Florence Malinga

Foreword

There has been remarkable progress towards some of the EFA goals since the international community made its commitments in Dakar in 2000. Some of the world's poorest countries have demonstrated that political leadership and practical policies make a difference. It is evident that far more needs to be done to get all children into school through primary education and beyond. Whereas many Commonwealth member countries have put in place accelerated measures towards achieving the two education MDGs, they cannot neglect the need for approaches that will sustain UPE well beyond the target deadline of 2015.

Indicators have suggested that most of Anglophone Africa achieved nominal UPE through 100 per cent gross enrolment ratios at some point in the past thirty years, and that slowdown or regression has taken place since then. Mobilisation towards UPE is an enormous financial and political burden, especially for those countries whose education indicators are the weakest. The leap to UPE is greater, and in most cases there are major challenges in terms of structural capacity. Initial acceleration through rapid expansion of the education system can become fiscally unsustainable. Quality can be compromised, and in time the rate of expansion is slowed, leading to a fall in attendance as confidence in the system starts to wane. These preliminary evaluations must also be taken into account in terms of the enormous funding gap that currently exists globally. Quite simply, current donor pledges are not enough to meet the requirements of developing countries to attain UPE. Drives towards UPE must therefore plan accordingly if gains made over the next ten years are to have any meaningful impact through longevity.

This study is intended for use by the Secretariat in advocacy for the two education MDGs. Experiences of regression from nominal UPE in Commonwealth Africa have strong resonance for present and future policies. Understanding why apparent success in attaining UPE has withered can benefit countries by feeding into National Education Strategy Plans, and can also help to inform those countries seeking to make significant steps towards UPE through 'bold initiatives' like school fee abolition.

The study has identified, analysed and evaluated the causes behind UPE slowdown and apparent regression through a detailed study in the selected countries of Ghana, Kenya, Zambia, Nigeria and Tanzania. The study included not only a historical analysis of attainment and subsequent regression from UPE but also had a strong contemporary applicability. It encompassed a comprehensive evaluation of lessons learnt, current policy considerations and means of factoring into broader initiatives towards solid attainment of UPE by 2015.

The study concludes that the last 10 per cent of children still out of school will be the hardest to reach. Enrolments are low, for instance, among the pastoral Fulani and other nomads in Nigeria (estimated at some nine million people) and among the Masai in Tanzania, as well as the people of Kenya's North Eastern Province. In Zambia, the very scattered low-density rural population has less opportunity for education than easy-to-reach urban children. In contrast, in Tanzania, urban children may be left out because there are not enough schools to cope with the numbers.

The report highlights the plans and strategies for maintaining UPE as derived from lessons of the recent past which include among others; strong political will, enshrining free UPE in the constitution, competent education planners and good reliable data and proper analysis of the financial implications for this massive expansion. The following are given as strategies for success of UPE programmes; adoption of a broad Education agenda, nurturing partnerships in provision, ensuring appropriate teaching and learning environments and paying attention to quality teaching and learning.

I would like to commend Council for Education in the Commonwealth (CEC) for a job well done by a team of highly qualified professionals in education. I would also like to recognise the significant contribution of Professor Keith Lewin of the University of Sussex, for his financial assistance through CREATE which enabled us to expand the study to two more African countries.

We are very grateful to the country contributors and particularly to Professor Lalage Bown who coordinated the study and acted as the editor of this book.

Finally, I wish to recognise the effort of colleagues at the Secretariat who contributed to this activity; Fatimah Kelleher (Programme Officer, Gender) and Florence Malinga (Adviser Education).

Dr. Henry Kaluba
Head and Advisor, Education
Social Transformations Programmes Division.

Contents

List of tables and figures

Tables

Figures and charts

Boxes

List of abbreviations

ADEA	Association for the Development of Education in Africa
AIA	Appropriations in Aid
BRAC	Bangladesh Rural Advancement Committee
CCEM	Conference of Commonwealth Education Ministers
CCM	Chama Cha Mapinduzi (The Party of Revolution) (Tanzania)
CDE	Children in Difficult Circumstances
CEC	Council for Education in the Commonwealth
CHE	Commission of Higher Education (Kenya)
CODESRIA	Council for the Development of Social Science Research in Africa
CPE	Certificate of Primary Education
CPP	Convention People's Party (Ghana)
CREATE	Consortium for Research in Education, Access, Transitions and Equality
CSACEFA	Civil Society Advocacy Consortium for Education for All (Nigeria)
DEO	District Education Officer
DFID	Department for International Development (UK)
DQAS	Directorate of Quality Assurance and Standards (Kenya)
DS	Deputy Secretary
EDB	Education Data Bank (Nigeria)
EFA	Education for All
ES	Education Secretary
FCUBE	Free and Compulsory Universal Basic Education
FPE	Free Primary Education
GDP	Gross Domestic Product
GDPpc	GDP per capita
GER	Gross Enrolment Ratio
GMR	Global Monitoring Report
GNP	Gross National Product
GOK	Government of Kenya
GPA	General Purpose Account
GPI	Gender Parity Index
GRZ	Government of the Republic of Zambia
HELB	Higher Education Loan Board (Kenya)
HIPC	Highly Indebted Poor Countries
IMF	International Monetary Fund

KCPE	Kenya Certificate of Primary Education
KCSE	Kenya Certificate of Secondary Education
KESI	Kenya Institute of Special Education
KIE	Kenya Institute of Education
KLB	Kenya Literature Bureau
KNEC	Kenya National Examination Council
LGEA	Local Government Education Authority
MDGs	Millennium Development Goals
MLHRD	Ministry of Labour and Human Resource Development (Kenya)
MOE	Ministry of Education
MOEC	Ministry of Education and Culture
NARC	National Rainbow Coalition (Kenya)
NCE	National Council on Education
NEEDS	National Empowerment and Educational Development Strategy (Nigeria)
NER	Net Enrolment Ratio
NIR	Net Intake Ratio
NLC	National Liberation Council (Ghana)
NRC	National Redemption Council (Ghana)
PDE	Provincial Director of Education
PEDP	Primary Education Development Programme (Tanzania)
PNDC	Provisional Defence Council (Ghana)
PS	Permanent Secretary
SADC	Southern Africa Development Community
SIMBA	School Instructional Materials Bank Account (Kenya)
SMC	School Management Committee
SPEB	State Primary Education Board
SUBEB	State Universal Basic Education Board
TANU	Tanganyika African National Union
TIVET	Technical Industrial and Entrepreneurship Training
TSC	Teachers Service Commission
UBE	Universal Basic Education
UN	United Nations
UNESCO	United Nations Education, Scientific and Cultural Organisation
UNICEF	United Nations Children's Fund
UPC	Universal Primary Completion
UPE	Universal Primary Education
UPN	Unity Party of Nigeria

Lalage Bown

Introduction and acknowledgements

Chapter 1

Kenneth Kaunda's story

The former President of Zambia, Kenneth Kaunda, tells the striking story of an episode in his childhood:

> 'The method of teaching young children in the 1920s was to gather them under a tree on which hung a cloth painted with the letters of the alphabet. I well remember sitting for hours under a shady tree chanting a-e-i-o-u, then forming the letters with my finger in the sand. We would smooth out a little area near where we were sitting and the teacher would wander round among the children correcting our letters. Each cloth was called *Nsalu* and when we had *Nsalu* one, two and three, we were promoted to the first class, when we were allowed to use slates.
>
> There was no free universal education at that time and every parent had to find half a crown a year. Just before my father died, I had been ill with the influenza and so was unable to attend the opening of the school. When I did at last present myself at school, the teacher asked me for my two and sixpence, and when I told him that I had no money, he sent me back to my mother to get the necessary half-crown. I ran sobbing to her, but she had no money in the house and she wept with me. Fortunately, a kind neighbour came to our aid and lent us the money, which was in due course repaid. For so small a thing in those days could a child forfeit the privilege of his life's education.'
>
> (Kaunda, K. D., 1962)

It is startling to realise that if the Kaundas' neighbour had not come up with the money, one of the major figures of twentieth century Africa would have been missing from history; and perhaps equally startling to realise that in many countries, and for many children of today, the situation is not so different from 'those days'. More than eighty years on, some schooling remains similar and there are still various obstacles in the way of many children getting an education of whatever style or quality.

This book describes an attempt to understand how African nations in the future can make sure that their children will not miss out – or risk missing out – on school.

Background to this project

In 1960, a year after the first Commonwealth Conference on Education (now the CCEM), members of the United Nations committed themselves to achieving Universal Primary Education (UPE) by 1980. At that time, and with many nations energised by a new release from colonial rule, the goal seemed not only desirable, but also achievable.

Commonwealth African countries made serious efforts to move towards it and some achieved substantial success. For reasons which will emerge in this book, they were unsuccessful in keeping up the impetus. There were several national and international attempts to revitalise their UPE programmes, including the Education For All (EFA) resolutions at the Jomtien Conference in 1990. For the early twenty-first century, the international educational agenda was set at the World Education Forum in Dakar, when a new goal was adopted: the achievement of UPE by 2015. Early in the decade, there were a number of forces converging which gave some cause for optimism. The African Union, the Commonwealth and the United Nations are all seriously committed to the effort and world opinion has been mobilised by such initiatives as the Commission for Africa and the work of international NGOs, including Oxfam and Action Aid. As a result, substantial new external resources were being made available to African education. With debt relief alongside, African countries therefore had more resources to put into UPE expansion.

The current backdrop of global recession, however, may have serious effects on national economies and on their capacity to capitalise on the additional resources provided and/or promised. There still is, in any case, a serious question as to whether, in the enthusiasm of international gatherings, Commonwealth African countries may have entered into over-ambitious undertakings. Given the realisation, reinforced by the studies in this book, that UPE programmes require quite long lead-times (e.g. it takes time to train teachers and build permanent classrooms), it may be that 2015 is an unrealistic deadline. The EFA Global Monitoring Report (GMR) for 2006 raises these doubts: 'Progress towards UPE has been slow overall since the World Education Forum in Dakar ... many countries still combine low enrolment ratios with insufficient capacity to accommodate all children. Ensuring that enrolled children remain in school until the last grade of primary schooling is a continuing challenge. ... Newly published data on learning outcomes suggest that average achievement levels have decreased in recent years in sub-Saharan African countries.' (Burnett et al., 2005). The report suggests that twenty-three African countries have a low chance of reaching UPE by 2015.[1]

Some of the nations currently struggling have in the past come close to UPE, at least in terms of Gross Enrolment Ratios. We need to understand why it fell apart. As Peter Williams has written:

> 'It somehow seems as if nothing is being learned from the past and as if yesterday's mistakes are being recklessly repeated all over the Continent [of Africa]. Whilst each situation has its own special features, it is worthwhile to revisit previous experience and draw appropriate lessons, adapting them as necessary to local circumstances. African Governments and their international collaborators must try to forestall possibilities of future regression and to ensure the suitability of UPE in Africa this time round, if they are to meet the goals to which they have committed themselves.' (in Beveridge et al., 2005)

The Council for Education in the Commonwealth (CEC) was aware that, for a number of reasons, governments (including ministries of education) have little institutional memory. Its research group has tried to reclaim that memory – in order to gain lessons from the past. The researchers aimed to answer the question: *How can Commonwealth developing countries, once having attained Universal Primary Education – assuming that they will be successful – maintain it?* This enquiry into the vicissitudes of primary education programmes in some diverse African countries was undertaken to learn from collective experience, for the benefit of Commonwealth and national policy-makers. The objects were to study what had happened in these selected countries and to look at what lay behind their achievements in UPE and at any setbacks they subsequently suffered. The focus was on educational policies, but the research project was framed in the awareness that education does not happen in a vacuum and that account has to be taken of various economic, political and social pressures which may affect the progress of educational provision.

Given that a whole range of factors will affect educational demand and colour educational provision, no-one would suggest that there is a single magic formula for arriving at UPE and staying there, but from detailed study of five very different countries, it was possible to arrive at some general lessons and some basic principles.

A general synthesis of the outcomes of the enquiry was contributed to the 16th Conference of Commonwealth Education Ministers, held in Cape Town in December 2006; and a short paper on it was presented to ministers there by Dr Gituro Wainaina, who was a member of the research group. This book gives a description of each of the case studies on which the synthesis was based and an extended discussion of conclusions. The case studies are to be found in Chapters 2 to 6 and the general conclusions in Chapter 7. The main work was carried out in 2006, in order to have a preliminary report available for the 16th CCEM at Cape Town. This joint document was presented by Dr Gituro Wainaina under the title *Attaining and Maintaining Universal Primary Education in Commonwealth Africa – Learning from Experience.* Since then, some of the data in some of the studies has been up-dated; but the team believes that in any case the work will maintain its value for some time to come, since these are longitudinal studies, showing trends and recurring phenomena.

Exploration of meanings

This was an open enquiry into what did and did not work, but in preliminary consultations some concepts were explored. To start with, the term UPE is problematic, owing to different ideas of universality and of primary education. Here *universality* has been taken to refer not to universal opportunity/access, but to *universal enrolment and attendance.* We have followed the GMR in using the definition of *primary education* of the International Standard Classification for Education (ISCED): 'Programmes normally designed on a unit or project basis to give pupils a sound basis in reading, writing and mathematics and an elementary understanding of subjects such as history, geography, natural sciences, social sciences, art and music. Religious instruction may also be featured. *These subjects serve to develop pupils' ability to obtain and use information they need about their home, community, country etc.* [our italics].' This may seem rather ambitious in the light of the kind of educational conditions described by Kenneth Kaunda and still sometimes extant; but it serves as a reminder of the richness of opportunity which primary education can promise and the italicised sentence indicates the expected benefits which pupils should derive from their primary schooling.

The advantage of this definition, based on educational purpose and content, is that it avoids technical matters such as age of entry and length of programmes; although it is to be noted that these technical issues have relevance to costs and that because of national differences in the coverage of primary education, international comparisons are not always easy. At the present time, a number of countries are melding primary education with some secondary studies and are using the term Universal Basic Education (UBE) instead of UPE. This is the case with Malawi and Ghana. Nigeria also uses the expression UBE, but with the meaning of universality of access regardless of age, and its national programmes of UBE include adults and out-of-school youth.

A third term in need of an agreed definition is *sustainability*, as a concept and as a goal. A serviceable one for the concept of educational sustainability would be: the achievement of provision sufficient to attain UPE and the conservation and development of that provision so that UPE can be maintained without overstretching available resources. There is still, however, the issue of sustainability as a goal. Many of the politicians who signed up to the goal of UPE in 2015 are no longer responsible for their national educational programmes, but their successors have to ask themselves: will the 2015 deadline be one at which a first cohort of all boys and girls of the relevant age has completed a course of primary education or one at which the entry to the first level will have reached 100 per cent? The answer is likely to be the latter, at best; and on these terms, no one can assume that the provision will actually be sustainable. This reinforces our contention that it is essential to have a primary education strategy in place based on an understanding of what factors are known to have contributed to or derogated from UPE in the past.

Design and plan of research

As already explained, the work focused on case studies of five countries: Ghana, Kenya, Nigeria, Tanzania and Zambia. They were chosen for their diversity. They are geographically spread, from East, South-Central and West Africa and they entered independence after the colonial period in very different situations. While Ghana, Kenya and Nigeria all had a sizeable educated class, Zambia had only 104 graduates. While Ghana, Nigeria and Zambia had the economic advantage of substantial mineral resources at the time, Kenya and Tanzania were less favoured, Tanzania having almost no financial reserves to fall back on. On the other hand, Tanzania perhaps had an advantage over the others when it came to the medium of education, having an indigenous lingua franca in Swahili; others had several dominant indigenous languages, none of which was used throughout the country (although of course Swahili was widely spoken in Kenya). In terms of administrative structures for delivering education, Nigeria was distinct from the others in its complex federal structure, within which different regional/state governments worked differing educational policies. In terms of politics, the ruling ideologies in the five countries ranged from African socialism and *ujamaa* to pragmatic capitalism. In all contexts, educational enrolment showed an upward trend over the turn of the 20th century; the diagram in the Appendix gives a picture of the changes in gross enrolment ratios between 1991 and 2004.

Three of these nations were studied in depth – Ghana, Kenya and Zambia – as there was relatively plentiful information about all of them: solid statistical evidence and continuity of data, so that it was possible to see trends. The two others were subjected to less intensive study. Despite the paucity of reliable data, it was believed to be important to gain at least some understanding of what happened in Nigeria, 'the Giant of Africa', just because of its size and significance in Africa. Tanzania also stood out, for a quite different reason; it had extremely strained resources, but still racked up considerable achievements in expanding education. Had time and funding allowed, it might have been illuminating to add other countries to the study, e.g. Malawi and Mozambique; other researchers may wish to take on the task.

The research team was made up of UK-based volunteers, all members of the CEC, each working with an African consultant from the relevant country. In four cases, the studies were carried out in close partnership; unfortunately, owing to communications difficulty, it was only possible to locate a Tanzanian scholar at a late stage and although he made valuable comments, the study (see Chapter 6) was entirely the work of the UK researcher. The whole project was carried out between April and September 2006. The CEC prepared an initial design, with a pro-forma set of questions to be investigated, to ensure at least minimum comparability. The questions covered the educational system, demographic issues, societal, economic and political factors in each case and the international context. After approval from the Commonwealth Secretariat, which provided the core funding, the team was assembled and a weekend workshop held in Dorking in July to do the groundwork on each of the papers. Additional funding was provided by CREATE, the major research consortium based at the University of Sussex. Research then involved consulting sources and experts in the various countries, the case studies were written up in September, then collated and the synthesis prepared in October for distribution in advance of the CCEM.

The speed of the project was only possible because of the researchers' depth of knowledge and good contacts among scholars in Africa and elsewhere, and because of the generosity of those scholars in making comments and suggestions.

Further work has been done on the case-studies, as said above, including several face-to-face consultations among the UK-based scholars and e-mail correspondence with African consultants. Within the team there has also been some peer appraisal. It should be stressed that this has all been done in a voluntary spirit, in the belief that the subject is of considerable public importance.

Acknowledgements

The Council for Education in the Commonwealth owes sincere thanks to many people. First, what has been written above shows that the researchers worked beyond any call of duty and overcame various problems of distance and communication. They were inspired with enthusiasm and bonded as a group at the Dorking workshop; and we are immensely grateful for the hospitality provided there so cheerfully by Peter and Julia Williams. Secondly, CEC and the research team owe a debt to the scholars mentioned above, whose names are listed inside the front cover. Thirdly, a significant element in the statistical analyses was provided by the UNESCO Institute of Statistics and special thanks for this data are due to Alison Kennedy. Fourthly, it was an imaginative gesture by Professor Keith Lewin of the University of Sussex to give the project a small grant from the CREATE funds, which enabled the enquiry to be extended to include Nigeria and Tanzania and also helped to put this book together.

Finally, the education section of the Commonwealth Secretariat was the main backer of this whole exploration. Their names are also listed at the front; but we must make special mention of the personal interest and commitment of Dr Henry Kaluba, with whom the CEC has had so much fruitful interchange.

Note

1   These countries were (Commonwealth countries in italics): Benin, *Botswana*, Burkina Faso, Burundi, Cote d'Ivoire, Djibouti, Egypt, Eritrea, Ethiopia, *The Gambia*, *Ghana*, *Kenya*, Madagascar, Mali, Mauritania, *Mozambique*, Niger, Senegal, *Swaziland*, *United Republic of Tanzania*, *Zambia*, and *Zimbabwe*.

Francis K. Amedahe and Balasubramanyam Chandramohan

Ghana – Towards FCUBE
(Free and Compulsory Universal Basic Education)

Chapter 2

Summary

This first case-study takes the recent educational history of Ghana, the earliest African country to regain independence from British rule and the one with, at the time, the strongest economy. It focuses on the experience of Ghana in developing and implementing strategies to achieve Universal Primary Education – UP(B)E. It maps the period from the 1950s to the present in terms of progress, achievements, external and internal drivers and factors that contributed to success and later regression in different aspects of UP(B)E. Based on this discussion, the study identifies particular areas, old and new, where ongoing efforts need to be made to achieve UPE goals, in terms of both enrolment and progression and with increased emphasis on quality.

Educational developments 1950s to 2006

General comments

In Ghana, since the colonial and later the transitional nationalist period as well as in the post independence era, education has been identified as the key to development. Generally, within the constraints of the economy at any particular point in time, successive governments made the effort to improve education at all levels.

Education in Ghana can be categorised into three main levels. Until the 1987 educational reforms, the first level of education included the primary (elementary), middle and/or continuation schools. In 1987, middle schools and continuation schools were jettisoned and junior secondary schools were introduced as a three-year stage following primary. The primary and junior secondary schools now constitute the basic education level in Ghana. At the basic level, the educational system of Ghana contains mission schools, public (mainly local authority) schools and private schools. The mission schools are managed by designated Educational Units on behalf of the government. The government funds both the mission and the public schools in terms of paying the salaries of teachers and supply of schools materials including textbooks. The local government authorities support public schools in terms of infrastructure.

The second level of education comprises secondary schools and technical institutes or their equivalent institutions. Universities and polytechnics are classified as tertiary institutions; in between them and the secondary institutions are various post-secondary institutions, some of which are now being upgraded to diploma-awarding colleges. This category of institutions includes teachers' and nurses' training colleges.

Ghana's educational history has been heavily influenced by political events – including changes of government involving coups and counter-coups – and by the instability and decline of the economy in the 1970s and 1980s, as shown in the brief commissions to review the educational sector and make recommendations for change. Some of the military governments had a short stay in power and consequently left hardly any meaningful footprint on the educational landscape.

Following the adoption of constitutional rule in 1993 coupled with a relative improvement in the economy in the 1990s, education received some attention, as shown in the implementation of the 1987 educational reforms. By 1996, the free universal compulsory basic education (FCUBE) programme was implemented. The gross enrolment rate at the basic level hovered around 80 per cent. Government continued its efforts to improve access to and quality of education in the 1990s and the early 2000s with the introduction of a capitation grant which sought to remove the school levies that partly accounted for the failure of some parents/guardians to send their wards to school, and also with the institution of a school feeding programme in selected schools in 2006. The country's education strategic plan targets universal primary completion in 2015.

Education in the Colonial and Nationalist Period (1950–57)

Formal education, otherwise known as the Western form of education was introduced into Ghana (then called the Gold Coast) in the early 17th century as a handmaid of Christianity to serve the primary needs of evangelism. The provision of formal education, initially, was a subsidiary function of European merchant companies. The first schools in Ghana were attached to the castles and forts which served as trading posts for the European merchants including the Portuguese, Dutch and later the English (Antwi, 1992).

Antwi (1992) notes that by 1950, on the eve of self-government, there were 2,904 primary schools in the Gold Coast Of these, 41 were directly run by the Government, while 1,551 were run by the missionaries and received government grants. The rest of the schools in the country were established and managed by private individuals, institutions and organisations. The total enrolment in all these schools was put at 271,954 (Nimako, 1976).

In 1951, the Gold Coast was granted internal self-government. The nationalist government of Dr. Kwame Nkrumah that assumed office in August 1951 introduced the Accelerated Development Plan (ADP) for Education, to provide for a significant expansion of education at all levels. In January 1952, tuition-free elementary education was introduced for children between the ages of 6 and 12. Essentially, this marked the modest beginning of what can be described as free primary education in Ghana.

The most outstanding result of the Accelerated Development Plan, according to McWilliam and Kwamena-Poh (1978), was the provision of half a million primary school places. Antwi (1992) notes that within the period 1952–57, primary and middle school places, taken together, tripled in number. On the eve of the independence of Ghana, Dr. Kwame Nkrumah declared that Ghana had a population of 5 million of whom nearly half a million were children enjoying primary education. Unfortunately, the goal of primary education for all was further away than had been thought because it turned out that the size of the population had been seriously underestimated. The 1960 census of Ghana, subsequently, showed that instead of 5 million, the population was actually nearer 7 million.

Independence and after (1957–66)

Ghana achieved full independence on March 1957 with Kwame Nkrumah as Prime Minister, leading the Convention People's Party (CPP). Later, in 1960, Ghana became a republic with Nkrumah as the first President. In education, the quantitative progress of the earlier years continued in the first years of independence. The number of approved primary schools rose from 3,571 in 1957 to 3,713 in 1959 and of middle schools from 1,311 to 1,394. Overall, the number of pupils enrolled in primary and middle schools combined doubled between 1961 and 1966 (Antwi, 1992); and according to UNESCO statistics, the gross enrolment ratio for the first level of education in Ghana (primary and middle schools, embracing the ages 6 to 15) rose from 38 per cent in 1960 to 69 per cent in 1965.

In November 1960, the President announced that fee-free compulsory primary and middle school education would be introduced in September 1961. Local Authorities were to continue to be responsible for providing buildings and it was reckoned that over 1,000 more schools would be required in September 1961. As a stopgap until new buildings were ready, a shift system was introduced with two daily shifts of four-and-a half hours each.

The immediate effects of the introduction of compulsory primary education were dramatic. Instead of the expected 1,000 new schools, 2,493 new primary schools were in fact opened in September 1961 and 219,480 children were enrolled in the first year classes. Just before this, in 1960–61, there had been 441,117 children in 3,514 public primary schools but within 2 years both these figures had doubled. By the fall of the CPP Government in 1966, the total had surged on to 1,137,494 children attending 8,144 schools (McWilliam & Kwamina-Poh, 1978). This development has been described by McWilliam & Kwamina-Poh as the high tide in the history of education in Ghana.

The post-independence CPP regime made considerable efforts to expand educational facilities at all levels, since education was identified as the key to Ghana's development. The expansion of educational facilities at the primary and middle schools called for the establishment of new teacher training colleges, most of which were phased out and changed into secondary schools after the overthrow of Dr. Kwame Nkrumah. During Nkrumah's regime, apart from paying the recurrent cost of teacher trainees, Government provided teacher trainees with allowances.

In furtherance of efforts to ensure attendance at primary and middle schools, the Education Act of October 1961 was passed. This Act established the post-independence legal basis for compulsory primary and middle school education for all children of school-going age. The Act replaced Governor Guggisberg's ordinances of 1925 and 1927, which had guided education in the colony and marked the beginning of universal free primary education in Ghana. The Education Act of 1961 empowered the Minister of Education after consultation with the Minister of Local Government to constitute local authorities into local education authorities (LEAs). The local education authorities were to establish, build, equip, and maintain all public primary and middle schools in their localities.

The Act declared education to be compulsory. According to Section 2: 'Every child who has attained the school-going age as determined by the Minister shall attend a course of instruction as laid down by the Minister in a school recognised for the purpose by the Minister'. A parent defying the law could expect to be fined up to £10 and in the case of a continuing offence to a fine not exceeding £2 in respect of each and every day during which the offence continued. The Act also made provision for education to be fee-free at the primary and middle school levels. Section 21 (1) of the Act states that: 'No fee, other than the payment for the provision of essential books or stationery or of materials required by pupils for use in practical work, shall be charged in respect of tuition at a public primary, middle or special school'.

Even though the Act made primary and middle school education tuition free and compulsory, the government was unable to enforce it because of lack of adequate resources and infrastructure to enrol all children of school-going age.

The legal basis of Ghana's education system was enshrined in later constitutions. The 1969, 1979 and 1992 constitutions of the Republic of Ghana clearly emphasise the role of the government in educating her citizens. For instance, Article 10 of the 1979 Constitution of the Republic of Ghana lays down, *inter alia*, that: 'The Government shall within two years after the coming into force of this constitution draw up a programme for implementation within the following ten years of free, compulsory and universal primary education (Clause 2). This Clause was repeated in the 1992 constitution in Article 38(2), providing the basis for the introduction of the free, compulsory and universal basic education (FCUBE) programme that was implemented in 1996.

The National Liberation Council (NLC) Regime (1966–69) and the Busia Administration (1969–70)

Dr. Kwame Nkrumah's regime was overthrown in February 1966. The new military administration of the National Liberation Council (NLC) under General Ankrah appointed two bodies, namely the Mills-Odoi Commission, to enquire into aspects of the educational system and the Education Review Committee. Among other things, the Mills-Odoi Commission proposed the establishment of a Teaching Service Division of the Public Service Commission and improvement of teacher remuneration and other conditions of service. These recommendations were later implemented. The Education Review Committee, on the other hand, 'streamlined education along the lines of the British system and upheld denominational supremacy and character building as the central theme of education' (Antwi, 1992).

The NLC regime in its three years of existence continued with the provision of educational facilities. However, a notable change brought about by the regime was the abolition of allowances to teacher trainees. The government still paid all the recurrent costs of the trainees. Other efforts were also made to improve education. As part of the effort, a two-year Development Plan was adopted in 1968, which stressed the need to improve the quality of education at all levels.

All the same, in 1966–67, after the overthrow of the CPP government, the enrolment fell back to 1,116,843 and was below the one million mark (at 975,629) by 1969–70. There was a corresponding decrease in the number of public primary schools from 7,913 in 1966–67 to 7,239 in 1969–70. Conversely, the figures for middle school education, which also showed rapid growth following the 1961 Act, did not full back in this period. In 1960–61, there were 1,234 public middle schools with a total enrolment of 145,377, while in 1965–66, there were 2,277 middle schools with 267,434 pupils. In 1966 67, the number of schools had grown to 2, 346, with 280,866 pupils. In 1969–70, the corresponding figures stood at 3,422 and 424,430.

In 1969, a new constitution was promulgated and the civilian Busia Administration assumed power in August 1969. The Busia regime was short lived. It was overthrown in January 1972. In its One-Year Development Plan, the Government did not place emphasis on primary education, but rather on the need to expand secondary schools to absorb the increasing number of middle school leavers and to strengthen the secondary level education to facilitate university education (Antwi, 1992).

Regime changes 1972–81

The decade of the 70s was marked by the rise and fall of several short-lived administrations, some of which paid attention to education, but whose influences on the system were rather sporadic. Only the National Redemption Council remained in power long enough to have an impact, both in following up earlier reforms and in developing new structures.

The National Redemption Council, headed by Colonel I.K. Acheampong, replaced the Busia administration in a military takeover in 1972. The Acheampong regime contributed to the development of education in a number of ways. Notable among them were: (a) the approval of proposals for a new structure and content of education which placed emphasis on vocational, practical and technical subjects throughout the entire pre-university education; and (b) a shortened duration of pre-university education from 17 years to 12 years, to enable the government to realise savings in educational expenditure. The Ghana Teaching Service that had been proposed by the Mills-Odoi Commission was first established in 1973 and was later changed to the Ghana Education Service, to embrace all teachers in pre-university educational institutions, as well as general managers of schools, supporting staff in educational institutions and all professional civil service staff in the Ministry of Education.

In 1978, the Supreme Military Council I was replaced by the Supreme Military Council II of Major-General F.W.K. Akuffo, which was in power for barely three months. The regime had little time to settle, let alone tackle educational problems before Flight-Lieutenant J.J. Rawlings and his Armed Forces Revolutionary Council (AFRC) swept it away in another military takeover on June 4, 1979. The AFRC regime existed for only three months and so hardly had time for educational development.

In September 1979, a new civilian administration came to power led by Dr. Hilla Limann. This regime was also short lived. The Limann administration, during its two years of administering the country, directed its attention to cutting down the costs of secondary education by taking a critical look at areas where some savings could be made.

The PNDC era and educational reforms of 1987

Flight-Lieutenant J.J. Rawlings returned to power in 1981, with the establishment of the Provisional Defence Council (PNDC). During the PNDC era, 1981 to 1991, measures were taken designed to improve the quality of and access to education generally in the country. These included (a) the restoration of state financial support for trainee teachers, (b) improvement in the supply of primary school textbooks and (c) the reform of the educational system.

As part of the process to improve education, the Evans-Anfom Commission on Basic Education was set up in 1986 to examine certain aspects of basic education in Ghana. The report of the commission noted, among other things:

* Approximately 27 per cent of the population of 6-year-old children in Ghana were not in school. The chief causal factor identified was inadequacy of facilities.
* The Education Act of 1961 that made provision in sections 1 and 2 for compulsory primary and middle school education had not been enforceable for mainly economic reasons, including the poverty of some parents resulting in their inability to provide the basic school needs of their wards as well as pay the fees and levies charged by the schools. A major factor, though, was that there was lack of adequate resources to ensure the attendance at school by every school-going aged child.
* The suggested timetable for the implementation of the compulsory primary and middle school education took the year 2000 as the target date by which Basic Education should be compulsory.
* Basic Education in Ghana could be defined as 'the minimum formal education to which every Ghanaian child is entitled as of right, to equip him/her to function effectively in the society'.
* Both Central Government and local communities should contribute funds to support Basic Education.
* About 97 per cent of the money voted for first-cycle education went to salaries of personnel. Only 3 per cent of the allocation remained to cater for the other requirements of schooling.
* District Councils were by law required to erect school buildings and maintain them and to provide equipment. Over the years, however, owing to the inability of many District Councils to perform these functions, they had had, in most cases, to be undertaken by the Central Government.

The commission recommended that the Central Government make allocations in the payment of salaries of personnel engaged in education and also make foreign exchange available for the importation of textbooks and other software for purchase by parents and guardians to improve the quality of teaching and learning.

The major elements of the reforms introduced the following year in 1987 included: the restructuring of the educational system to provide nine years of 'basic' education (6 years of primary followed by 3 years of junior secondary schooling) for all children, followed by three years of senior secondary and then four years of tertiary education. This structure reduced the duration of pre-university education from a maximum of 17 years (for the small minority of university entrants who had successively undergone six years primary, four years middle, five years secondary and two years sixth form although most transferred to secondary after one, two or three years of middle school) to a standardised 12 years. The reforms were intended, among other things, to provide increased access to education especially in the northern half of the country and in other areas where the intake was persistently low by making basic education available to every Ghanaian child. Once again, the intention was to provide universal free education. The reforms had been prepared as far back as 1974 during the Acheampong regime. The implementation of the reforms led to the construction of additional classrooms, renovation of existing structures, training of teachers and in-service training of teachers. The World Bank supported the reform programme with an amount of US$45 million.

The implementation of these educational reforms continued throughout the 1990s after the PNDC regime metamorphosed itself into an elected democratic government in 1992 and ruled the country until 2000 when it lost power to the New Patriotic Party (NPP).

An important development in the 1990s was the introduction of the free compulsory universal basic education (FCUBE) programme in 1995, which is a constitutional requirement. The FCUBE is a comprehensive programme designed to provide quality basic education to all school-aged children in Ghana by the year 2005. Specifically, the FCUBE programme addressed (a) quality of teaching and learning, (b) management for efficiency and (c) access and participation at the basic level. The access and participation aspect of the FCUBE programme focused on expansion of infrastructural facilities and services to enhance access for all children of school-going age, as well as emphasising girls' education.

A mid-term review study report of the FCUBE published by the Ghana Education Service implementation coordinating unit in 2002, for the period 1996–2000, indicated that there were increases in the number of schools and enrolments, both in public and private schools. The report showed that public primary schools increased by 9.5 per cent, while enrolment grew by 7.9 per cent. However, the GER for public primary schools showed a decrease slightly from 76.6 per cent in 1996–97 to 75 per cent in 2000–01 (GES, 2002). This was indeed an apparent slight regress, but it was attributed to the inability of the study to cover all the existing 110 districts. From the study report, one can conclude that modest gains were achieved in the implementation of the programme, on the whole.

New Patriotic Party – NPP (2000–2008)

The New Patriotic Party government, on the assumption of office in 2000, set up a committee under the chairmanship of Prof. Jophus Anamuah-Mensah to review Ghana's educational reforms. His committee submitted its report in October 2002. It recommended, among other things, a new basic education structure of 2 years kindergarten, 6 years primary and 3 years junior secondary school – a total of 11 years for the new basic education (Anamuah-Mensah et al., 2002). The government White Paper on the report accepted the proposed new structure but recommended that the junior secondary school should be named junior high school (MOEYS, 2004).

In an effort to improve on the efforts of their predecessors in terms of access, participation and quality of education at the basic level, the NPP government has, with effect from September 2005, instituted a capitation grant to basic schools. This is an amount of ¢30,000 per pupil enrolled in a school per year paid by the government to the schools in place of the school levies paid by parents and/or guardians (sports, cultural activities, development activities). With the coming into effect of the capitation grant, the government has abolished all school levies, the payment of which prevented some poor parents from sending their children to school. It has been estimated that enrolment at the primary level has increased by 14.22 per cent following the implementation of the capitation grant (*Daily Graphic*, June 9, 2006).

The enrolment rates calculated by the Institute of Statistical, Social and Economic Research (ISSER) in *The State of the Ghana Economy* indicate that the Gross Enrolment Ratio at the primary level was 87.5 per cent with the Net Enrolment Ratio of 59.1 per cent. At the junior secondary level the GER was estimated to be 70.2 with a NER of 31.6 (ISSER, 2006).

Other areas where efforts were made by the NPP government to ensure attendance at school by every child of school-going age include, among others, a school feeding programme and free transport to pupils to attend schools. The school feeding programme commenced in the 2005/2006 academic year in selected schools across the country. It ensures that pupils are fed with one nutritious meal during the school session, generally at lunchtime. It started on a pilot basis with 100 schools, 10 each from the 10 regions of the country. The programme, however, is not the first of its kind in the country. The Catholic Relief Services (CRS), supported by the United States Agency for International Development (USAID), had been operating school feeding programme in selected schools in the Northern Region of the country for some time before the Government stepped in, to promote improved enrolment. It has been reported that the government has spent ¢7 billion on the feeding of children, the setting up of kitchens and the provision of other inputs in 138 schools in the country (*Daily Graphic*, June 2, 2006). In the 2006–07 academic year, the programme benefited 975 public primary schools and over 440,000 pupils in all the 138 districts in the country. (*Daily Graphic*, September 5, 2006)

In 2008, in a straightforward democratic election, Dr Atta Mills was elected President; at the time of writing, he was continuing the efforts of his predecessor government.

Features and facets of primary/basic education

Teacher training

The teacher is the hub of any effective educational system. Thus the quality of an educational system is dependent on, and reflected partly by, the quality of teachers. Ghana's system of training teachers for basic schools expanded in the years since 1953. Under the

Accelerated Development Plan of 1951, emphasis was laid on the training of primary and middle school teachers. In February 1953, an Emergency Training College was opened at Saltpond and by the end of that year it had conducted five courses of six weeks and 298 pupil teachers (untrained teachers) had passed through its cocoa-sheds (McWilliam and Kwamina-Poh, 1978). Subsequently, Pupil Teachers' Centres were started in rented buildings in various parts of the country. In this way, about 3,000 pupil teachers attended the six-week course each year. By 1957, the number of pupil teachers in approved primary and middle schools had fallen to 9,688 from its peak of 11,055, as the output of the two-year training college (Teacher's Certificate B programme) began to overtake new primary and middle school openings. The Pupil Teachers' Centres were strongly criticised for attempting to train teachers in six weeks.

While in 1951 virtually all students in teacher training colleges were middle school leavers pursuing the Certificate B or A programmes, by 1961, the spread of secondary education provided a growing number of entrants to two-year post- secondary Certificate A programmes. By the beginning of 1960, out of 4,427 teachers in training 340 were products of secondary schools. As already noted, the Accelerated Development Plan gave encouragement to those entering the profession by allowing for the payment of salaries (allowances) to teachers in training. This system continued until the overthrow of Kwame Nkrumah in 1966 and was only restored in the early 1980s, to encourage more candidates and to support those in training. In order to provide guidance and control in teacher education for the primary and middle schools, the National Teacher Training Council of Ghana was set up in 1958.

As part of the implementation of the President's proclamation of fee-free compulsory primary and middle school education in 1961, local authorities were to continue to be responsible for providing buildings and over 1,000 more schools were required in September 1961. Again, as already noted, as a stopgap until new buildings were ready, a shift system was introduced, with two daily shifts of 4½ hours. The shift system prevails in some urban settlements. Its major disadvantage is the short instructional time as compared to the normal whole-day system. It also places strains on the teachers. By September 1960, there were about 12,000 trained and 8,000 untrained teachers (pupil teachers) in the education system. Following the announcement by the President of fee-free and compulsory primary and middle school education, it was planned to increase training college enrolment by 1,200 over the next 2 years to take care of the increases in the number of schools and classrooms.

In order to attract and retain teachers in the classroom, the government announced what had been described as the 'New Deal' for teachers in 1960. By this deal, the salary of Pupil Teachers was increased from £G102 to a scale of £G144 to £G180. Certificate A and B teacher received increases varying between £G35 and £G85 a year. In addition, 12 per cent of Certificate A teachers would be made Senior Teachers on £G500–700 a year and a new grade of Principal Teacher was to carry a salary of up to £G900. The President's intention was to create a teaching service that was second to none.

With the proclamation of fee-free primary education in 1960 and its implementation in September 1961, efforts were made to increase the number of trained teachers and also to make up for the decline in output caused by the ending of the Certificate B courses in 1962 following the decision that for middle school leavers, a 4-year Certificate A course should be the rule. The number of training colleges grew from 12 Certificate A and 19 Certificate B in 1961 to 82 Certificate A colleges in 1966. In this period, nearly 9,000 trained teachers qualified and the total numbers in the field rose by 28 per cent. But in the same five years (1961–1966), the number of pupil teachers went up by no less than 165 per cent and the proportion of trained teachers fell from 53 per cent to 35 per cent.

With the overthrow of the CPP government in 1966, the NLC government phased out some of the newly established teacher training colleges and turned them into secondary schools, because it was thought that there were going to be more trained teachers than would be required. But this proved not to be the case. There has been a perpetual deficit in teacher training in the Ghana for the basic level. Currently, there are 38 public teacher training colleges in the country. These are all post-secondary institutions that are being upgraded to Diploma awarding institutions. The process of upgrading the colleges is scheduled to be completed by 2010. The requirements for entry into the teacher training colleges are aggregate 24 or better in six subjects; three core and three electives at the senior secondary school level. The core subjects are English language, mathematics and science.

It is important to note that, despite the modest efforts to increase the number of trained teachers in the system, there has been a perennial shortage of trained teachers at the basic level since the 1960s. Even with the use of untrained teachers (pupil teachers), there has been always a shortfall. The problem partly stems from teacher distribution. Many trained teachers do not want to serve in remote and deprived areas. Serving in these areas often means living under harsh conditions, such as lack of potable water, absence of adequate medical facilities, no electricity, limited access to markets, poor dwelling facilities for the teacher and their families. Another dimension of the problem is the low level of remuneration of teachers. This accounts for the high attrition rate in the Ghana Education Service; teachers leave the service for greener pastures in other better-paying jobs. Coupled with the poor remuneration is the low social recognition given to teachers in the country.

A new development in tackling the perennial shortage of trained teachers is the institution of a new kind of untrained teachers training programme. This targets those untrained teachers already in the system by training them through a distance learning mode for four years.

The state and church schools – educational units

The Education Act of 1961 recognised the principle of freedom of religious belief and extended it. Section 22 of the Act reads:

* No person shall be refused admission as a pupil on account of the religious persuasion, nationality, race or language of himself or of either of his parents.
* No test or enquiries shall be made of or concerning the religious beliefs of pupils or students prior to their admittance to any school or college and
* No person attending a school as a pupil shall, if his parents object be required to

attend or to abstain from attending, whether in the institution or elsewhere any Sunday school, or any form of religious worship or observance, or any instruction in religious subjects.

By the Act, regardless of the management of a school, all schools are regarded as state-owned because the Government pays the teachers. The managers are, in fact, acting as agents of the government.

The Education Act of 1961 has been seen as having had the effect of stifling local initiative and the active interest of the denominational bodies in their schools (Antwi, 1992). By the middle of the 1960s, the growing protests of many parents, other interested citizens and members of various denominational bodies expressed through the mass media caused the NLC Administration to request the Ministry of Education to invite views from the public on the effects of the Act on the discipline of teachers, pupils, students and parents, and on the attitude of parents to education and religion.

The intention of the government to hand back to the denominational educational units their former schools absorbed into the public system was hotly debated by the mass media. This issue has still not been resolved. The Churches continue to ask the government to hand back the schools to them.

The Education Review Committee of 1966, established by the NLC, believed that the denominational bodies have a continuing and desirable role to play and proposed that they should be permitted to develop their philosophy of school management and concept of education of the young and that all institutions managed by them should be under their effective and immediate control within the general service conditions of the Ministry of Education.

The White Paper on the Report of the Education Review Committee rejected the dual pattern of school management and advocated its replacement by a unitary one. It pointed out that a unitary pattern would make for economy, simpler administration and efficiency and it recommended that the management of schools built, maintained and wholly financed from public funds should be vested in Management Boards/Committees on which Educational Units would be represented where necessary. The Mills-Odoi Committee of 1967, which was to review the structure and remuneration of the public services in Ghana, affirmed the government's position in the White Paper. Subsequently, efforts have been made over the past 35 years by Ghanaian governments either to absorb the denominations – educational units – into the public system or to relieve them of the responsibility of managing schools. In all cases, the denominational bodies have fiercely resisted these efforts.

From all indications, successive governments have been committed to ensuring equality of educational opportunity for all Ghanaians and also to efficiency and economy in educational provision, in order to maximise returns on educational expenditure. In pursuit of these aims, a report of the National Consultative Committee on Educational Finance appointed in 1975 recommended that district councils should take over the functions of the educational units and absorb their personnel where necessary. At present, the state is responsible for the payment of teachers' salaries as well as provision of infrastructure in terms of buildings and supply of textbooks in denominational (church) primary and junior secondary schools (except for those that are privately-owned and run).

Access, retention and drop-out

Studies conducted in the 1990s (Asare-Bediako et al., 1995, & BESIP, 1997) indicated that access and retention at the basic education level have been on the increase since the reform programme of 1987. Gross enrolment ratio at the primary level was 78 per cent in 1991/92. The ratio rose to 87.5 per cent in the 2004–05 academic year, as indicated earlier in this chapter. It is worthy of note that Gross Enrolment Ratios are not uniform across the country. Generally, they have been significantly lower in the three northern regions of the country even though in those regions, in an attempt to even out disparities and to promote the development, education up to the secondary level is free. There is also a continuing gender imbalance in both enrolment and retention rates.

Girls' education

Boys continue to outnumber girls in the education system generally, especially at the secondary and tertiary levels. A number of factors militate against girls' enrolment in schools. The factors include:

a   The high opportunity costs to families of sending girls to school and losing their contribution to domestic work and child-minding services;
b   The additional opportunity costs when families are poor and require these children to engage in farming, herding or petty trading;
c   Parental and community attitudes towards girls' education. This partly stems from cultural practices. These include early betrothal of girls, which means that those who start in school are withdrawn from it;
d   Teenage pregnancy, which is another cause of girls dropping out, particularly in rural areas;
e   Lack of comfortable access for girls (and women teachers), e.g. gender-sensitive facilities and security;
f   Lack of community action for girls' enrolment.

A study on *Gender and Primary Schooling in Ghana* under the auspices of the Forum for African Women Educationalists (FAWE) highlighted the problem: girls' enrolment has consistently lagged behind that of boys and the imbalance remained constant throughout the period 1991–92 to 1996–97.

Financing education

Since 1961, many African states including Ghana have been making efforts to expand their educational systems as part of their overall national development plans (Antwi, 1992) because of their conviction that education holds the key to development. By the Education Act of 1961, the government of Ghana declared a fee-free education at the primary and middle schools. In line with this policy, tuition at all levels of the public educational system was declared free, that is, it was borne by the government. At the basic and secondary levels, students paid minimal book-user fees every year.

These arrangements are still in place. In addition, the Ministry of Education subsidises the Basic Education Certificate Examination fee (formerly the Middle School Leaving Certificate) for junior secondary students. This is to make sure that no child drops out from the exam due to inability of the parents/guardians to pay the registration fee for the examination. The Ministry of Education also currently pays all recurrent costs of teacher training and provides allowances for teacher trainees. (As already noted, the provision of allowances for teacher trainees was discontinued during the period of the National Liberation Council Administration but later restored by the National Democratic Congress government led by Flt. Lt. Jerry John Rawlings).

As a result of governments' commitment to continued educational expansion, educational expenditures claimed, and continue to claim, a large, though fluctuating, share of government current expenditure. For instance, the government of Ghana in 1990, 1991, and 1992 allocated 22 per cent, 21 per cent, and 22 per cent of the national budget to education. Out of total education expenditure 43 per cent, 44 per cent, and 45 per cent respectively were allocated to primary education over those years (DeStefano, Hartwell & Tietjen, 1995).

An examination of educational expenditure in relation to the economy shows that for the years 1970, 1976 and 1978, the Ghana government's expenditure on education averaged 3.3 per cent of the gross national product (GNP). This expenditure was equivalent to an average of 24 per cent of the government's current expenditure (Antwi, 1992). Antwi further points out that, according to an official report issued by the government of Ghana in the 80s, the per capita expenditure on education had declined from $20 in 1972 to $10 in 1979 and to $1 in 1983 (using constant 1975 US dollars). Those were the years of economic decline that invariably affected expenditure on education. A World Bank Report (1996), Staff Appraisal Report on Basic Education Sector Improvement Programme noted that during the 1970s and early 1980s, the economy of Ghana had contracted by 2–3 per cent per annum. The decline had an impact on development and on the budget and thus inevitably on provision of educational facilities.

Government expenditure on education, however, varied with the educational levels. Antwi (1992) notes that a wide disparity was evident in the cost per student per year at different levels of education over the years. According to the Report of the Committee Appointed by the Executive Council of the National Liberation Council to advise Government on the future policy for financial support for University students in Ghana (1970), in the 1968/69 academic year the average recurrent costs per head for primary schools (6 years) was N¢120, that is ¢20 per annum, while that for middle schools was N¢80 – also ¢20 per annum. In the same year, public expenditure per head at the secondary level was N¢875, that is N¢175 per annum. At the University level for the same academic year, the expenditure per student on a course was N¢10,325, or N¢2,950 per annum. The annual unit costs at the university level were therefore 148 times the level of primary schools. This disparity is a dilemma for all governments providing for all levels of the educational system, but is particularly worrying in societies where only a very small proportion of the population have the opportunity of higher education.

More recently, according to the Ghana Education Service, in 2001, the recurring unit cost per pupil was ¢203 in the primary, ¢43,595 at the junior secondary, and ¢2,398,579 at the teacher training level. All these expenditures show a shortfall of between 56.2 per cent and 78.8 per cent from the planned expenditure (Education Review Report, 2002).

In 1984, the government launched the Economic Recovery Programme (ERP) with support from the IMF, the World Bank and other donors. Since launching the Economic Recovery Programme, the economy grew by an average of about 5 per cent annually or at around 2 per cent per capita. The macroeconomic situation was less favourable in the early 1990s. Despite a successful turnaround in fiscal balance, annual inflation exceeded 60 per cent in 1995 (World Bank Report, 1996).

Despite the financial difficulties which confronted the governments of Ghana over the years, each one continued to put emphasis on the importance of education in the development process, as reflected in the budgetary allocation for education. The World Bank Report in 1996 notes that Ghana showed, relatively, strong fiscal commitment to the education sector during the period of structural adjustment (1985–1995). Between 1990–1995, the proportion of the government's annual discretionary budget allocated to education averaged nearly 39 per cent on annual actual spending basis. The report (World Bank, 1996) further notes that intra-sectoral allocation since the educational reforms began in 1987 had been in favour of basic education that consistently received 60 per cent or more of the Ministry of Education's budget.

Since the late 1980's and 1990s, the government of Ghana has been provided with financial support for the educational sector following the implementation of the educational reforms in 1987. In the early 1990s (1990–1995), of the total amount of basic education recurrent expenditure, the government contributed about two-thirds, households about a quarter, and donors about 10 per cent (World Bank Report, 1996). The World Bank and the United States Agency for International Development (USAID) are among significant donors. USAID began providing support to the educational sector in Ghana in 1990. Most often the support of the Agency is limited to the primary level. For capital costs, districts were the major source of in-country domestic spending and, on average, they share the load equally with external aid partners. In terms of funding the education sector in Ghana, the donors provided 12 per cent in 1999, 6 per cent in 2000 and 9 per cent in 2001 (Education Review Report, 2002).

Two major sources of funding for districts in recent years are:

a   The District Assembly Common Fund (DACF), a centrally-distributed intergovernmental transfer of 5 per cent of the national tax revenue which was introduced in 1992; and

b   Funds generated by the districts themselves, with education levies accounting for most.

The government has been responsible mainly for recurrent expenditure, predominantly salary and administrative costs. For example in 1998, the Ministry of Education's share of the Ghana Government discretionary recurrent estimate was 33 per cent while the share for development was 3.9 per cent, a total of 36.9 per cent. In the same year, the allocation of the Ministry's recurrent budget by sectors and items show that the headquarters together with the subvented organizations received 4.6 per cent of the allocation, the Ghana Education Service (GES) received 83.3 per cent and tertiary education took 12.1per cent. Of the total recurrent budget for the Ministry, 86.3 per cent was earmarked for personal emoluments, leaving 13.7 per cent of the budget for non-salary items. Of the GES allocation, 88.1 per cent was also set aside for personal emoluments while 11.9 per cent was set aside for non-salary items (Ministry of Education, April 1998). At the basic level, the Governments spending on infrastructure and instructional materials has been minimal.

In 1995, there was a general shortage of instructional materials, especially in primary schools, and of trained teachers, particularly in rural areas. There was also weakness in the resource distribution system and the teacher posting system, resulting in considerable inequities between schools, regions and districts. (World Bank Report, 1996). These problems were partly due to absolute resource limitations.

From the foregoing sections, it is clear that Ghana's educational progress was hampered by severe economic difficulties in the 1970s and early 1980s. Following the acceptance of the structural adjustment programme by the World Bank in the 1980s, economic support was provided by the international bodies to help ensure Ghana's economic recovery, which reflected on the support for her educational programmes by late 1980s and early 1990s. Support for educational activities at the primary level is championed by United States Agency for Development (USAID), the Department for International Development of United Kingdom (DFID), German Technical Cooperation (GTZ) and the Japan International Cooperation Agency (JICA) to mention a few in recent years.

Private sector participation

Private sector participation in primary and junior secondary schooling has been rather limited till recently, as educational provision was seen as the preserve of the state. The figures for enrolment and number of schools for 2001–2002 provide a snapshot of the situation. During this period, 19.3 per cent of schools were in the Private category, and they accounted for 22.4 per cent of the total enrolment. 15.4 per cent of the junior secondary schools were private and they had a 14.3 per cent share of total enrolment. (Ministry of Education, 2002; cited in *Meeting the Challenges of Education in the Twenty First Century*, p. 255)

Commenting on the role of the private sector, a World Bank study pointed out that the private sector has 'limited government involvement and none from the Bank'. This statement should be treated with caution, since although there may be no direct public subvention, private schools benefit from such publicly-funded activities as teacher training and curriculum development. The sector had shown phenomenal growth to 20 per cent of primary enrolment compared to 5 per cent 15 years earlier. (*Impact Evaluation*, p. 27)

Voluntary Sector

Voluntary Sector organisations (VSOs) have emerged as key stakeholders in the educational development of Ghana. Some of them have strong links with overseas sponsoring organisations. They undertake small projects in specific parts of the country or focus on particular areas where the efforts of the state have not been fully successful. Also, they provide support that can reinforce the efforts of the government to make quantitative or qualitative improvements.

VSOs act as pressure groups highlighting areas of concern. For example, Action Aid International Ghana and Oxfam GB participated in the 2004 Global Action Week events in Ghana on the theme of 'Children Missing Out in School'. During the week a national lobby was held in Accra to bring together parliamentarians, policy makers, those missing school and students. 'Community Missing Out Maps' were produced to make the government 'indisputably aware of the exact areas in the north where help is needed to encourage children back into school.' (Abu-Gyamfi and Foster, p. 21)

The role of the diaspora in education

There are private initiatives from both within the country and from the Ghanaian diaspora that support schools with money or efforts to meet infrastructure needs or help individuals or groups of pupils. The role of the diaspora in educational development is on the rise especially as the remittances, globally, have increased faster than official aid from donor countries. Global migration trends have diversified diasporic destinations and new information technologies allow maintenance of links with the home country more than in the past. This interest might result in support for education at an individual level – through sponsorship to pay for educational expenses – or at an institutional level – to support educational institutions in their home towns/villages, for example. How far the current global recession will affect the scale of remittances from abroad, and as a result diminish this educational assistance, is not yet clear.

UP(B)E in Ghana: Why will it (not) succeed?

Commitment/political will

Both the government and the public are strongly committed to the notion/cause of UPE/UBE. Constitutional provisions provide the legal framework that underpins that commitment.

The commitment to universal basic education is an extension of the commitment to develop human resources. While notions of nation-building underpinned past initiatives, the current emphasis is on creating a well-educated population fit to compete in a globalised and globalising world. Comparisons with the rise of East Asian economies and the role of education in the process are cited in official documents:

> 'The rationale for an accelerated human resource development strategy for Ghana is based on the persuasive experience of countries that have made the transition to successful economic development. The evidence is strong that the basic level of education must be improved as the platform to sustainable growth and development. Asian countries with rapid economic growth had all achieved universal primary by the time they began their growth period. Today, Ghana has lower primary enrolment and literacy rates than the Asian countries had when

their economic growth began to accelerate ... . At the secondary level, however, Ghana's enrolment ratio of 39 per cent is quite high and compares favourably with Asian countries at the time of their take off. This is the basis of the argument for a high level of public resources to provide basic schooling and literacy.' *(Towards Learning for All, p. 2)*

The government in 2006 restated this rationale of education for economic prosperity in the context of globalisation: 'Ghana, in spite of severe economic constraints will continue to remain committed to efforts aimed at putting in place an efficient, credible and sustainable education system that will make the nation competitive in today's globalised economy which is increasingly becoming knowledge-driven' (Ghana Education System, last para).

Regional disparities

Regional variations in educational provision have their roots in the extension and consolidation of control by the British government during the colonial period in the 19th century. Three areas that had distinct political histories – Gold Coast, a coastal 'colony' established initially through an agreement with Fanti states, Ashanti, a colony by conquest, and the protectorate of the Northern Territories (NTs). Western Togoland, earlier a German colony, was administered by the British after 1918, alongside the then Gold Coast, first as a League of Nations Mandate and then as a UN Trust Territory; it was integrated into Ghana in 1957.

The governmental and missionary activities during the 19th century established 'the base of the educational system' (George, p. 7). When the British Government annexed Ashanti in 1901 and established the Northern Territories Protectorate in 1902, 'the population for which the Governor of the Gold Coast was responsible increased roughly by three times, but there was no corresponding increase for some years in the money available for such activities as education .... As it was there was no educational legislation for the Northern Territories until 1927, a generation later' (McWilliam, 1962, p. 34).

Regional variations can also be attributed to the prevalence of Christian missionary activities in the three regions, with the coastal regions having the most and the northern regions the least. Apart from being considered the 'right bodies to manage education' missionaries had more money than the government ... For example, ... in 1844 Thomas Birch Freeman during a single visit to Britain was able to collect £5,500 for the work of Wesleyan Mission on the Gold Coast – more than the Gold Coast Government's total revenue for that year' (McWilliam, 1962, p. 7).

The pattern of regional variations continued in the post-independence period. Even the increases in school enrolment in the post-independence nation-building of the 1950s and 1960s did not change the pattern. In 1970–71, for example, 'While Ghana had about 11 per cent of the total population in primary schools, about 5 per cent in middle schools, and 0.6 per cent in secondary schools ... [Northern and Upper regions] had less that 4 per cent of its population in primary schools, less that 2 per cent in middle schools, and less than 0.2 per cent in secondary schools' (George, p. 215).

Enrolment figures for 1994–97 in public primary schools by region and gender show the nexus between enrolment levels, poverty and gender disparities: 'Upper West, Upper East and Northern regions had the lowest number of enrolled pupils ... The three regions with the lowest enrolment also happen to be the three poorest in the country' (Avotri et al. p. 22).

The persistence of regional disparities continues into the 21st century, despite the successes of FCUBE and other measures. Table 2.1 shows the gross enrolment ratios of primary schools nationally and in the three Northern Regions of the country from 2001–02 to 2004–05.

Table 2.1. National and three regional gross enrolment ratios in primary schools

Indicator	2001–02	2002–03	2003–04	2004–05
National	90.4	84.5	86.3	87.5
Northern Region	66.4	70.5	70.5	71.5
Upper East	71.2	76.5	77.1	80.4
Upper West	63.1	70.3	74.1	77.3

Source: The State of the Ghanaian Economy in 2005, Accra, ISSER Publication

The government agencies are aware of the situation and efforts are being put in place to improve it. The problem is two-fold: to continue with expansion of provision for basic education (a problem of quantity); and to ensure that appropriate learning outcomes are achieved (a problem of quality). Admittedly, the challenge of achieving Universal Primary/Basic Education in Ghana is a difficult and complex one – arising out of the pattern of general and educational development set in the colonial period, and the inadequacy of colonial and post-colonial efforts to harmonise levels of educational access/uptake across the whole country.

Conclusions

Cultivating institutional memories of the past educational 'high tides' and retreats in their contexts, both external and internal and at micro and macro levels will be of great value to current and succeeding Ghanaian governments if they wish to lead Africa in the quest to achieve and maintain UPE successfully. Cycles of rapid expansion and drastic cutbacks have to be avoided in favour of a steadiness of approach. While external events, such as the oil shock and the recent global recession, are beyond national governments' control, it would make good sense to plan national education budgets 'for a rainy day' and avoid being pressured by outside agencies into sudden splurges.

In planning for the achievement of UPE by 2015, Ghana has some significant advantages. The constitutional obligation to free universal primary education is a cornerstone. With that assurance, the UPE/UBE initiatives in the country, in spite of political fluctuations, have been almost continuously backed by a strong political will and now also by a sense of urgency to find a rightful place for the nation in a globalising world. A good deal of work in the past fifty years by planners and reviewers is there as foundation for future progress. The Ghana Education Service has knowledgeable, experienced and committed staff, who usually remain throughout governmental changes. The basic structures are sound, in spite of the unsolved relationships with religious bodies, and the main stumbling blocks are well-known. There are problematic issues, such as how far it is safe to rely on external funding and when such funding is available, and how far can the country resist pressures from the donors.

Against this background, we would like to suggest the following guidelines for the future:

- The FCUBE programme, Ghana's flagship initiative, is well-structured to serve the children and parents of Ghana and to tap into internal and external funding. It is to be cherished;
- More work is needed to address social and historical/regional disparities. This should include a very serious effort to bring more girls into school and keep them there, with gender-sensitive facilities and positive incentives to guardians/parents. It should also include a new campaign to gain more uptake of schooling in the three Regions in the North which lag behind – e.g. extra payment to teachers who are ready to serve in remote areas and more involvement with local communities;
- New discussions might be valuable with representatives of the voluntary community and the diaspora organisations, to see if there are ways of rationalising their support, to channel it to the most needy sectors/areas;
- Finally, the whole system depends on the dedication and professionalism of teachers, without whom there will be no motivation for pupils to continue in school and no hope for improvement in the quality of education. It is critically important to increase the supply and standard of teachers, year on year.

Alba de Souza and Gituro Wainaina

Chapter 3

Kenya's three initiatives in UPE

Introduction

Since gaining independence in December 1963, Kenya has pursued a deliberate strategy that emphasised education as the key factor to development. Indeed, The Kenya Constitution, Sessional Paper No. 10 on African Socialism and various national development plans, recognised education as a means for promoting national integration among the various tribes and ethnic groups in Kenya[1]. Education was seen as a catalyst for political, economic and social advancement for individuals, through which human capital accumulation, essential for economic growth and national development could be attained. This belief made it imperative that Kenya had to pursue policies geared to the expansion and improvement of education for leaders of independent Kenya to sustain their political leadership.

It is therefore not surprising that each of Kenya's three presidents made an attempt to introduce Universal Primary Education (UPE) as part of their political agenda. Kenya's first President, Jomo Kenyatta, announced in 1972 that school fees for grades 1 to 4 would be abolished at the start of the school year in 1974[2]. This policy brought in its wake a surge in enrolment of children who had been excluded from the school system because of their inability to pay fees. However, the gains made were not sustained.

In 1978, President Daniel arap Moi became the second President of Kenya on the death of Kenyatta. He proclaimed that all school fees including building funds and other levies in primary schools should be abolished the following year, in 1979. In addition, arrangements were also made to start a programme to provide free school milk to all primary school children. These two decisions also resulted in a swell in enrolments. Again, this policy was not sustained as we shall see in the text of this chapter.

The third President of Kenya, Mwai Kibaki, succeeded Moi in December 2002 after a general election. The President's first policy initiative was to make primary education a focal point of his presidency. He immediately declared that 'Free Primary Education' (FPE) should be implemented in January 2003 at the start of the school year. By 2004 there was an increase of 1.3 million children over the previous year, representing an increase of 22 per cent over the previous year and a Gross Enrolment Ratio of 99 per cent. The current expansion to fulfil the EFA goal of free and universal primary education is still on-going.

This chapter on Kenya will look at the three attempts made at implementing UPE and will analyse the difficulties and shortcomings in policy and resources faced in each instance. It will discuss what lessons are to be learnt if UPE is to be sustained. But first, there will be an explanation of the current education system followed by the history of UPE efforts since 1963.

The present day

Structure. The current formal education system was introduced in 1984 and has an 8-4-4 structure consisting of 8 years of primary education (age 6–13), followed by 4 years of secondary education (14–17), leading to a minimum of 4 years for a general university degree (specialist courses take longer). At the end of the 8 years of primary education, pupils undertake the Kenya Certificate of Primary Education (KCPE) examination, the grades of which are used mainly to select and allocate pupils to secondary schools. At the end of the 4 years of secondary education, pupils sit the Kenya Certificate of Secondary Education (KCSE), which determines the grades for entry into university or to other post-secondary training institutions. Since 2004, pressure has been building from the public for the Government of Kenya (GOK) and the Ministry of Education (MOE) to consider 12 years of schooling (primary and secondary education) as being part of the basic education cycle. The 8-4-4 structure was introduced in an attempt to provide a vocational element in the last three grades of primary education to cater for the needs primary school leavers. This policy has not been wholly successful, partly from a curriculum planning point of view and partly from a lack of resources to maintain the vocational element.

Management. The management of formal education and training is mainly through MOE. Various other government ministries such as the Local Government, Home Affairs, Heritage and Sport, Health, and Labour and Human Resource Development, provide some sector-specific education and training. For instance, the Ministry of Labour and Human Resource Development provides technical education and training through Youth Polytechnics (post-primary education) and industrial training programmes (post-secondary education). It is also responsible for adult and continuing education programmes.

Policy, planning and the development of strategy for education rests with the MOE headquarters, although in many instances there has been considerable interference on education policy directly from the President. The MOE has eleven main departments:

- Administration and Finance
- Early Childhood Development and Pre-primary Education
- Primary Education
- Secondary Education
- University Education
- Field Services
- Planning and Development
- Formulation and Projects
- Inspectorate
- Legal matters
- Audit

In addition to the Departments, there are also semi-autonomous Government Agencies that come under the MOE. These are: The Kenya Institute of Education (KIE) responsible for curriculum development; The Kenya National Examination Council (KNEC)) which sets and marks examinations at the primary, secondary and technical and vocational level; the Commission for Higher Education (CHE) responsible for university education;

the Higher Education Loan Board (HELB), a body that determines the amount of the loan for university students, provides loans and collects repayments; the Teachers Service Commission (TSC) responsible for employment, deployment, salaries and all matters related to teachers once the teacher has been employed by the TSC; the Kenya Education Staff Institute (KESI) for training staff in MOE but which also provides training for other Government Ministries; the Kenya Institute of Special Education (KISE) which trains staff to teach children of various disabilities; and the Kenya Literature Bureau (KLB) responsible for printing and publishing books for schools.

Among the institutions listed above, those relevant to the success of UPE would be the TSC because it is responsible for the recruitment of teachers which it deploys throughout the country, and for dismissing teachers. It is also responsible for the welfare of teachers in schools, for the payment of their salaries and for arranging in-service training of teachers to improve their quality or to in-service them on new methodology and/or content. The KIE is responsible for curriculum development in all the sub-sectors of education except university – early childhood development, primary, secondary, teacher education and technical and vocational education. Curriculum for universities is done by the universities in collaboration with CHE and through linking with universities in other countries (mainly in the North). The KIE works closely with the Inspectorate and the KNEC.

The Permanent Secretary for Education is responsible for the proper functioning of MOE and is accountable for everything that happens within education and training. MOE is divided into two: the professional wing, and the administrative and managerial wing. The professional wing is headed by the Education Secretary (ES) and responsible directly to the ES are the Directors of Education for: Basic Education, Higher Education, Quality Assurance and Standards; and Policy and Planning. The functions that come under the District Secretary (DS) are: planning, budgeting and financing, and all personnel employed by the MOE at headquarters and those in the provinces and districts.

Education is decentralised from the central headquarters to the provinces, then to districts, divisions and zones. The Provincial Director of Education (PDE) is in charge of all educational services in the province and is responsible for carrying out the mandates and regulations issued by the Permanent Secretary. Below him is the District Education Officers (DEO) who are responsible to him for education in the district. Within each district there are Divisional Education Officers. The larger Divisions have Zonal Education Officers who have dual responsibility for school inspection and teacher development and support. In theory, decisions related to education at the local level can and should be made by the PDE or DEO. In practice decisions are made at the MOE headquarters or through the Provincial Commissioner who is from the Office of the President and is responsible to the President for the management of the province.

A brief outline of each sub-sector

Pre-primary education. In the past 20 years the programme has grown exponentially and has become significant in Kenya. It is for children between the ages of 3 to 5 – before starting primary school at the age of 6 years. The number of children attending pre-primary units in 1990 was 822,796 and there were 20,000 preschool teachers. By 2003, the number of children had increased to 1,207,276, representing a Gross Enrolment Ratio of around 30 per cent.

Before 1980, pre-primary education was the responsibility of Local Authorities, while agencies such as local communities, non-governmental organisations, and various Christian churches made a substantial contribution. In 1980, the Government assumed responsibility for the training of pre-school teachers partly because the social demand for pre-primary education was growing and partly because the quality of teaching and services provided varied so much that the GOK felt that it should step in and provide basic training for teachers at this level of education. In collaboration with donors, the GOK established the National Centre for Early Childhood Education and 14 districts were chosen to participate in the programme as District Centres for Early Childhood Education. The Kenya Institute of Education designed the curriculum, the syllabus and teaching materials.

The development of the facilities and the payment of teachers' salaries continue to remain the responsibilities of parents and the community. With the introduction of FPE in 2003, enrolment in Early Childhood Development programmes declined and this may be due to parents' perception that the cost of pre-primary education was high given that primary education was free.

There is talk of a policy initiative to mainstream pre-school as part of basic education and to integrate 4 to 5 year-old children into the primary cycle by 2010. Primary schools would have a pre-school facility and interested stakeholders would manage this facility. As there has been no clarity of how this would be financed, some donors are strongly opposed to this move.

Primary education. It is in essence the first phase of Kenya's formal education system and officially starts at age 6 in Grade 1 and is completed at age 14 in Grade 8. The curriculum is general – it has a wide variety of subjects to impart: literacy, numeracy, manipulative skills, and basic knowledge in history, civics, geography, literature and science. According to the KIE, primary education should develop the whole person, including the spiritual, mental and physical capacities; to appreciate and respect the dignity of labour and to develop positive attitudes and values towards society. Within cities and towns the medium of instruction is English. Outside towns, the first three grades are taught in the vernacular, with English introduced as a subject. After the third grade, the medium of instruction switches to English. In the last two grades of primary education, pre-vocational skills are introduced.

A diversified curriculum was brought in when the 8-4-4 system of education was introduced in 1984 consisted of 13 teaching subjects of which 7 were examined. The broad curriculum and the extensive selection of subjects required a large amount of resources – both in terms of the number of teachers who had to be trained to teach these subjects and in the actual materials used. The broad curriculum left little time and effort for students to study and master the core subjects to gain essential basic skills. Parents shunned the vocational subjects and, with the economy stagnating, there were less resources available to teach the pre-vocational subjects. An overhaul of the curriculum is currently being undertaken with emphasis placed on the core subjects.

Providing primary education to all has become central to the implementation of the

Poverty Reduction Strategy since the acquisition of basic literacy skills is seen as a means of expanding access to employment opportunities and sustainable livelihoods. The Government's policy was to achieve UPE by the target date of 2005 (but fell short of it) and also to attain Education for All (EFA) by 2015. It is continuing with the policy of providing free and compulsory primary education to all Kenyan children by working in partnership with national and international stakeholders in education to realise UPE and EFA.

The number of trained teachers employed rose from 17,682 in 1963 to 162,072 in 2006 (89,607 male and 72,465 female). During this period and especially since 1990, the number of untrained teachers has been significantly reduced from 61,659 in 1990 to 921 (634 male and 287 female) in 2006. Some of these untrained teachers are recruited directly by the school itself and on a temporary basis.

Recurrent expenditure at the primary level is predominantly personal emoluments in the form of teacher's salaries and other benefits. As a result of the 1997 teacher salary review, nearly 98 per cent of the primary education budget went on teachers' salaries and allowances, leaving less than 2 per cent for operations and maintenance (including spending on the school feeding programme)[3]. The lack of funds for curriculum implementation, for teaching and learning materials and equipment has been stark and the under-resourcing over a period of time has had a detrimental effect on the quality of many primary schools.

At the primary school level there has been significant improvement in the participation of girls. Girls made up only a third of the enrolment in primary schools at independence. By 2005 the proportion of girls had risen and the Gender Parity Index (GPI) for all grades in primary education stood at 0.99. Regional disparities in gender exist in Kenya. Although by 2005, the GPI had been realised at the national level, the disparities range from the remote disadvantaged semi-desert in the North Eastern Province, GPI of 0.71, (an intensely Muslim area where parents are reluctant to send girls to school), to Nairobi Province, GPI of 1.04 (far more girls at school than boys). The anecdotal evidence in Nairobi is that boys have been more disillusioned with the benefits and quality of primary school than girls and have dropped out of school, preferring to earn money in the streets. Also many of these boys are from the slum areas where they have to fend for themselves and school has not given them any credible alternative opportunities.

Secondary education. This consists of a four-year cycle from Form I to Form IV catering to students between the ages of 14 to 17. Apart from the traditional academic subjects for those who proceed to higher education, a vocational element (business and technical education) has been introduced to give a flavour of technical and vocational skills to those who do not proceed to university. But this has been unpopular with parents especially as there have been problems both with the design and the practicality of the curriculum. The vocational element has had the same fate as the primary education curriculum and is in the process of being revised.

There are three main categories of public secondary schools: national; provincial; and district secondary schools. The 17 national secondary schools are the best endowed with facilities and resources. Together they produce the most number of pupils for university –

and for this reason they are in the greatest demand. It is every parent's hope that their child will get admission to a national secondary school. Admission is by merit and a district quota has been established with the top achieving students gaining admission to the 17 national secondary schools. The provincial schools are a second best resort. The rest of the government schools are the district schools which vary in quality having limited provision and resources. A number of the district secondary schools were built through funds collected by the community through the vigorous *Harambee*[4] movement. These secondary schools have since been taken up by the Government. Annual fees charged for secondary education vary from the equivalent of US$100 to $300 a year.

Private secondary schools have mushroomed in Kenya and vary in quality. In 2006 there were 722 private secondary schools. Some of the good private secondary schools offer excellent curricula and extra-curriculum activities, have good and well maintained facilities, a more committed teaching force and are generally better than the national schools. They compete favourably for places at the national universities. The private schools at the lower-end of quality are mainly a money-making enterprise and in the last few years the Inspectorate and the Schools Registration Section have been monitoring these schools with a view to close the non-performing ones.

Expansion in secondary education has been tremendous. Between 1963 and 2006, enrolment grew from 30,000 to 1,030,080 and the number of schools expanded from 151 to 4,247. By the end of the period, the number of teachers employed was 49,105. Of the total enrolment in 2006, girls accounted for 47 per cent of enrolment and the GER for the same year is 32.4 per cent. The transition rate from primary to secondary schools has also increased from 44.6 per cent in 1990 to 60 per cent in 2006.

Policy priorities for secondary education are geared towards increasing access to secondary education, especially for girls and for disadvantaged groups such as the disabled, AIDS orphans, street children and Children in Difficult Circumstances (CEDC). A bursary scheme had been established to provide support for children from economically poor backgrounds but it was not well targeted, supervised and lacked transparency. As it was often given to cronies of those administering the scheme, MOE is currently reviewing the programme. Due to the increased number of pupils attending primary schools, it is the policy of the Ministry to increase transition rates to secondary education by 70 per cent, 80 per cent and 90 per cent by 2008, 2012 and 2015, respectively.

Technical education. Technical education in the MOE is offered at the tertiary level at the National Polytechnics. There are 4 national polytechnics with a total enrolment of 10,472 in 2001. The national polytechnics are at the apex of technical training and provide courses leading to diplomas and degrees.

The Harambee Institutes of Technology, now known as the Institutes of Technology (IT) were built by communities as part of the *Harambee* movement to provide some post-secondary training to those who did not get into the national polytechnics or university. Most of the subjects taught initially were business education, secretarial skills and some level of computer training as these were low on recurrent cost. A number of the better-endowed ITs now offer courses in electric engineering, mechanical engineering, building and carpentry. The courses offered are not at the same level as the national polytechnics.

Technical, Industrial and Vocational Education (TIVET) is also offered by the Ministry of Labour and Human Resource Development. The Village Polytechnics, mainly funded by the community, with subsidy from MLHRD, offer courses in artisan and crafts for post-primary students and secondary school drop-outs. The Institutes of Technology offer courses at the post-secondary level, some of which are similar to those offered at the ITs. In addition, courses are also offered to firms for individuals who have started working and need a proficient course to boost their skills.

Teacher education and training: *Primary teachers*. There are 29 public and 8 private colleges that offer pre-service education and training to teachers of primary schools in a two-year residential course. In 2003, there were 16,794 students enrolled in state teacher training colleges (51 per cent were female) and the 8 private teacher training colleges enrolled about 4,500 students. Annual output of qualified teachers is in the order of 10,000. The public colleges operate below their capacity of approximately 18,000 (about 1,500 places not used). Apart from providing an in-service two-year full time residential course, the public teacher training colleges also provide a three-year distance learning and part-time residential course to up-grade and up-date teachers in the service. A quota system for admission exists to provide regional balance and provision is made from those in disadvantaged areas to be admitted with lower grades. The current recruitment criteria have no special emphasis on subject grades, resulting in poorly qualified teachers particularly in science and mathematics.

Secondary teachers. There are two public secondary school diploma teachers' colleges that offer a pre-service course of 3 years. There are 5 universities (4 public and 1 private) offering degree programmes leading to a Bachelor of Education degree. The degree programme is 4 years.

Kenya appears to be one of the few Sub-Saharan African countries not suffering from a lack of trained primary school teachers. Currently the supply of teachers outstrips the demand. Not only are there surplus trained teachers graduating from teacher training colleges, there is also the budgetary implication if all these teachers were employed – paying their salaries and pension. There is a strict code, based on classrooms, of how many teachers can be deployed to each school. Schools may wish to have additional teachers to cope with the number of primary school children but they have to pay the salaries of these teachers from school funds. Many of the public primary schools cannot afford them. The dilemma of surplus primary school teachers became particularly acute in 1995 when the supply of trained teachers outstripped the actual demand for them. The MOE and the Teachers Service Commission were forced to change its statutes on its recruitment policy in 1997. Previously, every trained teacher was guaranteed employment in schools. After 1997, the recruitment and deployment of teachers was decentralised and made dependent on the number of vacancies in that year in the district. In addition, there were stipulations on the employment of these teachers. One was that teachers employed would serve in that specific school and district for a minimum of 5 years before being considered for a transfer. This was designed to regulate the deployment of teachers whereby urban areas had teacher-pupil ratios of 1:20 while the rural areas, particularly those in arid areas, had teacher-pupil ratios of 1:45. Prior to the third attempt at UPE in 2003, the national pupil-teacher ratio was around 1:31, very favourable for a country in Sub-Saharan Africa! Anecdotal evidence suggests that Kenyan trained teachers are getting jobs in other Africa countries, particularly in Eastern and Southern Africa, where the demand for trained and qualified teachers is high. Teachers also had substantial increases in their salaries over a two year period between 1996 and 1998. The new regulations are to make it imperative for schools and teachers to be utilised efficiently.

University. It is the apex of Kenya's formal education and training system. In addition to preparing high level manpower for national development, the universities also undertake research, development and dissemination of knowledge.

Enrolment at university has been steadily increasing since the establishment of the University of Nairobi in 1970. By 1980 the University of Nairobi could no longer cope with the demand for university admissions and between 1985 and 1992 there was an unprecedented expansion in capacity. Six universities were established and enrolment jumped from 9,044 in 1985 to 43,290 in 1992. As a result of this rapid expansion, most universities lacked adequate teaching facilities and materials, adequately trained lecturers and the necessary social amenities such as student and staff housing and related facilities.

The demand for university education continues unabated. One reason is the low transition rate of 4 per cent from secondary to university and this has resulted in the mushrooming of private universities to fill in the gap. At the time of writing, there were 17 private universities (6 private universities have been officially accredited, all varying in quality and in the type of degree offered. Total enrolment in public and private universities is about 72,000 students; annual intake in public universities of students with some public subsidy is around 10,000 and there is also an annual intake of 4,000 self-sponsored students, who bear the whole cost themselves. In addition, the private universities enrol about 6,000 annually.

In the public universities, undergraduate education generally consists of a 4-year course culminating in a Bachelors degree; specialist courses such as medicine may take 6 years. Supervision of universities is assured by the Commission for Higher Education (CHE).

Cost-sharing exists at the public universities. MOE pays around US$1,270 per student and students pay US$500. Self sponsored students pay fees ranging from around US$2,400 for an Arts degree to $5,400 for Medicine.

The three attempts at UPE

In order to discuss UPE and the three efforts made, it is necessary to review the context of the importance of education to Kenyans which has its roots and determination in the colonial era.

The colonial era

Education in Kenya was segregated and stratified along the lines of race, gender and creed. The central government provided education to all European children whose parents were working in Kenya. Some provision was made to African schools (it was argued that there were insufficient resources to provide education to all African children) and some provision to Asian schools. Christian missionaries and local communities were left to fill in the gap. Although the central government did provide some grants to schools, which were supplemented by the missionaries' own resources, there was a shortfall and fees had to be charged to make up for running the school, providing teaching materials and equipment, furniture and construction[5]. In addition to paying fees, parents had to buy text books and exercise books for their children.

The curriculum was also affected by the segregation mentioned. There were three types of curriculum – one for the European schools, another for the Asian schools and another for the African schools. European and Asian education had a 7 year basic cycle while African education had an 8-year cycle made up of two cycles of 4 years each. Those who passed Grade 4 and wished to continue with education could go on to Grade 5. In addition, African education had an over-emphasis on practical learning as compared to the broad-based academic education offered in both European and Asian schools. The response of the Africans to this was to build their own schools in opposition to the government schools and their policy – thus started the Independent Schools based mainly in the Central Province in Kenya. By 1952 there were over 400 Independent Primary Schools[6] funded through self-help and it laid down the foundation for community participation in education through the *Harambee* movement, once independence had been achieved[7]. The significance of the Independent Schools was to highlight the importance of education, something that future heads of government and politicians wanting to rise to prominence could not ignore. Indeed, it had political undertones with distinct political consequences.

Post independence period – from December 1963 onwards

The Kenya African National Union (KANU), the political party that won the elections, had Universal Primary Education in its manifesto: 'every child in Kenya shall have a minimum of seven years free education' (Kenya African National Union 1963 and 1969). When Jomo Kenyatta became the first President of Kenya, reform in education began. The ruling party explicitly stated that the government would be guided by the principle in the KANU manifesto. Within two weeks of the party taking over from the colonial administration, the government appointed Professor Simeon Ominde to undertake a review of the segregated education system and propose a way forward for all ethnic groups. Professor Ominde produced the Kenya Education Commission Report in 1964 which recommended a unified system offering one curriculum that would foster national unity and the creation of the critical mass of human capital required for national development. Policies to integrate the various ethnic groups were also undertaken, one of which was to pay fees to those African families whose children had the basic education requirements to enter primary or secondary schools but could not afford the fees in former European or Asian schools.

Reviews of the Kenyan education and training system have since been undertaken periodically (about every 10 years), or if there is a particular issue to look into. The Government usually appoints a committee, a working group or a commission to review, advise and suggest recommendations to the Government[8]. This practice has kept education in the forefront of the minds of the public. Some milestone reports are: the Report of the National Committee on Educational Objectives and Policies in 1976, which focused on redefining Kenya's educational policies and objectives; the Report of the Presidential Working Party on the Second University in Kenya, which led to the introduction of the current structure of education the 8-4-4 system; the Report of the Presidential Working Party on Education and Manpower Training for the Next Decade and Beyond in 1988 which focused on education financing, quality and relevance; and, finally, The Report of the Commission of Inquiry into the Education System of Kenya in 2000, which recommended an integrated curriculum but which the government did not accept due to cost implications. Its recommendation on reviewing all the curricula in primary and secondary education has been adopted and is being implemented.

As indicated earlier, at Independence primary education was almost exclusively the responsibility of the local communities or non-governmental agencies such as local churches and was under the jurisdiction of the former colonial Regional Authority. In 1966, the Kenya African National Union, with its centralist tendencies, needed to weaken the Regional Authorities particularly as some of the Provinces had voted and were aligned with the opposition party, the Kenya African Democratic Union (KADU). The strategy used was to move primary schools to the newly formed Local Authorities (different name but similar functions to the Regional Authorities) and at the same time remove the revenue base of the Local Authorities. De facto, the control of primary education became dependent on central government subventions through the Local Authorities.

The government merely wanted to extend influence and control over those who were responsible for primary schools. During this period it was preoccupied with and was giving priority to post-primary education in order to facilitate the Africanisation of middle-level and high-level positions in the economy (Republic of Kenya, 1966). It took over the best secondary schools, which became government-maintained schools (government provided funding for capital and recurrent expenditure and had a say in admissions) and Kenya's first university was established in 1970, the University of Nairobi – which was wholly funded by the government. A snapshot of government financing to education illustrates this point. In 1969 the unit cost of primary education was 0.31, while that of secondary education was 38.84, and university was 541.55.

By the 1970s Africanisation was well under way and secondary and university education were well established. The government was then in a position to give primary education the attention it deserved and to enable KANU, (the party still in government) to fulfil their independence manifesto and pledges.

As discussed above, the jurisdiction over primary education had been passed on to Local Authorities, who paid a small grant to schools and this was topped-up with contributions from religious bodies and through fees payable by parents for the running and maintenance of schools. The amount of fees charged varied from school to school depending on the facilities (library and stock of books, swimming pool, sports field, etc.), and the number of subjects taught and the number of teachers and staff employed. Wishing to make the provision of education more homogeneous, the government made its second move in 1970. Primary schools were to be designated as either private schools with no funding from the government or public schools i.e. eligible for some funding by the central government. As many of the missionary and community run schools were dependent on the Local Authorities for the payment of teacher's salaries, they opted to become public schools. The MOE took over the control of the administration and the provision of school revenue and with this move, the financial cost of primary education, including teachers' salaries, was shifted to the MOE. The effect of the take-over on the Government's financial responsibility can be seen in the following figures: in 1969, the primary education budget was K£397,441, representing 5.04 per cent of the total recurrent budget for education; in 1970, the cost of education jumped to K£3,212,670, representing 25.97 per cent of recurrent expenditure on education, or an increase of over 700 per cent over the previous year.

With the aim of speeding up the progress of universal primary education, President Jomo Kenyatta announced the removal of fees in primary education, starting in 1974. The section below will discuss the circumstances, the policies and the outcome of the First Surge in primary school enrolments.

The first attempt – 1974

Nine years after independence, in 1973, President Jomo Kenyatta announced that from 1974 tuition fees would be abolished for the first four grades of primary education. The first four grades were chosen because this had previously been a cycle in itself for African schools in the segregated education system prior to independence (as described earlier, African primary education was 8 years with two 4-year cycles), and had then been replaced with a 7-year cycle. The four years of free primary education would to encourage those outside the school system, for whatever reason, to enrol in schools thereby giving them a flavour of primary education. It must be remembered, that at this time, children were needed to help their parents either at work or in the household and some parents had to be persuaded to send their children to school.

Enrolments in primary education had been growing steadily but slowly (Chart 3.1). In the 10 years of independence from 1963 to 1973, enrolment grew from 891,553 to 1,816,017 children in primary schools. Enrolment was growing at an annual average rate of around 7.5 per cent. However, with the announcement of free primary education for Grades 1 to 4, the enrolment rate between 1973 and 1974 increased dramatically to 49 per cent in one single year! In actual numbers, enrolment grew from 1,816,017 children enrolled in 1973 to 2,705,878 in 1974 – almost a million more children attended school. The following year in 1975, the growth rate fell back to the pre-announcement time and is recorded as 6.5 per cent.

Over the next few years the enrolment growth tapered off. While in absolute terms there was a modest increase in numbers, there were many who dropped out of school and many of those outside the school system did not enrol. Why were these gains not maintained?

a   *Government inability to sustain the finances.* In its enthusiasm to take over primary
    schools, which previously had been partly financed by religious bodies and the
    community, the government had taken on a financial burden which it was not able

to sustain at levels that schools themselves were able to sustain. Teacher's salaries took much of the budget and there was little left to give schools for operations and maintenance. Quality of education took a nose-dive and parents withdrew their children from school.

b   *Demand on parents to construct schools.* Parents and the community were responsible for constructing the additional schools and classrooms where necessary. While some school management committees allowed those parents who could not afford to pay in monetary terms to contribute in labour, other school committees insisted on the monetary payment of building fees as being conditional to enrolment and attendance. Parents who could not afford to pay for school building funds withdrew their children from school.

c   *Over crowding of classrooms and the effect on quality.* The expanded enrolments meant that, until additional classrooms were built, school children had to be crammed into the existing classrooms, putting a strain on teachers as pupil-teacher ratios rose. The quality of education was compromised in those schools that had high pupil-teacher ratios. To remedy this situation, untrained teachers were hired. Total teacher recruitment increased by 22,000 in one year – from 56,543 in 1973 to 78,340 in 1974. With the output of teachers colleges at around 1,500 trained teachers a year, the 21,797 additional teachers required in 1974 were recruited largely from a pool of untrained people willing to teach, thus began a pool of untrained teachers. The total number of untrained teachers in the system grew from 5,411 in 1973 to 26,208 in 1974. By the following year, 1975, the number of untrained teachers had risen to 31,284, bringing the proportion of untrained teachers to trained teachers in primary education to 37 per cent, that is over one-third of the existing teaching force was untrained. While the Kenya National Union of Teachers insisted that untrained teachers provided reasonable education, it was clear that quality of education had plummeted and that parents preferred to have their children as child labour/domestic labour, where they could be earning some money instead of wasting their time and money in school.

d   *Introduction of levies.* With the realisation that facilities could not be maintained, schools gradually began to impose levies on parents – officially the levies could not be referred to as fees, since these had been abolished by Presidential decree. Parents were levied on school maintenance and development costs. In addition, parents had to buy school books and equipment. The children of those who could not afford the levies dropped out of school.

e   *Fees re-imposed in Grade 5.* Data shows that when fees were encountered in Grade 5, children dropped-out of school (Somerset, 2007). Although school fees were only US$8 per annum, it had clearly acted as a deterrent to school participation for children from low-income families (ibid., Somerset). Poverty associated with the cost of education contributed to parents withdrawing their children from school.

Chart 3.1. Enrolment (thousands) in public primary schools 1963–2006

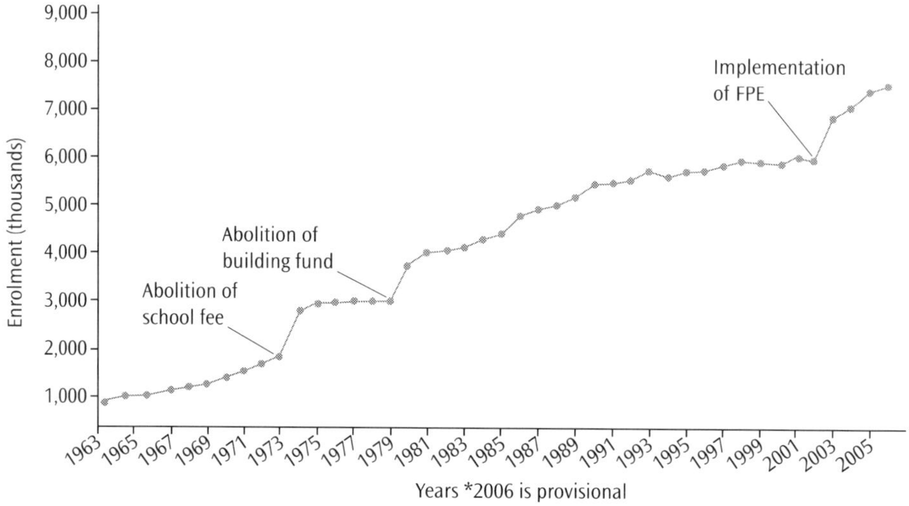

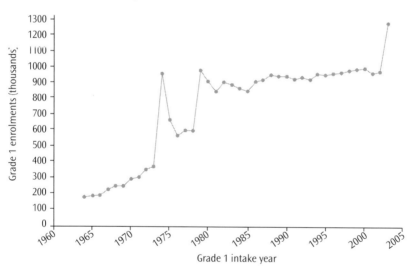

Source: Somerset, A. (2007) & MOE Education Statistical data * Provisional

Chart 3.2. Grade 1 Primary school enrolment 1963 to 2006

Source: Somerset, A. (2007) & MOE Education Statistical data

The second attempt – 1978

Between 1975 and 1978, parents and the communities bore the cost of building schools, building teacher's houses and buying text books for their children, while the Government paid for teachers' salaries. During this period many schools had increased their building levies to cope with the increase in enrolments. To add to the financial burden of parents for new school buildings and classrooms, construction costs unfortunately escalated during this period due to higher oil prices, restrictions being imposed on private credit to combat mishandled coffee boom money, and the closure of the Tanzania border (East African

Kenya's three iniatives in UPE

Community break-up), leading to tighter import restrictions[9]. Classrooms that had previously cost US$1,300 in 1974 were costing about US$ 3,900, over three times as much by 1978 (ibid., Somerset). Schools transferred these increased costs as higher building levies on parents, who were now paying between five and ten times as much as the original tuition fee that had been abolished. Parents who had more than one child at school, often had had to remove some siblings to enable at least one child to attend school.

In 1978 President Daniel Arap Moi became Kenya's second president, after the death of President Kenyatta. Having come from the ranks of being a primary school teacher before entering politics and being nominated the Vice-President a few years after independence, he was aware of the hardship and problems parents faced. The following year in 1979 he announced that primary education from Grade 1 to Grade 7 would be free and that schools could no longer collect building levies from families whose children had enrolled in schools. Funds for building schools could only be raised through the joint effort of the community and not households, giving a fresh impetus to the *Harambee* movement. In addition, he also introduced the free school milk scheme, whereby children would get a packet of milk twice a week to improve their nutrition. The School Milk Scheme was introduced in schools in 1981 and the Scheme lasted until 1998.

Enrolments surged for a second time, rising from 2,994,894 in 1978 to 3,698,246 in 1979, an increase of 703,352 or 23.5 per cent. It showed that the financial burden on parents had been great. Those children who had dropped out of school at re-entered the school system at every grade and it was not uncommon to find boys with sprouting beards sitting with 7 year-old children. The profile of children over the age of 8 years old in Grade 1 can be seen in the table 3.1. below. In Grade 1 alone there was an increase of 63 per cent in enrolment.

Table 3.1. Age profile of Kenya Grade 1 enrollees in 1978 and 1979

Age	1978	1979	Percentage increase 1978 to 1979
6 years	260,500	339,200	30
7 years	220,900	364,300	65
8 and 9 years	106,200	230,400	117
10 years plus	11,500	43,400	278
Total 6 to 10	**599,100**	**977,400**	**63**

Source: Somerset 2006

It is also interesting to note from the table above that while the number of 6 year olds increased by only 30 per cent, the number of children of 8 years and above increased by 395 per cent, the largest increase being among those over the age of 10 years. This indicates that it was the out-of-school children who took advantage of the no school levy policy, most probably because they were unable to afford to pay the levies.

The MOE accommodated this increase by hiring only a modest number of teachers, unlike the first surge in 1974 when thousands of teachers were recruited. In the second surge, teachers recruited increased from 90,391 in 1978 to 92,827 in 1979, an increase of 2,436 or only 3 per cent. The expanded primary school enrolments were accommodated through increased class sizes. Pupil-teacher ratios rose from 33.13 to 39.84 during the same two years. There was a public outcry and the social pressure to recruit more teachers became political. In the following year, the government gave in and allowed the Teachers Service Commission in 1980, to recruit 9,662 more teachers, most of whom were untrained. Pupil-teacher ratios dropped to 38.31 and continued dropping gradually until they were 30.4 in 1995.

Enrolments continued to increase like the 1974 group at a steady but slow pace. GER reached a peak of 95 per cent in 1985 but by 1990 it had fallen to 88.8 per cent and on the eve of the third surge in 2002, it had declined to 87.6 per cent. Drop-out rates were also high particularly between Grade 1 and 2 , which had a rate of 26 per cent. By the time the 1979 cohort reached Grade 5, nearly 45 per cent of the children had dropped out of school; similarly, by the time the 1986 cohort had reached Grade 7, only 32.2 per cent of the original cohort remained (Somerset 2006).

Why did enrolment level off when school fees and building fees had been abolished? The attainment of UPE failed despite 'free primary education' and a state-funded scheme to supply free milk to primary school children due to a number of reasons:

a *Very large class sizes.* Additional teachers had not been recruited in time and the increased school population was accommodated through increased class sizes. These classes were too large to teach and very little learning took place. Students, disillusioned with school, dropped out.

b *Basic classrooms and facilities were lacking.* Temporary class rooms were constructed, which were wholly inadequate for the purpose. The lack of facilities was even worse in Grade 1. Grade 1 was considered not to be as important as the higher grades and in many instances the former Grade 1 classrooms became Grade 5, 6 or 7. Grade 1 children were taught in the open air (under the shade of trees) or in the school corridors. There was an increase of 63 per cent in Grade 1 between 1978 and 1988. It was the over-aged children in this category who became disillusioned with education and dropped out – perhaps for the second time.

c *Lack of teaching and learning materials.* The lack of adequate class-rooms was compounded by the lack of adequate teaching and learning materials. The employment of additional teachers meant that more funds had to be sought for teachers' emoluments. The Government had increasingly narrowed its contribution to four main line items: Of the total primary education budget, 92 per cent was for teachers' salaries and benefits; 6 per cent to the provision of school milk (ended in 1988); 1.4 per cent to boarding schools in the Arid and Semi-Arid areas; and 0.6 per cent to school equipment (Republic of Kenya 1988, and Appropriation Accounts 1990/91). By 1998, with salary increases being awarded to teachers, their pay alone took up 98 per cent of the entire primary school budget with only 2 per cent left for boarding schools in the Arid and Semi-Arid areas and for teaching and learning resources. MOE was unable to provide teacher's manuals or books, nor even basic teaching tools such as chalk and dusters. School teachers reported that chalk was kept in the head teacher's office and each teacher was given a piece of chalk in the morning and had to account for its usage at the end of the class.

d   *Untrained teachers and poor quality of education.* The untrained teachers were given the lower grades to teach. Often they had no prior training and were recruited from the ranks of unemployed secondary school leavers. These school leavers were not committed to the teaching profession but accepted employment as teachers as it provided them with a means of earning their living. Parents became disenchanted and kept their children at home, especially girls and young children who had to walk long distances to school.

e   *Child labour.* In some areas of Kenya (Nyanza, Eastern, Coast and Central Kenya) the opportunity cost of parents sending their children to school was very high. This is because labour is needed in the coffee, tea and sugarcane plantations, fishing, sand harvesting, quarrying, etc. Therefore, if there is very little learning going on at schools, children drop out of schools to engage in the workforce to supplement household incomes (MOE Workshop Paper[10]).

f   *Pre-vocational element not well designed or planned.* In changing the structure of education from a 7-4-2-3 to an 8-4-4 system, President Moi instructed that a vocational element be introduced in the curriculum. The KIE was either unprepared or did not have the capacity to prepare the curriculum and train teachers. The design had flaws, and the implementation had problems with very little guidance and instruction for teachers, head-teachers and the Inspectorate. Implementation was by trial and error and very clumsy. Parents did not want it. Parents wanted education to have core academic subjects, which would hold their children in good stead when leaving school and were unhappy with the new curriculum. In addition, the MOE did not have the funds to pay for vocational education (the practical content is very expensive). The cost of the materials for vocational education was gradually shifted to parents who took their children out of school.

g   *Impact of the primary school league tables.* The KNEC calculated league tables in 1978 which established merit orders based on the Certificate of Primary Education (CPE) scores at two levels of aggregation – first at the District Level and then within each district at the school level. It became a major public issue – politicians, government officials, unions and newspaper editors joined in the lively debate. Trophies were established to give recognition to schools that performed best (Somerset 2007). To enhance the position of the school in the district, school principals had to ensure that the mean scores of all the candidates taking the CPE examination were high. It became advantageous to the school that the academically weaker children, by repeating the previous grade, would hopefully rise up to the standard required for the CPE examination and could move on to the final primary school class. Parents of weaker children were opposed to their children having to repeat, and those who felt strongly about it and could not afford to have their child repeat and stay longer at school, withdrew their children from school.

h *Cost-sharing gradually began to creep in again.* With a lack of budgetary provision from the MOE for the running and upkeep of schools, schools began to fall apart. Because funds for running and maintaining schools was only permissible through the *Harambee* movement, the Parents-Teachers Association put pressure on parents to contribute to the maintenance of schools through *Harambee.* Parents from economically poor backgrounds felt victimised for being forced to contribute to *Harambee* funds because in many instances their contribution was made a condition for the admission of their children to school. Parents who could not afford to contribute to the *Harambee* pulled their children out of school. The report of the Presidential Working Party on Education and Training for the Next Decade and Beyond (1988) recommended the introduction of cost-sharing. Other than teachers' emoluments, parents, through the Parents Teachers Association, and with the help of the community, were responsible for primary education.

i *Poverty.* The Second Poverty Report in Kenya (2000) reported that 56 per cent of Kenyans lived on or were below the poverty line. According to this report 30.7 per cent of the children out of school cited poverty as the main reason for not attending school. Further evidence of poverty was found in the Arid and Semi Arid Lands where household food security is a problem. The World Food Programme provides a school meal to children in these areas to encourage their parents to send them to school. When food was not delivered to schools (poor transportation and/or organisation), enrolment dropped and schools were closed (MOE Workshop Paper). Parents took their children out of school to help in household activities (collecting firewood, bringing water, looking after younger siblings, or assisting with the grazing of livestock). This gesture also highlights the value that parents place on schooling – which should be that learning is taking place which will be beneficial to their children, but clearly it is not.

j *HIV/AIDS.* HIV/AIDS has emerged as another cause of school drop-outs. When parents have become too sick to provide for their children, the older children are forced to leave school to take care of their parents and their younger siblings. The younger ones are eventually removed from school because there is no money to pay fees.

Parents' reaction to Education during the Moi era could be summed up as disillusion, disenchantment and disappointment. It is no wonder that the GER fell from 95 per cent in 1985 to 87.6 per cent in 2002.

The third attempt – 2003 – on-going

President Mwai Kibaki succeeded Moi in December 2002 after a general election. It was the first time since independence that an opposition party had won the national political election and could form the government. Kibaki and the National Rainbow Coalition (NARC) broke 40 years of political dominance by one political party that had ruled Kenya. While Kibaki was in opposition, there was a growing national and international consensus (various lobbies of mulit-lateral and bi-lateral agencies, international NGOs and civil society groups) that NARC should take action immediately to fulfil Kenya's commitment of achieving the EFA target of UPE by 2015 through abolishing school fees and levies. In its manifesto published in 2002, NARC pledged that it would provide free and compulsory primary education to all children. Kenya was a signatory to the Jomtien and Dakar agreements.

On taking over the reins of government, President Mwai Kibaki's first policy pronouncement was to make primary education a focal point of his presidency. He immediately directed that 'Free Primary Education' (FPE) should be implemented in January 2003 at the start of the school year.

President Kibaki inherited an education system that was crumbling and of poor quality and the brave decision he had taken had not been planned for. There were just a few weeks from the time the national elections were held (end of December) and the swearing in of the new government in January 2003, when Kibaki made his Acceptance Speech in which he talked about free primary education. The beginning of the school year for primary and secondary schools in January also added to the planning crisis.

Events have been recorded thus: 'On Saturday, 4th January, the Minister for Education clarified the pre-election pledge – no child would be required to pay any form of fees or levies to any public primary school, and that every child regardless of age should report to the nearest public primary school for admission' (MOE Workshop Paper 2006). The new academic year was due to start on 6th January 2003 and the Minister put together a task force and summoned them to a crisis meeting on the same day, Saturday, to work out the strategies for the implementation of Free Primary Education (FPE) programme. No provision in the existing budget had been made for FPE (the Kenya financial year is from June to July) and the government could not wait until the end in June 2003 to allocate additional funds to primary education (the school academic year is from January to December). With no budget or any formal plans, the policy was seen as a mirage and wishful thinking of a new and inexperienced government. The fear was that quality would also be compromised.

Two days later, on 6th January, those who had been out of school reported to the closest school as the announcement, indicated. Expansion in primary education again jump-started for the third time with enrolments in public primary schools increasing from 5.9 million in 2002 to 7.2 million in 2004 (an increase of 22 per cent), representing a GER of 99 per cent (102 per cent girls; 97 per cent boys – MOE Census Data). Universal and free primary education in 2003 opened the school system to everyone who wanted a primary education – both over-age and under-age people came into primary school. One person who made headlines was an 82 year old the man, a Mr Kimani Ng'ang'a, who started primary education at Grade 1 and would not be persuaded to attend adult literacy classes because according to him, adult literacy was under-funded and lacked material and qualified teachers. In 2007 he was still in school, in primary Grade 5.

Between 2003 and 2007, UPE or rather FPE (Free Primary Education) has continued to expand, has continued to be a government priority and has continued to receive government support. How has the government organised it this time to make it work and what did it do differently?

a *Professionals from outside the government were included in the Task Force.* Membership was drawn from a cross-section of stakeholder groups (civil society organisations, education professionals, Faith Based Organisations, the media, NGOs/INGOs, multi-lateral and bi-lateral aid agencies).[11] By including NGOs and aid agencies, the MOE ensured that it would get the best range of advice and the best deal with civic society.

    i   NGOs and Aid Agencies boosted the capacity of MOE and Treasury officials by working alongside them to assist with realistic plans, to identify potential problems and to attempt to solve them or to work around them.

    ii In addition, the move to bring aid agencies into the planning process right at the beginning, transferred responsibility for the success of the programme onto them. Organisations represented in the Task Force were the first to offer financial assistance to the fledging programme. They also arranged to form a coalition with other donors to support the programme.

    iii The media also felt that they could not be critical about the plan or the government because they too were responsible for the implementation of the ambitious programme.

b *Participatory approach.* The Task Force involved the community at the grass roots at the outset of the planning programme and empowered them to take ownership of the programme.

    i   The media were used to publicise FPE; its implication, expectations and potential impact to the communities

    ii At the local level, the communities were involved in the planning and decision making process. Local plans were designed incorporating short-term strategies that the communities could support.

    iii The MOE sent its officers to the field to work with the local Education officials and to carry out a rapid assessment of the situation on the ground and to collect data to inform the planning process.

c *Resource mobilisation.* The government, together with donors and interested stakeholders, embarked on a rapid resource mobilisation exercise for the programme.

    i   A technical team was formed and it determined an acceptable unit cost for financing FPE.

    ii Actual funds harnessed were:

        a Supplementary funds from the government were released to facilitate the programme until the end of June – approximately US$31.6 million was disbursed. Another US$6.8 million under emergency funding was provided by the government;

        b DFID gave an initial grant of US$21.1 million; UNICEF gave US$2.5 million;

        c Financing during the year came from: The World Bank US$50 million to increase institutional capacity and for instructional materials; DFID, together with SIDA, gave an additional US$10.6 million; WFP US$13.9 million; OPEC US$9.9 million; there were other smaller donations from Oxfam (GB), Action Aid, etc.;

        d A fund was started for well-wishers who wanted to support the FPE programme and during the first year a total of US$10,500 was collected.

d *Funds sent directly to schools from the MOE.* The 'good practice' experience of the Dutch government in two districts in Kenya was replicated. Each school had to open two bank accounts (some schools had never had bank accounts and consequently there were teething problems with the accidental interchanging of numbers etc). The MOE signed an agreement with the commercial banks requesting minimal charges to schools. By electronically transferring the funds directly into the schools' bank accounts from the MOE headquarters twice a year, the funds by-passed the Provincial and District offices (where leakages and irregularities could occur), thereby safeguarding the totality of the funds.

e *Parents-Teachers committees set up.* Every school had to have a School Management Committee, which consisted of the head-teacher as secretary and the rest of the members were elected by parents from the school's Parents Association. A unit cost per school grade had been identified and parents were informed that the funds their school was to receive depended on the number of children in each grade multiplied by the amount. This was the capitation grant. Each child was to receive a certain number of text books, exercise books, pens, pencils and a compass set. Anecdotal evidence indicated that if children went home without the stipulated number of books, pens etc., parents came to the school to demand to know what had happened and threatened the head and teachers that they would report them to the government. Such was the extent to which the media and the government had galvanised parents and the communities. A clear lesson was that parents appeared to be the best custodians of their children's education once they were empowered.

f *The two school accounts.* (i) The School Instructional Materials Bank Account (SIMBA). The total amount the school received was based on the number of children in each class multiplied by the unit cost of that grade. To ensure transparency, the signatory to the account was not a member of the SMC but was accountable to it. Heads were also in-serviced on the accuracy and promptness of reporting enrolment to the MOE, without which funds could not be disbursed. (ii) The second account was the General Purpose Account (GPA) which was for operation and maintenance expenses of the school. Neither of the two accounts was for teachers' salaries.

g *Transparency in the use of the funds.* Each school had to draw up charts on manila paper (also sent to schools). One chart had enrolment by class and gender; the second chart had the school accounts on it for the SIMBA, and a third chart had the GPA on it. These were to be displayed either outside the head's office or in the head's office at all times. Inspectors and MOE officials could visit schools at random and check enrolment and the use of the funds. The system has worked well and the MOE has agreed that it would be in use every year.

h *There were two notable champions during the third attempt.* The first two attempts at UPE did not have champions and hence they failed. The third attempt has been steered in a dedicated manner by Professor George Saitoti, who has a credible track record for being able to steer difficult reforms. He is a mathematician by profession and has a good understanding of educational issues such as finance, access and quality of education (he was previously Minister of Finance and is well versed in the relationship of education to GDP, and education and the productive sectors). He made a vigorous attempt to engage with interested stakeholders and donors and has taken a personal interest and ownership of the implementation on FPE. He went abroad and met with various donors to obtain sufficient funding to cover at least seven years of the implementation of FPE during which it is expected that the domestic capacity to finance will have grown[12]. Professor Karega Mutahi, Permanent Secretary to the Ministry of Education has also been a driving force to implement FPE and has travelled throughout the country listening to people's problems in the implementation process and trying to remedy the problems. The two champions in the Ministry – the Permanent Secretary and the Minister of Education – worked in harmony and were determined that FPE would succeed; the success so far should be credited to the two of them.

The impact of FPE

Teachers. The number of teachers rose marginally on the third attempt. Total number of primary teachers rose from 172,424 in 2002 to 176,887 in 2004, an increase of only 2.4 per cent. The MOE was unable to employ additional classes for the expanded primary population because of the need to contain the wage bill. At the time of writing, there was an IMF freeze on employing teachers and a ceiling was being imposed on the recruitment of all civil servants. According to the freeze, total MOE salaries, including teacher remuneration, should not exceed 5.2 per cent as a percentage of GDP. It has been argued that there are two reasons for this. One is that education spending in Kenya as a percentage of GDP is estimated as 6.6 per cent compared to 3.6 per cent for Sub-Saharan Africa. These expenditures are skewed towards wages and salaries. The second reason is that pupil-teacher ratios are low, particularly at secondary level – estimated to be at 21:1 in 2005[13].

The non-recruitment of additional teachers in primary education has apparently increased the efficiency of the utilisation of teachers. Teacher-pupil ratios rose from 31:1 in 2002 to 40:1 in 2004. In Kenya, the supply of trained teachers is greater than demand

Table 3.2. Teachers in public primary schools and pupil-teacher ratios 2002–04, Kenya

Province	Number of teachers			Pupil-teacher ratio		
	2002	2003	2004	2002	2003	2004
Coast	10,398	10,527	10,783	35.1	43.6	48.8
Central	24,176	23,709	23,303	33.0	35.8	36.5
Eastern	36,386	36,815	36,573	31.5	35.0	36.9
Nairobi	4,117	4,007	4,189	35.3	48.1	48.5
Rift Valley	44,685	46,897	46,603	33.1	36.8	38.1
Western	21,933	22,718	22,753	40.1	46.1	48.0
Nyanza	29,467	30,611	31,205	34.4	41.9	40.3
North-Eastern	1,262	1,288	1,478	38.2	50.0	45.6
Total	172,424	176,572	176,887	34.1	39.1	40.3

Source: Ministry of Education and the Teachers Service Commission

and there is a surplus over 600,000 trained teachers. However, it has to be noted that national teacher-pupil ratios are deceptive. Great disparities exist. The ratio of 40:1 is the national average which does not reflect the true picture in marginalised and economically poor areas. Highly populated areas such as those in the urban slums and some rural areas have high class sizes – some schools are over-crowded and have a ratio of 100:1. In the more sparsely populated affluent urban areas, class sizes are much lower. In particular, class sizes in the North-Eastern Province of Kenya (situated in the semi-desert) are low, due to the scattered nature of the nomadic population.

The MOE is aware that the quality of education has taken a nose-dive with the rapid quantitative expansion of primary education. To arrest the situation, it created the Directorate of Quality Assurance and Standards (DQAS), to work with the Kenya National Examinations Council (KNEC) to carry out a national assessment in all districts. It had yet to report at the time of writing.

Repetition, drop-out and completion rates are also being closely monitored. Initially, the MOE put a stop to repetition but parents complained that their child had not grasped the subject content of the previous class and an automatic promotion meant that they would be even worse off. Due to parental pressure, the MOE has capitulated and has made allowances for the weaker primary school children to repeat.

One unexpected phenomenon has been the growth of private primary schools. With the increase in class sizes in the state system, compounded by the re-entry of pupils who had previously dropped out of school for several years, the quality of education has fallen. Pupils, who have re-entered school, have relapsed into semi-literacy and teachers are finding it difficult to cope with the large variation of the learners. Attention given by the teachers to the new entrants means that they cannot give adequate attention to those who were in school and have progressed in the school grades. Learning for the latter has been compromised. Consequently, parents who can afford to pay fees in private schools have removed their children from public schools and put them in private schools that have moderate class sizes and where teaching and learning is visibly taking place. So great has been the exodus to private schools that enrolment in one year grew from 187,966 in 2002 to 253,169 in 2004, an increase of 34 per cent! Staffing has not been a problem as there is a surplus of teachers in the country. Anecdotal evidence is that private schools now have a choice in their recruitment of teachers and that they are able to recruit them at a lower salary than they would have been able to a few years ago. Thus, one of the results of expanded primary school enrolment has been the mushrooming of private schools in Kenya. On the other hand, in the poorer areas, some private primary schools, which did not offer a good education have closed down because parents transferred their children to public schools after the announcement of free primary education.

Education expenditure

The performance of Kenya's economy improved in recent years. After experiencing declining trends in macroeconomic performance from the late 1980s right through the 1990s till 2003, the country gradually picked up and real growth rates rose from a low of 0.6 per cent in 2002 to 3.6 per cent in 2003, to 4.9 per cent in 2004 and 5.8 per cent in

2005. The growth has been attributed to the priority macroeconomic policies pursued by government within the Economic Recovery Strategy for Wealth and Employment Creation (ERS) framework.

The importance that the government has given to education can be seen in the high investment allocated to the sector. Education in Kenya has continued to receive one of the highest public spending allocations. Total education expenditure as a percentage of GDP rose from 6.2 per cent in 2002/3 to 6.6 per cent in 2005/6 representing 29.6 per cent and 25.8 per cent of total government public spending in the respective years.

Most of the funds allocated to primary education has been in the form of recurrent expenditure (96.4 per cent in 2004/5)[14], leaving capital development expenditure with less than 4 per cent at the time of rapid primary school expansion. The implication of such a small percentage being devoted to capital development has meant that most of the physical infrastructure in primary education was financed either by households or through external support, even though FPE was meant to be free with no parental obligation. The situation changed in 2005/6, when the share of the capital development budget increased from 3.6 per cent to 7 per cent, due in the main to the external support from development partners for the Kenya Education Sector Support Programme[15], which was accepted by the donors in 2005 as being robust and viable for increased investment.

External support for education through Donor Appropriations in Aid (AIA) has been small compared to what the government has put in the pot. It has been estimated that donor funding to FPE has been around 6 per cent to 8 per cent of total expenditure on Free Primary Education effort. The main donors to FPE are the World Bank and the UK government. DFID is the major player but exact figures have been difficult to obtain as it also handles the consortium money in the Fast Track Initiative. UNICEF has a tranched programme and the World Food Programme provides the food which the GOK distributes.

With the increased resources spent on the provision of instructional materials (text book, exercise books and a compass set) for each primary school pupil, there is the beginning of a change in the primary school recurrent budget. Teachers' salaries and emoluments as a percentage of the recurrent budget have been falling. In 2002/3 teacher's salaries comprised 96.18 per cent; in 2003/4 it was 81.2 per cent; in 2004/5 it was 81.36 per cent and in 2005/6 it was 80.2 per cent. The measures show that inputs other than teachers' salaries are being injected into the schools system to improve quality. A recent study in 2006 showed that the provision of instructional material and the teacher in-service programme has had a positive impact on quality. Using the KCPE 2003 results as the base year, the study has established that KCPE scores for schools in economically poor districts increased by 1.7 per cent between 2003 and 2005[16].

Conclusion

The Government remains fully committed to the successful implementation of the FPE. Financially, the government has increased its allocation to the MOE's budget over the next four years. The Medium Term Economic Framework 2006/7 to 2009/10[17] shows what the MOE has been allocated for each year: 33.1 per cent; 34 per cent; 36.4 per cent and

35.4 per cent of the total government budget – over one-third of government spending is being devoted to education. The MOE is also aware that quantitative expansion has been undertaken at the expense of quality. Together with its development partners, it is taking measures to remedy the problem, bringing in external professionals to boost its capacity for qualitative improvement, which includes an in-service programme for primary teachers in content and methodology to make the curriculum more relevant, as well as making resources such as text books available to pupils. Measures to increase access through the building of schools with help from Kenya's development partners and well-wishers have also been undertaken. The success is also due to parents who have continued to be involved in the running of the schools that their children attend and to ensure that their children actually receive the books they are entitled to. Anecdotal evidence also suggests that it is difficult for teachers to be moon-lighting or to be absent from school without a good reason, as parents demand to know why a class does not have a teacher. In those areas where there is a school feeding programme, parents have mobilised themselves into groups and volunteer to cook the mid-day meal. Finally, the entire FPE/UPE programme has been underpinned with the recovery in Kenya's economy. Economic growth was expected to sustain the expanded primary school enrolments; but the latest world economic events may put a brake on some of the government's more ambitious plans.

Notes

1 All information pertaining to education is from the Ministry of Education, unless otherwise cited.
2 All statistics in this paper are from the Planning and Development Department, Ministry of Education, Government of Kenya, unless otherwise stated.
3 World Bank Report, 2004.
4 *Harambee* is a Kiswahili word meaning 'lets pull together'. Money is raised by a group of interested stakeholders inviting people to get together to contribute/pledge funds towards a project.
5 Lillis, K. 1986
6 Mutua, R. 1975
7 Mwiria, K. 1985
8 The Ominde Commission of 1964 was followed by: The Education Act (1968) (Revised 1970); The Report of the National Committee on Educational Objectives and Policies (1976); The Report of the Presidential Working Party on the Second University in Kenya (1981); Report of the Presidential Working Party on Education and Manpower Training for the Next Decade and Beyond (1988); The Report of the Commission of Inquiry into the Education System of Kenya (2000); Sessional Paper No. 1 of 2005 on Policy Framework for Education, Training and Research in Kenya (2005).
9 T.C.I. Ryan. Email communication on 7th September 2007.
10 Ministry of Education Paper for Workshop on 'Building on What We Know and Defining Sustained Support', held at the Hilton Hotel Nairobi, 5–7 April 2006.
11 Ibid.
12 Email communication from Professor T.C.I. Ryan to Alba de Souza. He was a former lecturer at the University of Nairobi, former Economic Secretary to the Ministry of Finance, and currently consultant to the Governor of the Central Bank of Kenya.
13 Draft Paper on Efficiency of Government Education Expenditures in Kenya. March 2007.
14 World Bank (March 2007). Draft Paper on the Efficiency of Government Education Expenditures in Kenya.

15 The KESSP 2005–10 was the first programme prepared as a Sector Wide Approach (SWAp) for Education planning and financing reflecting levels of support by donors).

16 Ministry of Education (2006). Delivering Quality Primary Education and Improving Access: An Impact Evaluation of the Instructional Materials and In-service Teacher Training Programme.

17 Document which has guided GOK spending and covers government financial commitments.

Fidelis Haambote and John Oxenham

Regaining momentum towards UPE in Zambia

Chapter 4

The current context

Introduction

Zambia gained independence from British colonial rule in 1964. In that year, the Gross Enrolment Rate (GER) in primary schools was estimated at about 58 per cent. Between then and 2004, 40 years, the population grew by a factor of three from 3.7 to11.5 million people, while enrolments in the country's primary schools grew by a factor of 5.9, from 378,417 to 2,251,000 pupils. By 2004 then, the estimated GER had in fact reached 99.9 per cent with a gender parity index (GPI) of 0.96 – a more than creditable achievement.

Moreover, in between those two dates something even more remarkable had occurred. By 1983 – within 10 years of independence – the GER had risen to 100 per cent, 105 per cent for boys, 95 per cent for girls[1]. Clearly, there had been a momentous achievement. Some data from a 1984 report will serve as a summary of the remarkable growth of enrolments and transitions during those early years of independence.

Primary enrolment: annual rate of increase, 1964–81 at selected grades (%)

	Grade 1	Grade 5
1964–70	11.8	20.7
1970–76	3.05	6.3
1976–81	3.3	4.0

Source: Coombe and Lauvas. 1984. p. 9

However, 1983 saw the peak of success in maintaining progress in terms of both absolute figures and ratios. Thereafter, although enrolments continued to grow, they grew more slowly than the population of school-age children. By 1999, the GER had declined to 75 per cent. The gap between population and enrolment growth grew so large that the World Bank's Country Assistance Strategy paper of 2004 observed that schooling levels were higher among the 40–45 year old group than among the 20–25 year olds. (See Table 4.1. for the statistics 1964–2002).

In this chapter, we will explore the factors that help explain why Zambia could not maintain the nearly two decades of success; and why, after another nearly two decades, the country seems to have resumed a successful path. First, however, it will be helpful to sketch the context in which the country has had to operate.

Table 4.1. Growth of total primary school enrolments, Zambia 1964–2002

Year	Total primary enrolment	Percentage increase
1964	378,417	
1965	410,093	8.4
1966	473,432	15.4
1967	539,352	13.9
1968	608,893	12.9
1969	661,281	22.6
1970	694,670	5.0
1971	729,801	5.1
1972	777,873	6.6
1973	810,234	4.2
1974	858,191	5.9
1975	872,392	1.6
1976	907,867	4.1
1977	936,816	3.2
1978	964,475	2.9
1979	996,597	3.3
1980	1,041,938	4.5
1981	1,073,314	3.01
1982	1,120,935	4.4
1983	1,195,274	6.6
1984	1,261,587	5.5
1985	1,349,212	6.9
1986	1,378,022	2.1
1987	1,391,561	0.9
1988	1,426,135	2.5
1991	1,461,206	2.5 [over 1988]
1998	1,557,000	6.6 [over 1991]
1999	1,555,112	−1.0
2000	1,590,000	2.2
2001	1,626,000	4.6
2002	1,732,000	6.5
2004	2,251,000	29.9 [over 2002]

Land and people

To help explain educational development, it is important to remark on two facts. First, Zambia is a landlocked country, surrounded by no fewer than eight neighbours. Second, it covers a land area of 752, 614 sq. km. with an estimated population in 2007 of some 11.7 million people. The first fact has impacted education through the civil wars that raged at different times in five of its eight neighbours from 1960 onwards. It demanded preoccupying attention and the priority allocation of resources to national security.

The second fact involves a very low population density of about 15 persons per sq. km. As just over half the people live in the rural areas, the distribution is scattered, with the attendant implications for the distribution of primary schools and access to them.

More than 50 per cent of the population is below 15 years of age, a fact that implies that the government's goal of a Universal Basic Education (UBE) of nine years would require some three to four million places in primary and basic schools.

A fourth fact is that the estimated population growth rate during the 1960s was about 3.4 per cent (it has since declined to 1.7 per cent and to 1.2 per cent for the age group 0–4 years). To keep the supply of primary education growing at a pace that would both absorb the inherited backlog and simultaneously provide sufficient places for the rapidly increasing numbers of young children meant either that the share of primary education in the budget would have to be enlarged at around five per cent annually, or that the economy would have to grow at a higher pace than the population. As will be seen later, neither condition was satisfied.

Languages and culture

Zambia is home to 73 recognised languages. Their existence implies a multiplicity of traditions and cultural practices which could affect education. The government uses seven major ones for the purposes of public communication through the mass media and for the preservation of indigenous lore. However, it declared English as the official language of the country from the onset of independence and the medium of instruction in all grades of school. While this policy has almost certainly had negative effects on the learning of many children, especially on those from rural and poor families, it has made a significant contribution towards fostering a sense of national unity. Since 1996, however, a revised policy has begun to mitigate those negative effects by using a Zambian language as the medium of instruction for the first two grades, changing progressively to English so that English becomes the medium by Grade 5.

Zambia is fortunate in having no population groups whose way of life or religion makes them resistant to schooling in principle. On the other hand, some portion of relatively low daily attendance ratios and higher than average rates of drop out in some rural areas could stem from local traditions and cultural practices, such as initiation and circumcision ceremonies for boys, or early marriages for girls.

Economy

At independence, the government's revenues came almost wholly from the country's copper mines and were sufficient for the country to be ranked as 'middle income'. The oil crises of the 1970s, the consequent world economic recession and the accompanying fall in copper prices saw the economy steadily decline. Twenty-five years of heavy government borrowing from abroad and the failure of successive stabilisation and structural adjustment programmes to stimulate and diversify the economy finally led to the 2000 World Bank estimate that 82 per cent of Zambians were living below the poverty line of US$1.00 a day.

In 1964, most waged and salaried employment was in the public sector and total waged employment accounted for about a quarter of the labour force. Most of the population made their livings through subsistence agriculture. The protracted economic decline coupled with continued population growth has meant that the proportion of people in subsistence agriculture has actually increased, as waged/ salaried employment in 2000 occupied only about ten per cent of the work force.

Since 2000, the economy has recovered somewhat and has been growing at a slightly faster pace than the population. The government's development budget, however, remains dependent on external donors and financiers, while the recent success in qualifying for debt relief under the HIPC[2] initiative has brought additional funds for investment in education and health. The recent global downturn may, of course, have an adverse effect.

School structure

In operational terms, Zambia currently has three levels of formal education. The first or basic level comprises nine years – Grades 1 to 9. Children are expected to enter Grade 1 at age seven and to reach Grade 9 at age 15. The basic level has three sub-levels. Grades 1 to 4 are termed 'lower basic', Grades 5 to 7 are termed 'middle basic', while Grades 8 and 9 are 'upper basic'[3]. The distinction persists because some schools, mainly in the rural areas, are still able to offer only the lower basic course. Transiting to more distant middle or upper basic schools means that some children, the majority girls, continue to drop out on completing Grades 4 and 7.

Those who do very well in Grade 7 have a chance of being selected for the traditional secondary schools, which offer the Junior Secondary Grades 8 and 9. The majority, who do less well in Grade 7, continue into Grades 8 and 9 of the upper basic course.

Although the Basic Schools and conventional secondary schools both offer Grades 8 and 9, the Ministry of Education acknowledges, 'Basic schools are normally the same schools that offered Grade 1–7 but have now been extended to offer Grade 8 and 9 in the same schooling environment with little improvements made to the school in terms of either appropriate infrastructure or facilities appropriate to that level or grade. Some of the Basic Schools have inadequate teaching materials and teaching staff. Basic Schools located in the rural areas have a high likelihood of their pupils failing to proceed or cope with the lessons in grade 10 to 12 classes'. (*Ministry of Education Strategic plan 2003–2007*). In effect, there are currently two tracks in junior secondary school, one superior to the other.

Zambia aspires in due time to provide a 9-year Universal Basic Education (UBE), but is for the moment focusing on UPE, which comprises Grades 1 to 7 only.

The second level of education is Senior Secondary, which comprises the final three Grades 10 to 12 and is subject to tuition fees. Pupils in Grade 9 of the Basic Schools are eligible to take the national exam that qualifies them for entry to Grade 10.

The third level is post-secondary or tertiary education and includes three universities and a number of technical institutes.

Many years of over-use of school buildings, through multiple sessions and large classes, coupled with the near-absence of public funds for school maintenance and repairs, have left most schools in an unacceptably poor physical condition. Almost half the rural schools do not have their own source of safe drinking water, while urban schools have grown well beyond their planned size, but without any commensurate increase in sanitary facilities.

Since 1991, the liberalisation and privatisation of the economy has created an environment in which participants in educational provision now include the government, communities, enterprising individuals, religious organisations and secular non-governmental organisations (NGOs). There has been an increase in alternative provisions of basic schooling. The economically well off have tended to enrol their children in private schools, while the less fortunate use the government system, where it is available, or, where it is not, have set up community schools.

In terms of actual provision, in 2004 there were 6,796 Basic Schools, of which 4,409 were government-run (64.9 per cent). There were 174 grant-aided schools, 143 church schools and 252 private schools. The known Community Schools were 1,388, which made them the second largest provider of basic education[4]. In addition, there were 430 unclassified schools and a number of Interactive Radio Instruction Centres (IRI).

According to UNESCO's Global Monitoring Report for 2007, some 380,000 children entered Grade 1 in 2004. This number represented 110.0 per cent of the estimated number of 7-year olds in the country [Gross Intake Ratio]. However, the children actually aged 7 years were a minority in this group, so that the Net Intake Ratio (NIR) amounted to only 39.0 per cent. On the other hand, the long-standing gender disparity in favour of boys was reversed by a small margin: the NIR for boys was only 38.0 per cent, while that for girls was 41.0 per cent, yielding a Gender Parity Index (GPI) of 1.06.

As indicated earlier, the Gross Enrolment Ratio (GER) in 2004 stood at 99.0 per cent, with 101.0 per cent for the boys and 97.0 per cent for the girls, a GPI of 0.96. However, the GPI had improved to the desired 1.0 for the Net Enrolment Ratio (NER), which stood at 80.0 per cent for both boys and girls. The ratios implied that some 435,000 children of primary school age were not in school in 2004, 51 per cent boys and 49 per cent girls.

In terms of efficiency, the percentage of repeaters across all seven grades in 2004 was estimated at a moderate 6.9 per cent. The survival rate to Grade 5 in 2003 was thought to be 98.5 per cent, and to Grade 7, 66.2 per cent.

As regards the supply of primary and basic teachers, approximately 5,000 new teachers graduate per year from the 14 Colleges of Education operated by the Ministry of Education. Of these, 12 train teachers for Grades 1–7 and two train for Grades 8 and 9. In 2004, total enrolment in the 12 primary colleges was 8,762, an increase of over 50 per cent from 2003. Females constituted 51.4 per cent of the student body.

Since 2003, the colleges have been following the Zambia Teachers Education Course (ZATEC) at basic level, designed to meet the demand for teachers. Instead of the traditional two-year residential programme at college, ZATEC students receive one-year intensive training in college and spend their second year in school teaching and at the same time studying courses taught by distance methods.

The pupil-teacher ratio in basic schools is reckoned to average 43:1. However, it is possible that this comparatively favourable ratio arises from calculating it on the basis of two shifts per class per day. If that is so, the actual ratio would be in the region of 80:1, with one teacher serving two classes each of some 40 pupils. All serving teachers are classed as fully trained and qualified, with 48 per cent of them being female.

Quality in terms of learning attainments is also reported to be improving, partly due to the introduction in 1999 of the Zambia Primary Reading Programme. An evaluation in 2002 found that reading levels among pupils of Grades 1 and 2 were dramatically above their expected grades in Zambian languages and at the appropriate grades in English. There are hopes that, as more teachers become more proficient in the methods of the programme, national assessments will find continuously rising outcomes.

The gradually improving economic situation, the benefit from qualifying for debt relief and the cooperation from more than a dozen international partners have helped the country to begin to ameliorate the long standing shortage of textbooks and instructional materials in the primary schools[5].

In short, the current reported status of primary/basic education permits strong hopes that very soon every child in Zambia will be able to start and complete at least seven years of schooling with sufficient attainments in the basic skills of reading, writing and written calculation in the official national language to enable a decent life well above the poverty line.

The next section will trace the progress that Zambia had made in the first two decades of independence, but which faltered during the two subsequent decades.

Outline history of UPE efforts 1964–2004

The primary system at Independence

The goal of UPE/UPC is not new to Zambia. Its pre-independence leaders took part in UNESCO's Addis Ababa educational conference of 1961, which promised education for all African children by 1980. On taking power in 1964, the new government followed up that promise by stating, 'We are pledged to the pursuance of the policy of compulsory education and free tuition for all children up to Form II'. At that time, the pledge covered ten years of schooling, eight for the complete primary course, plus two years of secondary school. The existence of the pledge signalled two important facts. First, the government recognised the importance of a scholastic education for every child. Second, it aimed, even in 1964, not at Universal Primary Education, but at an extended Universal Basic Education. As first steps, in 1966 it consolidated the eight-year primary course into seven years of full-time education starting at age seven and ending at age fourteen and its First National Development Plan 1966–70 aimed to provide school places for all seven year-olds by 1970.

Primary education in 1964 comprised an initial two years of half-day school in what were termed Sub-A and Sub-B for five and six-year old children, followed by four years in what were called Standards 1, 2, 3 and 4 for children aged seven to ten years. These six years constituted the 'lower primary' course, which followed the UN belief that it would enable most pupils to master the arts of reading, writing and arithmetic sufficiently to retain and develop for the rest of their lives. They were, in effect, the basic education of the time and even before independence were tuition-free[6], with texts and instructional materials supplied by the state. However, they were not compulsory. Indeed, as the available schools could accommodate less than 60 per cent of the eligible age group, immediate compulsory schooling was simply not feasible.

The assumption of sufficient and permanent literacy by the end of the first six years of primary education (two half-time, four full-time) was the basis of two policies for the remaining two years of the course. As resources were always limited and as additional education was assumed to be not strictly necessary for a still largely agrarian population, the provision of places for the final two years of primary school, Standards 5 and 6[7], were allowed to lag behind lower primary: fewer places were available in Standard 5 than in Standard 4. In effect, selection and competition entered the education system very early. The second policy required those who chose to continue their education to contribute to its costs through tuition fees. There was thus selection both by academic ability and by ability to pay.

In 1964, the national transition rate from Standard 4 to 5 was approximately 75 per cent. The new government planned that from 1966 it should be 100 per cent for all urban areas and 75 per cent for the rural regions. The government also significantly reduced the financial costs by immediately abolishing tuition fees for the upper primary Grades 5–7.

A second selection point came at the end of the three-year upper primary course: on the basis of attainments in a national examination, children were selected for the lower secondary course of Forms 1 and 2. In 1964, only 4,639 of the approximately 13,000 (35.7 per cent) pupils in Standard 6 in 1963 succeeded in gaining entrance to Form I. The new government planned to increase access to secondary school in step with expanding primary enrolments and graduations, so that by 1974, the numbers of successful entrants to Form 1 had risen to 19,254 – a fourfold increase in ten years.

The selection for junior secondary was followed two years later by selection for senior secondary or Forms III, IV and V. Then came selection for Form VI (pre-university), and after that selection for a university, which had to be abroad, as the country had no university of its own until shortly after independence. In 1960, the chances that a child entering Grade 1 would enter Form VI were 1 in 1,000. Not surprisingly, at independence, only just over 100 Zambian nationals held university degrees.

Ownership

As in many former colonial territories, school education for the indigenous peoples in Zambia had begun not with the government, but with Christian missionaries[8]. Although each church ran its own network of schools and was responsible for staffing, it benefited from the government's subsidies through teachers' salaries and teaching materials. There were also some private schools. By 1964, the majority of lower primary schools in the rural areas were built and maintained by their communities with some help and supervision from their local governments. In the urban areas, municipal authorities were responsible for building and running the schools. The Ministry of Education supplied teachers for both sets of schools and supervised their quality. The less numerous upper primary schools of Standards 5 and 6 were usually run either by a mission or the government.

By the early 1990s, the inability of the government to sustain the supply of schools began to force communities into building and running their own schools once more. Initiatives arose all over the country, not just in the urban areas. Known as Community Schools, these establishments are community based, owned and managed. They strive to meet the primary or basic education needs of pupils who cannot enter government schools. Representatives of the initiating community organise and manage them.

Alongside the Community Schools, some Interactive Radio Instruction Centres (IRI) have arisen. They are innovative distance learning programmes that use radio for instruction, facilitated by a mentor. The target pupils are similar to those of the Community Schools. Indeed, some of the Community Schools follow the IRI as a methodology for teaching.

Both Community Schools and IRI Centres demonstrate the desire of communities to ensure an education for their children. The children who access these schools:

- are over-aged and cannot be enrolled by government schools;
- cannot afford school costs, even though government schools are within reach;
- are in peripheral, mostly rural, areas with no other school in the vicinity;
- care for aspects of education, e.g. issues of faith, which the government system does not;
- feel that the frequent and prolonged strikes by teachers in government schools make it impossible to obtain an education of adequate quality.

Typically, these schools do not charge fees and do not require their pupils to wear uniforms or even shoes. Teachers in Community Schools and mentors in the IRI Centres are mostly volunteer young women and men with Grade 9 or Grade 12 backgrounds from within the community. Funding for the schools is provided by a number of international organisations, NGOs, church organisations, and community self-help initiatives.

In 1995, UNICEF took a hand and imported advice on running 'non formal primary education' from the experience of BRAC[9] in Bangladesh. The growth of community schools has been phenomenal: in 1996, 55 schools were known to exist, whereas in 2006, more than 3,000 were estimated to be operating all over the country. The Ministry of Education now recognises Community Schools and is committed, when resources permit, to assist them in accordance with the Education Policy. (*ZCSS Strategic plan: 3*)

Currently then, there are four categories of basic schools: government, aided, private and community.

The primary curriculum

In 1964, the primary curriculum was widely regarded as irrelevant. The majority of families lived by subsistence farming, but the curriculum was geared to language, knowledge and skills more relevant to urban and government occupations. Shortly after independence, in the interests of promoting national unity and at the risk of undermining good quality teaching and learning, English was made the language of instruction in all grades and the language policy was reinforced by posting primary school teachers to schools outside their own language areas, so that they had to insist on English.

The first effort at reform began in 1969 and ended in 1977 with the virtual rejection of efforts to make the curriculum more relevant and practical. The only concessions were the formation of 'Production Units' to supply the schools' – and teachers' – needs for fresh food and a 'Practical Studies' project supported by the Finnish government.

The next major reform came in 1996 with the introduction of the new Zambia Primary Reading Programme mentioned in Section 1. It addressed the tension between the desirability of launching children into reading and writing through their mother tongue and the need for them to master the national official language, English. Highly encouraging results in the piloting led to the adoption of the programme in all basic schools in 2003.

Simultaneously, the Ministry of Education began a fresh effort to adjust the curriculum. It published the new 'Basic Education Curriculum for the Lower Basic and Middle Basic Grades 1–7'. The intent is to realign the curriculum to focus on elements of education that are cardinal for further learning notably the development of literacy, numeracy and personality. The curriculum also comprises five learning areas with curricula and content common to all schools: Literacy and Languages, Mathematics, Integrated Science, Creative and Technology Studies, and Social and Developmental Studies. A sixth learning area, Community Studies, will derive its curriculum and content from a school's local community and environment. The revised syllabuses for the six learning areas are outcome-based, learner-centred and oriented to continuous assessment.

Supplying schools, teachers and teaching materials

In the early years of independence, the need for new schools and classrooms was so large and urgent that the Ministry of Education formed its own building agency to deal with the work involved and to move at almost break-neck speed. To help accelerate the process, responsibility for identifying where schools were needed and for selecting sites was devolved to the provincial and district administrations.

So successful was this drive, despite local deviations, that within four years, the Ministry of Education felt able to claim that sufficient Grade 1 places were available for all seven year olds. The 1969 Census estimated that there were between 112,000–119,000 seven year-olds in Zambia, while Grade 1 enrolment numbered 125,000 and climbed to 127,131 in the following year, 1970. Indeed, it appeared that the number of places in all four grades of lower primary closely matched the 7–10 year age group[10]. Further, the primary school Grade 6/7 output had grown 'from a mere 13,000 in 1964 to 67,000 in 1970 – a magnificent expansion of opportunity'. (Coombe, 1970. para. 58.152)

On the other hand, despite the cheering news from the census and enrolments, the drive was showing signs of fatigue. In 1970, the Ministry managed to open only 27 new Grade 1 classes, sufficient to accommodate at most 1,500 additional pupils. But 5–6,000 new 7-year-olds needed places. Schools were already having to organise themselves in double shifts to accommodate the press of new enrolments. Pupils in the lower primary classes of Grades 1 to 4 were being rationed to only three hours of tuition per day – a virtual reversion to the pre-independence half-day of Sub-A and Sub-B that now affected four years of schooling, not just the first two years. Concerns about the depressing effect on the effectiveness of learning were subordinated to the drive to accommodate as many children as could be squeezed into classrooms and into a school day.

Also, after a good start, the rate of progression from Grade 4 to Grade 5 in all the regions had fallen behind the target. (See Tables 4.2 and 4.3.) The government had planned that, by 1970, 82 per cent of Grade 4 leavers should be able to continue on to Grade 5. In 1968-69, the rate had been 82.3 per cent, but by 1972–73 had slipped to 75.5 per cent. The shortage of Grade 5 places was particularly acute in the rural regions. Whereas the capital city and the Copperbelt had progression rates of over 90 per cent in 1970, three of the rural regions had fallen below 60 per cent.

**Table 4.2. Flow table of primary Grade 4–5 progression, by sex and region %
1968–69, Zambia**

Region	68–69 Boys	68–69 Girls	68–69 Total
Copperbelt	101.5	96.0	98.8
Kabwe	83.0	78.5	81.1
Lusaka	100.4	94.9	97.8
Southern	81.6	73.0	77.7
Luapula	80.5	66.4	74.2
Northern	78.5	68.3	74.1
Eastern	73.7	61.6	68.7
N-West	89.6	80.5	86.2
Western	81.2	69.3	75.9
ZAMBIA	**85.8**	**77.9**	**82.3**

Source: Ministry of Education Annual Report for 1968–69, Lusaka, 1975

**Table 4.3. Flow table of primary Grade 4–5 progression, by sex and region %
1972–73, Zambia**

Region	72–73 Boys	72–73 Girls	72–73 Total
Copperbelt	100.7	98.0	99.4
Kabwe	76.7	73.2	75.1
Lusaka	102.5	97.6	100.1
Southern	80.7	77.2	79.1
Luapula	62.4	53.8	58.6
Northern	61.5	50.6	56.8
Eastern	64.7	47.4	57.4
N-West	82.6	71.9	78.2
Western	76.7	68.2	72.9
ZAMBIA	**78.3**	**72.1**	**75.5**

Source: Ministry of Education Annual Report for 1972–73

Regaining momentum towards UPE in Zambia

Similarly, the proportion of pupils continuing to Form 1 had declined from 41.5 per cent in 1966–67 to 23.4 per cent in 1969–70. The explanation was a combination of rising Grade 7 enrolments and a serious interruption in the building programme for secondary schools.

By the time of the First National Education Conference in late 1969, there seemed to be general acceptance that the country would be able to provide just seven years' primary education for all, and even that not immediately. The goal of nine years of universal basic education would have to be postponed. This acceptance received official recognition eight years later in the 1977 document on educational reform.

Despite the setback and disappointment, by 1977, the net enrolment ratio (NER) for the primary school age group in Grades 1–7 was reckoned at around 80 per cent (See Table 4.4). On the less positive side, the Ministry had to acknowledge that, whereas in 1970, there were sufficient Grade 1 places to accommodate all seven-year-olds, there were now places for only 85 per cent of the age group. And even there, the persisting backlog of children older than seven years taking up places in Grade 1 meant that less than 40 per cent of the actual seven-year-olds were in Grade 1. The population had been growing too fast for the Ministry to keep pace. A persistent downward trend in the economy and general restraint on public spending had necessitated a reduction in expenditures on new primary schools. In the urban areas, some municipalities reported that they were so short of places that one-third of their children could not go to school, even though several schools had gone beyond double shifts and introduced triple shifts in their efforts to accommodate public demand. Some schools reported pupil–teacher ratios as high as 80:1.[11]

Table 4.4. Grades 1–7 enrolment as proportion of estimated population aged 7–14 years Zambia, 1977

Region	Boys	Girls	Total
Copperbelt	72.8	71.3	72.0
Central	75.4	70.3	72.8
Southern	114.2	102.4	108.3
Luapula	107.6	89.8	98.8
Northern	100.3	77.5	89.0
Eastern	96.4	71.0	83.9
North-western	109.6	82.4	96.0
Western	92.7	81.3	87.1
Total Zambia	**89.5**	**77.8**	**83.7**

In the country as a whole, one-quarter of the pupils enrolled in Grade 4 could not find places in Grade 5. The progression rate from Grade 7 to secondary Form 1 in 1970 had been planned for 27 per cent: in 1977 it turned out to be less than 20 per cent.

If the supply of schools and classrooms had failed to keep pace with the growth of the population, the story for trained primary teachers was more cheering. The supply of teacher training institutions was continuously expanded and special training of just one year for lower primary teachers had been introduced, so that in 1977, 86.6 per cent of the teachers were qualified, leaving about only one in seven less than fully trained. On the less cheering side were two aspects.

First, pupil–teacher ratios were deteriorating: in 1973, the ratio had climbed to an average in lower primary schools of 62.8 pupils for every teacher, with the urban Copperbelt reporting 67.7 and the rural Northern region 57.8. For the upper primary schools, the overall national ratio was a little better at 47.7 pupils for every teacher, but here with the rural Eastern region reporting the highest ratio at 50.5 pupils per teacher and the equally rural Western region reporting the lowest at 44 pupils per teacher.

Second, the majority of untrained teachers were to be found in rural schools, as their fully qualified colleagues with their families preferred urban postings. For instance, in 1973, whereas the capital, Lusaka, had 89 per cent of its primary teachers trained, the Northern region had only 69.3 per cent.

By 1981, the situation had worsened. The government was no longer able to keep the supply of new teachers abreast of growing numbers of the primary school age cohort. Larger numbers of untrained teachers were recruited to teach in primary schools. They received short initial training courses, but most proved unable to teach the Zambia Primary Course effectively. Quality naturally suffered. Migration to the urban areas exacerbated problems there, so that it was not uncommon in cities like Lusaka, Ndola and Kitwe to find classes of more than 50 pupils, and even in a few cases 70 pupils. Triple sessions, introduced as an emergency measure, began to look more and more permanent.

Nevertheless, in 1983 the Gross Enrolment Ratio had peaked at an overall 100 per cent: it clearly reflected a continuing high demand. Even so, in 1986 the Ministry of Education felt that the combination of stalling enrolments, the increasing backlog of children receiving no schooling, the continuing high rate of population growth – enrolments were growing at around two per cent against the population's rate of 3.2 per cent – and the bleakness of the economic outlook made it necessary to revise its targets. Increases in the number of classrooms and the number of teachers were not keeping pace with even the two per cent growth in enrolments, so that severe over-crowding and deterioration of facilities were on the rise, while pupil-teacher ratios and pupil-teacher time were worsening. In the face of all this, plus the scarcity of teaching materials, the teaching force had grown demoralised and lost its motivation to teach well.

In 1986 the Ministry therefore suggested that the realistic aim was to achieve UPE, Grades 1–7, by the year 2000, with only a minimal advance towards UBE or nine years of 'basic' education. More specifically, the Ministry planned to achieve by 2001 a net enrolment of 80 per cent for Grades 1–7, 35 per cent for Grades 8 and 9, and 25 per cent for Grades 10, 11 and 12 – secondary education[12].

Six years later in 1992 the Ministry of Education estimated that by 1996, 4,114 extra teachers and 3,657 extra classrooms would be needed just to maintain the status quo: it aimed to provide 4,400 teachers per year, but only 2,225 were produced. Indeed, instead of increases, statistics show a decrease in the number of teachers: in 1996, there were 40,488 teachers in public schools, in 1998 there were 38,840 and by 1999 there were 37,117, a drop of 8 per cent.

Several factors explained the high attrition rate: overcrowded classes, multi-grade classes in some rural schools (with no training to prepare for its challenges), poor conditions of service – by 1999 the starting salary of a primary school teacher was $660 per year, a sum less than the meals allowance paid to university students and 25 per cent below the government's own official poverty line for two adults and four children – a lack of housing particularly in rural areas and inadequate provisions for the security of single female teachers. In addition, the HIV/AIDS epidemic was taking its toll both in terms of sick leave and death, and in making teachers more unwilling to serve in areas with poor medical facilities.

If teachers were in short supply, the supplies of learning and teaching materials were even shorter. A report in 1990 observed, 'As Kelly's 1987 figures show, expenditure on teaching materials and general expenses accounted for 22 per cent of public recurrent expenditure on primary education in 1970, 15.6 per cent in 1975, 7.8 per cent in 1980 and 3.5 per cent in 1986 (of which zero was allocated for teaching materials in that year). Moreover, in real terms the expenditure per primary school student fell by 60 per cent between 1970 and 1986'. For some years now the institutions given responsibility of supplying school materials had not been able to keep up with the needs of the schools, while the distribution system also often broke down, so that large quantities of textbooks simply piled up in warehouses.

By 1989, only 44 per cent of rural 7–13 year-olds were actually attending school, a percentage only marginally better than when the government had taken over from the colonial regime 25 years earlier.

Organisation

As already mentioned, in 1964 a single Ministry of Education controlled all levels and types of education and training from primary through to university and vocational and technical schools. By 1980, the growth of the system had led to a perception that the Ministry was overloaded. It was therefore split in two, with one part having responsibility for 'Basic Education and Culture', which included secondary education both general and vocational/technical, the other taking over post-secondary and higher education. The reversion in the 1990s to a single ministry in charge of all education suggests that the division of labour did not produce the results hoped for.

Nevertheless, the single ministry has devolved the detailed day-to-day running of all basic schools directly to District Education Boards, by-passing the regional and district governments. The latter had performed disappointingly in the past, diverting education budgets to other purposes and siting schools for political advantage rather than educational need.

Financing

Shortfalls in supplies of schools, teachers and materials and the decline in quality were very likely due to the decline in the government's allocations to primary education. 'Moreover, in real terms the expenditure per primary school student fell by 60 per cent between 1970 and 1986 ... . The key indicator in this respect is that education's average share of total public expenditure in constant prices has fallen from 14 per cent in the 1970s to eight per cent over the past three years.' (Coombe et al. 1990, p. 11)

The Educational Reform Implementation Programme of 1986 attempted to respond to this and, in the context of structural adjustment, strongly favoured cost-sharing at all levels. It proposed parental payments for teaching materials and for all costs (especially boarding, but not for tuition at the primary and basic levels), the introduction of some form of tuition fees at secondary and tertiary levels, the mobilisation of local authority levies and the encouragement of private and aided schools. 'As from May 1986, all primary and secondary school boarders were to pay fees ... .'

In 1989, a FINNIDA mission observed:

'Within the limitations of the adjustment programme, the government's current educational priorities may be stated as:
[1] to reverse the decline in quality and access to education,
[2] to shift educational expenditure in favour of primary education, especially among the poorest.' (At that time, the expenditure per university student was 186 times that of a primary school student.)

The outcomes of 'cost-sharing' and the resolutions and priorities noted by the 1989 FINNIDA mission may be gauged from the situation a decade later, when a 1999 National Assessment Survey found instruction in lower primary grades 1–5 reduced from five to three hours daily and its preliminary findings indicated that only 3 per cent of the 1999 Grade 5 pupils had attained the desirable mastery level. In fact, only 26 per cent of these pupils had reached even the minimum mastery levels, doing so poorly indeed as to be functionally illiterate in English.

Retention rates had also declined: of 1000 children enrolling in 1990, only 770 remained until Grade 5 and 683 until Grade 7. The situation was worse for girls: of 1,000 rural girls enrolled in 1990, only 510 remained in Grade 7 in 1996.

It appeared that cost-sharing had neither attracted more resources nor improved quality. On the contrary, it had pushed the goal of UPE further away.

In 2002, the government had made arrangements with the international community that enabled it to reverse the cost-sharing necessitated by structural adjustment and reintroduce free primary education. As a result of this step, the government was able to report that, in 2003, enrolments in primary schools had risen by six per cent, as compared with the two per cent of the three preceding years.

Resurgence

In dramatic contrast with the history of decline and disappointment between 1983 and 2001, the years since 2002 have seen a resurgence of the momentum towards UPE. Tables 4.5 and 4.6 give the statistics and projections reported by the Zambian Ministry of Education[13]. The rate of growth in enrolments over the past six years rivals that of the years immediately following independence in 1964. As would be expected, the urban regions experienced the highest increases in enrolment, with the very rural and sparsely populated North Western and Western provinces responding more slowly.

Table 4.5. Enrolment in Grades 1–9, by gender in Basic Schools from 2000 to 2005, Zambia

Year	2000	2001	2002	2003	2004	2005
Female	864,682	951,377	1,023,327	1,101,949	1,218,611	1,391,988
Male	942,072	1,025,055	1,104,711	1,184,666	1,300,530	1,460,382
Total	**1,806,754**	**1,976,432**	**2,128,038**	**2,286,615**	**2,519,141**	**2,852,370**
% Change		9.4%	7.7%	7.5%	10.2%	13.2%
% Av. Change					8.7%	9.6%

Table 4.6. Enrolment in all schools in Grades 1–9 by gender and province, 2005, Zambia

	Male	Female	% (F)	Total	% of Tot.
Central	163,709	155,430	48.7%	319,139	11.2%
Copperbelt	251,167	257,076	50.6%	508,243	17.8%
Eastern	158,546	149,283	48.5%	307,829	10.8%
Luapula	116,090	104,767	47.4%	220,857	7.7%
Lusaka	162,840	169,167	51.0%	332,007	11.6%
N. Western	93,966	85,482	47.6%	179,448	6.3%
Northern	210,381	185,176	46.8%	395,557	13.9%
Southern	204,783	193,695	48.6%	398,478	14.0%
Western	98,900	91,912	48.2%	190,812	6.7%
National	**1,460,382**	**1,391,988**	**48.8%**	**2,852,370**	**100.0%**

The major policy interventions that removed some of the barriers to education included:

* The abolition of all fees and charges for Grades 1–7, making primary education completely free of direct costs to families.
* Making school uniforms optional and prohibiting the exclusion of pupils who cannot afford uniforms.
* Accepting the validity of alternative modes of education, mainly through recognising community schools and Interactive Radio Instruction Centres.
* The proposed abolition of the Grade 7 examination, which would make entry to Grade 8 almost automatic (but the exam persists and still governs entry to the better secondary schools).
* Permitting the re-admission of pregnant female pupils, who had previously been barred from continuing with their schooling.

The two tables also show that the GPI is also healthy, even though not yet perfect: in 2005 girls made up 48.8 per cent of the enrolments across the country. However, Table 4.6 reveals that rural girls are still worse off than their urban sisters. In the two most urban regions, Copperbelt and Lusaka, girls formed slightly more that fifty per cent of the enrolments, whereas in the rural regions their ratios vary between a low of 46.8 per cent in the Northern and a high of 48.7 per cent in the Central. The facts that the gap has been closed in the towns and is relatively small among rural communities suggest that Zambia was well advanced towards the goal of gender parity by 2005, even if it had not quite reached it.

The very large increases in enrolments have of course advanced the GER and NER to the point where in 2005 they regained and even surpassed the levels of 1983. Figure 4.1 reports that the GER for boys and girls are respectively 108.4 and 102.7, with the NER in Figure 4.2 reported as 94.0 and 92.3. If these increases are sustained and if drop out rates between Grades 1 and 7 can be kept low, Zambia should achieve the goal of Universal Primary Completion well before 2015, the year envisioned by the Millennium Development Goals.

Figure 4.1. Gross enrolment ratio in Grades 1–9 by gender and year, Zambia

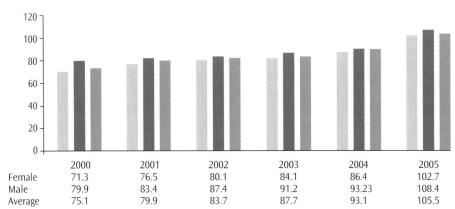

	2000	2001	2002	2003	2004	2005
Female	71.3	76.5	80.1	84.1	86.4	102.7
Male	79.9	83.4	87.4	91.2	93.23	108.4
Average	75.1	79.9	83.7	87.7	93.1	105.5

Figure 4.2. Net enrolment ratio in Grades 1–9 by gender and year, Zambia

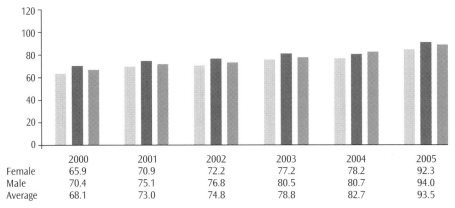

	2000	2001	2002	2003	2004	2005
Female	65.9	70.9	72.2	77.2	78.2	92.3
Male	70.4	75.1	76.8	80.5	80.7	94.0
Average	68.1	73.0	74.8	78.8	82.7	93.5

The improvement of conditions since 2000 led to the 2004 data reporting 45,970 teachers, 47.8 per cent of them female (see Tables 4.7 and 4.8 for their distribution across institutions and provinces). Counter-balancing this positive news, the sharp increases in enrolments caused the teacher-pupil ratio to deteriorate from 1:46 in 2001 to 1:52.7 in 2004. This is attributed to teacher loss and non-recruitment of trained teachers. The capital city, Lusaka, had the most favourable teacher-pupil ratio of 1:47. The rural provinces were less favoured, with the worst off being Northern at 1:77[14].

In 2003 the Ministry of Education published its '*Strategic Plan 2003–2007 and National Implementation Framework'*. The document reconfirms the government's determination to achieve increased and equitable access to quality education at all levels. The measures

Table 4.7. Teachers in Grades 1–9, Zambia, by agency and province

Province	GRZ	Grant Aid	Private	Church	Community school	Total
Central	4,090	81	115	34	315	4,635
Copperbelt	7,525	169	1,110	243	501	9,548
Eastern	3,496	179	80	53	582	4,390
Luapula	2,940	38	21	33	289	3,321
Lusaka	4,694	130	1,238	235	542	6,839
North Western	2,559	73	31	3	171	2,837
Northern	4,183	180	56	87	663	5,169
Southern	4,902	208	209	135	704	6,158
Western	2,803	26	18	50	176	3,073
Total	**37,192**	**1,084**	**2,878**	**873**	**3,943**	**45,970**

Table 4.8. Teachers in Grades 1–9, Zambia, from 2000 to 2005

	2000	2001	2002	2003	2004	2005
Female	17,558	18,258	19,886	20,012	21,955	24,199
Male	19,366	19,535	20,602	21,534	23,806	26,416
Total	**36,924**	**37,793**	**40,488**	**41,546**	**45,761**	**50,615**
% Change		2.4%	7.1%	2.6%	10.1%	10.6%
% Av. Change					5.6%	7.6%

include the abolition of schools fees, support to alternative modes of delivery and the introduction of bursaries to cater for the most vulnerable.

The Ministry proposed to undertake:

- Sensitising communities to the importance of educating girls, women, orphans and the vulnerable;
- Distributing grants to all government and recognised community schools based on unit cost, learner population and equity-based criteria;
- Providing infrastructure and learning materials;
- Providing bursaries for orphans and children with special needs for basic essentials like clothing and weekly boarding facilities for those without adequate home-based care.

The Ministry expected these measures to bring about substantial and sustained increases in enrolment in basic schools and to reduce both the numbers and the percentages of out-of-school children. The data it reported for 2005 suggest that its expectations were realistic.

As part of its new strategy, the Ministry of Education in 2003 moved towards setting up a decentralised system of educational materials procurement. To ensure that educational materials are provided in sufficient quantities and in good time to schools, the Ministry now involves the private sector in supplying books and other educational materials directly to schools. A list of 'Approved and Recommended Books' for all schools has been circulated to the schools and publishers. The responsibility to purchase the books has been transferred to the schools, which receive termly grants for the purpose. The publishers, book sellers and the Educational Materials Unit have to deal directly with the schools. Gradually, the schools are being re-stocked with the full range of books and other teaching resources.

Clearly, despite the setbacks, the Ministry of Education, with the support of its many external supporters[15] is succeeding in regaining momentum towards UPE of good quality. In sum, despite nearly 20 years of disappointing progress and frustration, Zambia is on track towards the achievement of Universal Primary Education, possibly even before 2015, the target date of the Millennium Development Goals.

The following sections consider the range of factors that contributed to the trough of disappointment in the nearly 20 years following 1983.

Social factors

This section considers the social factors that may have supported or hindered Zambia's drive for UPE. They include the demand by parents and children for schooling, their views on the purposes and uses of schooling, their expectations of what constituted a sound schooling, parents' reasons for withdrawing their children from school or agreeing to their leaving before the completion of the primary course, and children's reasons for dropping out from primary school.

Population distribution

As the first section noted, an important factor that affected social views on schooling is the distribution of Zambia's rural population. Prior to independence it was very thinly spread in relatively small settlements across a large area. Most people made their livings through subsistence agriculture, using the slash-and-burn approach, which meant that villages would move their sites from time to time. Siting schools to serve sufficiently large and stable groupings of people was difficult, which meant that for many people distances from schools were relatively great.

Since 1964 the population has trebled and the rapid rate of urbanisation has brought nearly half the people – 44 per cent – into towns. This latter fact has both facilitated access to and efficiency in the use of schools and simultaneously put the government under huge pressure to provide urban schools. Double and even triple shifts have been introduced and persisted with the effort to afford every child an education. The problem for education in the towns then is not one of demand, but of supply. The problem in rural areas is more ambiguous: parents do want schools for their children, but where the population is scattered, the children locally available may not be sufficient to fill the four grades of a lower basic school.

Ways of life

In some countries, the ways of life of some population groups have made it difficult to provide schooling for their children. Nomadic pastoralists and itinerant fishers are among the better known examples. Zambia had and has no such groupings. Neither does it have desert or especially mountainous regions that resist human settlement. Despite shifting agriculture and scattered patterns of settlement, the population was relatively immobile and increasingly open to the principle of sending their children to school. However, particularly among rural groups, concerns about the safety of daughters, tendencies to use children for domestic labour or to send boys to protracted circumcision and initiation rites were factors that militated against regular attendance and transiting to higher grades in more distant schools. Also, the preference of some communities – particularly in the rural Eastern, Central and Southern provinces – to marry off their girls at an early age, as they attracted a higher dowry and to avoid the danger of pregnancies outside wedlock contributed to dropout[16]. In effect, initial demand is strong, but other priorities can affect the attendance and perseverance of minorities of pupils.

Religion

Similarly, in some countries, religious beliefs have been a factor in a people's reluctance to send their children to what were seen as proselytising Christian or simply alien schools. This was not a factor in Zambia, where none of the numerous ethnic groups of Zambia held beliefs that were antagonistic to schooling, Christian or secular.

Gender disparities

Although gender disparity has been a feature of primary education in Zambia, it is clear that it has never been as severe as experienced in some other countries. At independence, girls already comprised 43 per cent of primary school enrolments, a GPI of 0.75. The first section showed, however, that in new enrolments in primary/basic education and in transitions to secondary education gender parity has been achieved and even exceeded. In other words, there have been no ingrained or institutional forms of resistance to schooling girls, although there have indeed been socio-economic and institutional factors that have hindered their perseverance to the completion of courses.

Dependency on government

Until 1964, rural communities were called upon to build and maintain classrooms and teachers' houses, if they wished the government to open a lower primary school (Grades 1 to 4) for their children. Then, for more than 20 years, the government accepted full responsibility for supplying schools and teachers. Although the people may well have become more dependent on government for primary schools, the emergence of Community Schools in great numbers since the 1980s suggests that such dependency as exists is not absolute.

Schooling only as a means of access to wage/salary employment

It is sometimes suggested that demand for and perseverance in primary school would have been stronger, if Zambia had experienced better economic growth and a more rapid expansion of waged and salaried employment. Assessing the precise force of such a suggestion is impossible without data from appropriate studies. However, perhaps the most powerful evidence of the relative unimportance of the link between primary education and the wage/salary employment market is the steady growth of school enrolments contrasted with the failure of the market to grow: indeed it shrank drastically as a proportion of the labour force, as Section 1 documented: whereas primary enrolments almost quadrupled between 1964 and 2002, the number of waged and salaried jobs virtually stagnated. If the demand for salaried jobs and the demand for education were highly correlated, a similar stagnation in enrolments would have followed, possibly after some time lag. Further, the leaps in enrolments that have occurred since 2000 have not been matched by similar leaps in the numbers of available jobs. The inference is that the demand for primary/basic education could now be quite independent of the demand for waged and salaried employment.

Kelly provides perhaps the best summing up of public attitudes to education:

> 'Despite the best efforts of teachers, supervisors and administrators, the quality of the education provided declined ... . Nevertheless, public confidence in education as an instrument of development remained high. Even the most indigent people did not question the need to make substantial sacrifices so that their children could have a school education. They willingly paid for school supplies, additional school facilities, and heavily school-related expenses (such as uniforms). As the economic situation worsened, people's faith in the ability of education to deliver them and their children from the oppression of poverty increased. As wage employment became scarcer, people attached greater store to educational credentials as the necessary, if not always sufficient, passport to such employment.'
> (Kelly, M.J. 1991. p. xi)

'Relevance'

There was an argument that one of the factors that promoted drop-out was the irrelevance of the primary school curriculum. The failures of proposals in 1976 for a more practically oriented curriculum, of the Production Units to affect the taught curriculum and of a 20-year Practical Studies programme all suggest that for the Zambian public in general 'relevance' was not an important issue.

Drop-out

Rates of drop-out can at least in part reflect dissatisfaction with education. At least in this respect the basic schools of Zambia appear to satisfy the vast majority of their pupils. Figure 4.3 shows the statistics reported on drop out from the full basic course of Grades 1 through 9 for the years 2000–05. Even in 2000, the rate was small in comparison with other countries – no more than five per cent for the girls and just over four per cent for the boys. By 2005, the rates were reported to have declined to just three per cent for the girls and two per cent for the boys.

Figure 4.3. Drop-out rates in Grades 1–9 by gender and year, Zambia

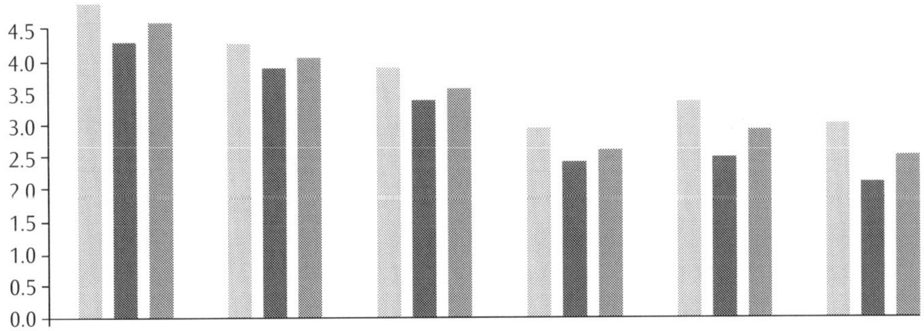

	2000	2001	2002	2003	2004	2005
Female	4.9	4.3	3.9	2.9	3.4	3.0
Male	4.3	3.9	3.4	2.4	2.5	2.1
Average	4.6	4.1	3.6	2.6	2.9	2.5

HIV/AIDS

HIV/AIDS is estimated by now to have infected 15.6 per cent of those aged 15–49 (23.1 per cent in urban areas and 10.8 per cent in rural). However, the pandemic cannot be blamed for the disappointment of not achieving UPE in the 1980s. It had not taken hold by then and the education system had in any case been experiencing difficulty previously. Also, the reported leap in primary/basic enrolments since the removal of all direct financial barriers to schooling in 2002 underlines the relative unimportance of the disease as far as enrolment and perseverance are concerned.

That said, its likely impact on the quality and effectiveness of education cannot be discounted. Frequent and prolonged absences by teachers – and even deaths[17] – on the one hand, and on the other, absences by pupils who need to look after sick parents or orphaned siblings reduce contact hours and learning.

Conclusion

The information available suggests that no unambiguously social factor – as distinct from economic or political factors – contributed to the failure of primary school enrolments to keep pace with population growth between 1983 and 2000. The enrolments have continued to mount steadily over the 43 years since independence and have leapt upward during the past five years. The data provided in the preceding chapters make it very clear that most of the parents of Zambia, urban and rural, have wanted and still want their children to be educated in school.

Economic factors

Zambia entered independence with reserves of foreign exchange – some £400 million – that represented nearly 20 years of annual recurrent expenditure under the colonial regime. Between 1964 and 1974 the economy was buoyant and expanding. A sharp increase in the world price for copper in 1967 enabled the government to levy an additional 100 per cent windfall tax on the copper companies and emboldened it to nationalise them in 1969. It was able to sustain its investments in all levels of education and to continue its work on improving the infrastructure for water, roads, transport and communications. The rate of economic growth might have been even greater but for the difficulties and sharply increased costs caused by the unilateral declaration of independence by Southern Rhodesia in 1965[18].

However, the oil crises of 1973 and 1979 and the consequent long contraction of the world economy brought the price of copper down drastically, so that the government's tax revenues began shrinking. Worse, the actual output of copper also began to decline, shrinking revenues further. The government's efforts to make the agricultural sector more productive and to diversify the rest of the economy made disappointing headway, so that the government soon found that it was spending much more than its income. Indeed, 'By 1976, the country was being rocked by economic and financial crises unparalleled in its history.' (Carmody, p. 38)

In its drive to accelerate development, the government had augmented its own resources by borrowing heavily against future revenues from copper and the returns to its new investments. It reckoned that, as in the past, the slide in the price of copper would be short-lived and that there would be a return to prosperity. On the contrary, 'Zambia's economic decline has been persistent. Despite several stabilization packages in the 1970s and structural adjustment programmes in the 1980s, real growth has been negative on average since 1973. GDP per capita at constant 1977 prices plunged from K439 in 1971 to K313 in 1984 and K287 in 1987.' (Coombe et al. 1990, p. 1) Both rural and urban incomes fell by 50 per cent as agriculture stagnated, waged/salaried employment declined from 23.9 to 9.8 per cent of the work force and the wages on offer shrank in real terms 'in the formal sector ... real average annual cash earnings in 1988 (excluding fringe benefits) had plunged to 15 per cent of their 1980 level. Proportionately the highly skilled groups have lost most.' (Coombe et al. 1990, p. 5) Between 1987 and 1991, the work force grew by more than 11 per cent, whereas total wage employment increased by just over three per cent. By 2002, per capita income had declined from US$752 in 1965 to US$351, a fall of 50 per cent. In that year, the proportion of people living in absolute poverty stood at over 70 per cent, while the revenue base of government expenditure had fallen from 30 per cent of the national product in the 1960s to less than 20 per cent in the 1990s.

Table 4.9. Inflation in Zambia, 1986–94

Year	Inflation %
1986	35.0
1988	64.0
1989	154.3
1990	124.3
1993	200.0
1994	27.3

The government's 'deficits have been financed by foreign borrowing which has made Zambia the most indebted country in the world relative to GDP per capita'. (Coombe et al. 1990, p. 3). They also generated galloping inflation, as Table 4.9 shows.

The resultant rural and urban poverty, aggravated by the HIV/AIDS pandemic, has left the country with a life expectancy now estimated at 33 years – compared with 54 years at the end of the 1980s.

The stagnation in Zambia's economy began to be reversed in 1999. In the years since then, the national income per capita has attained modest increases of approximately 1.4 per cent annually. In 2001, Zambia began to receive debt relief under the Highly Indebted Poor Countries Initiative (HIPC) to the extent of 6 per cent of the total approved budget. Under this initiative, the money for debt servicing was shifted to the social sectors, i.e. education and health. In 2005, the government satisfied the conditions for debt relief under the HIPC initiative and had much of its debt cancelled. Although it is still too soon to assess the long term effects on the education system, the rapid response of enrolments to the new expenditures and the removal of all direct costs are very encouraging.

Figure 4.4. Education allocation as a percentage of the GDP, Zambia

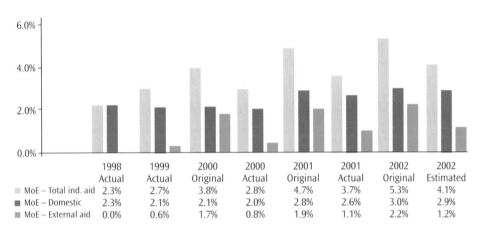

	1998 Actual	1999 Actual	2000 Original	2000 Actual	2001 Original	2001 Actual	2002 Original	2002 Estimated
MoE – Total ind. aid	2.3%	2.7%	3.8%	2.8%	4.7%	3.7%	5.3%	4.1%
MoE – Domestic	2.3%	2.1%	2.1%	2.0%	2.8%	2.6%	3.0%	2.9%
MoE – External aid	0.0%	0.6%	1.7%	0.8%	1.9%	1.1%	2.2%	1.2%

On the other hand, it is clear that the economic reverses and apparent mismanagement that the country suffered over that quarter of a century were bound to hinder the government's drive for UPE. Indeed, even in 2002, the government could not engage a number of new primary teachers to replace those who were about to retire, as it was unable to pay the retirement benefits of the latter. To pull the government out of its predicament, the government of the Netherlands offered a grant to pay off the retirees. The wonder is that enrolments in primary and secondary schools kept growing at all.

It seems clear that the economic factor of plain and deepening poverty explains why many parents could not send their children to school or continue to keep them there; and that the economic factors of falling revenues and mounting debt explain at least part of the government's failure to sustain the drive for UPE.

Political factors

Between 1964 and 1974, the early years were years of plenty – the government honoured its pledge to achieve UPE. However, when economic conditions turned and remained adverse, the competition between priorities became harder for the government to resolve and the social services, including primary and secondary education, tended to lose out. As late as 2001, the budget allocation to education in Zambia remained the lowest in the Southern African sub-region. Although a good deal better than the eight per cent of 1990 at just over 20 per cent of the total disposable budget, it compared poorly with the 25–30 per cent in neighbouring countries.

Armed conflict

The country was blessed with relative stability in terms of political rivalries and struggles for power and never suffered a military coup. On the other hand, Zambia shares borders with no fewer than eight other countries and at different periods there were instability and armed conflict on five of them – Mozambique, Zimbabwe (Rhodesia), Namibia, Angola, and Congo (Zaire). Indeed, severe trouble began in 1965, when the Unilateral Declaration of Independence by the Smith regime in Southern Rhodesia severed Zambia's routes to the sea. Additionally, in the struggle against apartheid South Africa, Zambia was a front-line state. The military and other security forces naturally took and retained a high priority for financial resources and were in a position to insist on it.

Socialism

Second, the government had chosen a one-party, socialistic path to development. That entailed state control over the productive sectors. This led not only to a large civil service and largely loss-making state corporations, but also to substantial subventions to the organs of the ruling party. The government's interest required that it maintain the levels of employment in these bodies, if necessary at the expense of other services.

Inappropriate decentralisation

Third, the government followed a pattern of decentralising decision-making that placed a good deal of discretion in the hands of local political offices. Inadequate safeguards against abuse led to a situation where 'Party functionaries were given sinecures at all levels of state operations and the total cost of financing such activities was more than the budgetary allocation by Parliament to education and health combined. Indeed, money allocated to education and health by Parliament was largely diverted to party functions by provincial accounting units. This led to a very rapid deterioration of the education services'. (Carmody, 2004, p. 37)

High level manpower

Fourth, in 1964, Zambia had only 104 Zambian university graduates. Therefore, the government gave a very high priority to the development of what was termed 'high level manpower'. Pre-eminent among the institutions charged with producing this manpower was the University of Zambia, which opened only in 1966. From its early days, its students attracted privileged treatment. This treatment helps explain why, as late as 1999, primary school teacher starting salaries of $660 per year were less than the meals allowance for university students and, on top of that, 25 per cent below the government's official poverty line for two adults and four children.

Kelly had this to say: 'Within the education sector, political decisions tended to divert resources away from the primary, secondary, teacher training and technical education levels and toward the university. Unit costs at the primary level fell by over 25 per cent and by over 50 per cent at the secondary level, but at the university they rose by more than 40 per cent. ... in the allocation of resources between educational levels, and within each level, between functions, too much was devoted to the refined needs of too few at the higher level, and too little to the general needs of too many at the lower level.' (Kelly, M.J. 1991, p. xiv)

In 1989, the expenditure per university student was 186 times that of a primary school student. Ten years later in 1999, the Basic Education Sub-Sector Investment Project (BESSIP) noted that in terms of unit costs, one university student was still absorbing on average the equivalent of the resources for 127 primary school pupils. (See Table 4.10)

Table 4.10. Percentage change in unit expenditures, Zambia, 1975–84

Level	1975–79 to 1980–84
Primary	−19.9
Secondary	−25.7
Teacher Trg	−13.8
Tech. Ed.	−13.9
University of Zambia	+21.3

Source: Kelly, M.J. (1988)

Lack of champions

An institutional factor that may have facilitated the relegation of primary and secondary education in the priorities of the government was the President's custom of rotating ministers and civil service heads frequently. The practice certainly prevented the build up of expertise in the Ministry of Education. It had the additional effect of slowing the formation of an informed body of influential practitioners who could lobby effectively to maintain the priority of primary education and UPE in the allocation of resources. Local civil society and community organisations were too thin on the ground to act as an effective counter-weight to the government's distraction from UPE.

International dimensions

As noted earlier, UNESCO's Addis Ababa educational conference of 1961 promised education for all African children by 1980. It based the promise on the understanding that virtually all the governments of Africa would be able to rely on international help. Zambia was no exception, for ever since independence its education system has used funds and expertise from a range of external sources, bilateral and multilateral, in efforts to expand and to improve its quality at all levels. Examples have been mentioned in previous chapters. However, the external assistance did not prove as generous as UNESCO and the conference might have hoped. As the British Chancellor of the Exchequer, Gordon Brown, said in December 2004 to the American Council on Foreign Relations in New York:

'Recall the past promises:

- the promise in 1970 that all developed countries would set aside 0.7 per cent of their national income for development aid;
- the promise of primary education for all made in 1990 in Jomtien (Thailand) and re-affirmed in 2000 in Dakar (Senegal);
- the promises at the World Summit for social development in 1995 on eliminating poverty.

Promises which all have one thing in common – they have all been broken.'

For Zambia, one consequence of the under-fulfilled promises was that protracted economic difficulties forced the government into relying much more heavily on borrowing from the IMF than it had intended. Unfortunately, mismanagement led to the unsuccessful stabilisation programmes of the 1970s and the structural adjustment programmes of the 1980s. Coombe and his team observed in 1990, 'Adjustment failed for many reasons; contradictory demand management instead of direct stimulation of production and investment, over-optimistic forecasts of copper prices and production volumes, the inability of the Zambian Government to meet its declared commitments, inflexible labour markets, and the low priority accorded to the social sectors in programme design'. (Coombe et al. 1990, p. 1)

The documentation indicates that the international financiers were as interested in promoting primary/basic education and in reducing poverty as the government declared itself to be. There is, of course, the probability that the measures required by the financiers, especially the push for cost-sharing, underestimated the impact of sheer poverty and were inappropriate for Zambian conditions. Unfortunately, the hypothesis cannot be fully tested, as the earlier pattern of inconsistent implementation continued even with a change of government in 1991, when the worsening economic situation prompted a second attempt at structural adjustment. That was again inconsistently applied and had little effect.

Only in 1999, and again with much advice and financial help from the international community, did the economy begin a recovery that appears to have taken hold. As noted earlier, economic growth was been steady, if modest, over the six years up to 2007, at between four and five per cent per annum. On a per capita basis, that is approximately 1.4 per cent per annum. As also noted, the government has been able to satisfy the conditions of the HIPC, which has relieved it of a substantial burden of debt repayments and which has insisted that it spend the extra funds now at its disposal on the social sectors of health and education.

Inferences, conclusions and lessons

The broad conclusion must be that political decisions forced partly by economic factors, partly by economic policies, partly by inconsistency, partly by forms of corruption and partly by armed conflict in neighbouring countries largely explain Zambia's failure to attain UPE. As long as the money was available, the government was willing to allocate it to building schools and supplying teachers and teaching materials. It was also willing to agree that debt relief should be allocated totally to education and health. However, when money was scarce, other priorities took precedence both in central government and in the decentralised agencies of the regions.

Economic growth

Therefore, a first lesson seems to be that governments need to maintain economic stability and promote at least enough economic and purchasing power growth to keep pace with population growth. In Zambia's case, the halving of the population growth rate from 3.4 per cent in 1964 to the current 1.7 per cent should help make economic betterment more sustainable. Economic growth must enable the government to pay public servants wages that are above the poverty line.

Advocacy

A second lesson seems to be that the education sector needs a very strong corps of advocates to prop up political will in maintaining the priority of primary education. Frequently rotating ministers of education and the civil service heads of ministries of education is unlikely to enable the formation of such a corps.

A country's political and administrative cadre are likely to have a strong interest in maintaining the university sector, even at the expense of secondary and primary education. A corps of advocates for primary schooling is needed to resist this bias and to insist on a holistic view of a properly balanced education system.

Accountable decentralisation

Part of this lesson is that one precondition for sound decentralisation must be effective accountability. In this regard, a recent World Bank study of targeted subsidies found that, where there was strong direction, there was 100 per cent delivery of the subsidies to their target populations. In contrast, where decentralised agencies were allowed some discretion, target populations actually received only 40 per cent of their entitlement. Effective systems of monitoring and accountability must be in place.

Strong demand

Third, in a society like Zambia's, there will be no lack of parental demand for schools – on the contrary. It is striking that, although about 70 per cent of Zambia's population lives below the absolute poverty line of $1.00 per day, the schools are full and rates of attendance and transition high. However, poverty does inhibit participation: the 6–7 per cent surge in primary enrolments following the abolition of fees and other charges in 2002 stemmed from the children of poor and rural families. It may indeed be the case that a minority of parents and children, 'the last ten per cent', will ignore, reject or be unable to take up opportunities even of free schooling, but this will not be true of the overwhelming majority.

Community support and partnerships

On the contrary, in most communities local leaders will always be ready to make an effort to mobilise finance, labour or other resources to ensure at least some educational opportunity for their children. The spontaneous appearance and rapid expansion of Zambia's community schools attest to this. It may be then that the fourth lesson is that governments should refrain from shouldering complete responsibility for the provision of schools, but should instead examine how parents and their communities, both urban and rural, can be encouraged to participate in ensuring that enough schools and classrooms exist for all the children, but always without raising barriers for the poorer groups.

Notes

1 The Net Enrolment Ratios were of course rather lower, running in the 70s and 80s for both females and males in 1983. The discrepancy between the GER and NER in 2002 was rather smaller than in 1983.
2 HIPC – Highly Indebted Poor Countries.
3 Historically, Grades 1–4 constituted 'lower primary', Grades 5–7 were 'upper primary', while Grades 8 and 9 constituted 'Junior Secondary'. The change of terminology reflects the long held aim of affording nine years of basic education to every child.
4 The actual number is thought to be slightly more than 3,000.
5 For instance, the provision of books in English for basic schools went up from 947,988 in 2003 to 1,323,118 in 2004, an increase of approximately 40 per cent.
6 However, parents were expected to provide uniforms for their children and, where they lived far from a school, to furnish their children with food and cooking utensils. Also, communities and their local governments – mostly tribal 'Native Authorities' in the rural areas and municipalities in the urban- were expected to provide the buildings, many of them 'pole-and-dagga' or sticks, mud plaster and thatch.
7 The grades of Sub-A and Sub-B were abolished, while the full primary course was extended to seven years. Lower primary then comprised four years or grades and upper primary three.
8 Schools for European and mixed-race children had been separate before the formation of the Central African Federation in 1953 and, until the demise of the Federation in 1963, had been the responsibility of the federal government –and much more generously funded. At independence in 1964 they came under Zambian government control.
9 BRAC – Bangladesh Rural Advancement Committee.
10 On the other hand, the Census reckoned that only 42 per cent of Grade 1 places were occupied by seven year olds, and only 59-62 per cent of the seven year age group were in school at all. In effect, the disparity between the Gross Enrolment and Net Enrolment Ratios was wide. Of course, this in no way detracts from the magnitude and success of the Ministry's drive to provide the schools and classrooms. On the contrary, it simply illustrates the pervasive, powerful and determined demand for education on the part of young people who had lost out under the colonial regime.
11 1979. The Effect of Population Growth on the Development and Cost of First Level Education in Zambia. A.N. Mehra – Lusaka. Manpower Research Unit. Institute for African Studies. University of Zambia. Report no. 4, Table 2
12 As it turned out, even that modification in target proved too optimistic: in 2001, the total enrolment of 1,774,909 pupils in Grades 1–7 turned out to be a GER of 84 per cent, with the NER at 68 per cent, i.e. 12 per cent behind the modified target.
13 It is notable that the Zambia Ministry of Education has been able to report the statistics for 2005 so swiftly. In the 1980s and 1990s, the public might have to wait for up to five years for this kind of information.

14 The situation might have been better, if the government had not decided in 2002 to use its budgetary leeway to increase the emoluments of existing public servants, rather than hire 5,000 newly graduated basic school teachers.

15 Zambia's education system received help from the governments of Denmark, Finland, Ireland, Japan, the Netherlands, Norway, Sweden, UK and USA (the Netherlands and Ireland currently lead the donor consortium for education) as well as UNESCO, UNICEF, the World Bank and many NGOs.

16 The Ministry of Education reported that in 2005 1,405 girls in urban basic schools and 7,706 girls in rural basic schools had to suspend their education because of pregnancy.

17 Whereas 457 teachers in government basic schools died during 2002, as many as 787 did so in 2005 (53 per cent men, 47 per cent women).

18 For more than 15 years, Zambia had its traditional supply routes of fuel and other supplies cut off, so that imports had to come more expensively by air or at considerable delay via Tanzania on relatively poor roads. Eventually, the new TanZam railway, built by the Chinese and completed in1975, helped to offset the loss of the rail-link through Zimbabwe and South Africa.

UPE and UBE in a federal system – What happened in Nigeria

Chapter 5

Preliminary

The three previous chapters have provided in-depth and detailed studies of the UPE experience of three countries, one from Western, one from Eastern and one from Southern Africa. This chapter and the next are designed to add two outlines – of Nigeria as the most populous African country and Tanzania as a case where scarce resources did not inhibit educational development. For reasons of time and resource constraints, these two cases were not studied so deeply, but the research team believe that the narratives that follow will enrich and illuminate the whole issue of sustaining and maintaining UPE.

Uniqueness and complexity of Nigeria

Nigeria presents a unique context for study of universal primary education (UPE), with its huge population, federal style of government and numerous thrusts towards UPE. It not only has Africa's largest population (2006 estimate of 140 million), but must also contend with over 350 distinct languages and two main religions, Islam and Christianity unevenly dispersed in the north and south respectively thereby, creating a cultural north/south divide. As a federal republic, Nigeria has a president and states administered by elected governors and federal and state houses of assembly. Ministers in the federal and state governments are appointed by the president and governors respectively and are not often elected members of the assemblies.

This chapter examines briefly the ups and downs of UPE in Nigeria in the light of the country's geographical, social, and political complexity. It considers the extent of success of UPE to date, notes lessons learned for sustainability and that may inform future policy.

Accordingly, we present a broad outline of the education policy climate in Nigeria, highlight the country's uneven 'education topography' then sketch a history of the country's UPE adventures, and the lessons from those experiences. This is followed by a more detailed focus on the Universal Basic Education (UBE) programme currently being implemented. We note the UBE goals in the broader context of global Education For All (EFA) initiatives, teething problems, and achievements so far. Finally, we consider the concept of sustainability and how best to apply it in the Nigerian context with a view to leading to the ultimate success of the UPE/UBE initiative.

Education policy climate

Before considering the education policy climate, it is necessary to highlight some statistics that illustrate the context against which Nigeria is trying to achieve UPE (and universal basic education); it is one of poverty and ongoing mass illiteracy, neither of which is evenly distributed across the country. The sheer numbers make any kind of educational initiative a huge logistical nightmare and one requiring vast sums of revenue as well as slick administration at the three levels of government. Data are sourced from the 2006 Global Monitoring Report and summarised in Box 5.1 below.

Box 5.1. Statistical data for Nigeria

Total population 2002*	120,911,000
Annual growth rate 2000–05	2.5%
Life expectancy	51 years
GNP per head 2002	$300
Population living on less than $2 per day	90%
Adult literacy rate	66.8%
Number of illiterates 2002	Over 22 million

*Recent estimates suggest a population of over 140 million.

Education is a responsibility shared by the three tiers of government in the Federation of Nigeria, that is, the federal, state and local governments. The constitution of the country refers to this as belonging to the concurrent legislative list, meaning that both the federal and the other two tiers of government can legislate on it. This is in contrast to some subjects which are on the exclusive legislative list such as Defence, which is the sole preserve of the federal government.

In the years since independence in 1960, Nigeria has gone through a number of changes in government, including over 30 years of military rule, as well as a number of changes in government structure, although it has retained a federal system throughout. From a federation of three regions at independence, it has been divided again and again, until there are now 36 States and a Federal Capital Territory. Each State has a number of local governments and there are at present 774 local governments. From 1952 (the year of limited self-government) to the first military coup in 1966, the three regions (East, West and North) enjoyed a great deal of autonomy. The period is often referred to as that of 'a weak centre and strong regions'. Education during the period was a strongly regional affair, particularly at the primary and secondary levels. Competition was a feature of the relationship between the regions and was especially keen in the field of education.

The first military coup was followed swiftly by another that installed General Yakubu Gowon as Head of State. The ensuing civil war, in which the Eastern Region attempted secession as the state of Biafra, was bitter and bloody, ending in the defeat of Biafra in 1970. Then followed a period of political instability with a succession of military and semi-military regimes; the succession of military leaders included General Murtala Muhammad, General Olusegun Obasanjo and culminated in the deeply unpopular General Sani Abacha. During this long period of military rule that ended in May 1999 government was characterised by a very strong centre and relatively weak States. The situation is explained largely by the unitary command structure of the Army, and also by the economic weakness of the States.

In the pre-military coup era, the States had a much stronger control over the revenue accruing from the export products originating from their geographical territory (an arrangement known as the 'derivation principle'). As the economy became more dependent on one single export, oil, the military rule altered this arrangement to the advantage of the centre (the federal government). Civilian rule has not significantly altered the military-era revenue allocation formula but State governments are asking for greater devolution of power and a consequent increase in control over resources.

Just as military rule, whatever its failings, had the salutary effect of keeping Nigeria one it has also helped with the emergence of a unified National Policy on Education; first published in 1977, it was a late outcome of a national curriculum conference held as far back as 1969. All three tiers of government subscribe to the ideals of the national policy, even though there has been a tendency to emphasise its framework (the 6-3-3-4 structure), rather than its substance (the major reforms the policy was intended to effect such as diversification of secondary level curricula and continuous assessment).

The States still enjoy a large measure of autonomy and, in principle, a State can carry on the business of education in its own way. The system does however provide for a coordinating mechanism, which operates at two levels: the professional and the political. For an initiative from any quarter to become nationally accepted, it has to go through professional screening by the Joint Consultative Committee on Education (JCC) and then be subjected to political backing by the National Council on Education (NCE), a forum of the thirty-six State Ministers (Commissioners) of Education and the Federal Minister.

In spite of this apparently neat coordination arrangement, the practice has been dominated (since the advent of military rule) of 'knocking down' education policy on the citizenry. This is a practice by which new policy is announced by the authorities with the clause 'henceforth, the following will be the policy'. Such announcements are sometimes followed (but hardly ever preceded) by some form of policy dialogue, often termed consultation, with major stakeholders. How consultative this process actually is may be questionable. Meanwhile, the day-to-day running of primary schools is in the hands of the local governments, notwithstanding some federal interventions noted below.

One major management policy change that began with the military, and which was 'knocked down on the citizenry' was the proliferation of education sector parastatal organisations. These were executing agencies for a number of government education programmes such as teacher education, universities and primary education. By 1999, when the country returned to civilian rule, there were 21 education sector parastatals. These included special commissions for example nomadic education, teachers' colleges and, in due course, Universal Basic Education. While the main government structure was, as has been said, one of horizontal tiers, there were a number of vertical arrangements cutting through the State and local jurisdictions.

Another major change was the occasional assumption of responsibility by the federal government for state-owned tertiary institutions. This extended to the federal government intervening heavily in the management/ownership of secondary institutions, some 108 'unity colleges', as at the last count. A further extension of the federal intervention syndrome was the decision of the Babangida regime of the 1980s to intervene directly in primary education and adult literacy programmes. Responsibility for these programmes had hitherto belonged to the third tier of governance, the 774 local governments. National parastatals were accordingly established.

As noted earlier, these tendencies to centralisation have continued under civilian rule, in much the same way as has the habit of launching policies before they have been democratically X-rayed. This was to become the subject of legal challenges by State governments and impinged on the smooth take-off of the Universal Basic Education (UBE) programme that was launched in 1999.

An uneven education topography

In terms of natural vegetation belts, Nigeria can conveniently be divided into two broad zones. These are the equatorial forest (South) and the tropical grassland (North). The South faces towards the Atlantic Ocean and has for many centuries had international communications via the sea, while the North faced the Sahara desert and its main communication routes were towards North Africa. The Northern zone represents about two-thirds of the whole land area of the country. The two zones had two broad types of pre-colonial experience; they were in the early days of British rule, two distinct 'protectorates' (with Lagos as a Crown Colony) until they were merged into a single protectorate in 1914. They were administered in two different ways by the colonial government, and remain in many ways distinct socio-cultural, economic and political zones nearly five decades after independence. Further, in addition to the actual distinctions, there are quite serious divisions of perception by one ethnic group of another.

The North witnessed the penetration of Islam around the 14th century. It was home to the great Jihad of the early 19th century and nourished a flourishing Islamic empire at the advent of colonialism early in the 20th century, when it became known as the (British) Protectorate of Northern Nigeria. It was then administered by 'indirect rule', a system in which traditional authorities exercised direct control over the people, while the British authorities supervised from a comfortable distance.

Indirect rule was also applied in the South, but the native authorities did not enjoy the same level of autonomy as their counterparts in the North. The South had come under strong Christian missionary influence before the advent of British rule. Christian evangelists recognised that they could influence the children by getting them to school and thereby hoped to influence the parents. Thus the missionaries spread literacy (both in English and indigenous languages) and laid the foundation for primary schooling.

By the time the British colonial government began officially to promote western-type formal education, there was already fertile soil for its ready acceptance and spread in the South. In the North, the soil was not as fertile, perhaps because of the initial antipathy of those steeped in the Islamic learning traditions towards western-style education (Bray, 1981). By 1965, there were 12,234 primary schools in the south compared to 2,743 in the north and nearly two and a half million pupils enrolled in the south compared to less than half a million in the north.

This educational imbalance is not simply a pedagogical issue but one with strong political undertones. Education power has to some extent translated into economic power, and a very strong current in Nigeria's political power play has been about avoiding a situation in which all the powers (educational, economic and political) are enjoyed by (or vested in) the same geographical zone.

This has been translated into educational policy in two ways: firstly the classification of some parts of the Nigerian federation as educationally disadvantaged States and, secondly and related to this, the adoption of a quota system (better known as federal character) into student admission to federal government institutions. Federal character is also in force in every other aspect of national life, it is a feature of the constitution, and there is a Federal Character Commission to enforce its provisions.

There is also a realisation in Nigeria that the division into North and South was too simplistic and too broad to reflect the diversity and complexity of the country. Therefore, the term 'geopolitical zones' has crept into national political discourse, and Nigerians have come to accept that one certain way to ensure equity in development activities, in the distribution of federal government patronage, in determining who holds specific political offices and so on is to have representation from all six geopolitical zones. The map of Nigeria in Figure 5.1 below illustrates the division of Nigeria into six geopolitical zones.

Figure 5.1 Map of Nigeria, showing the six geopolitical zones of Nigeria, the 36 States and the Federal Capital territory

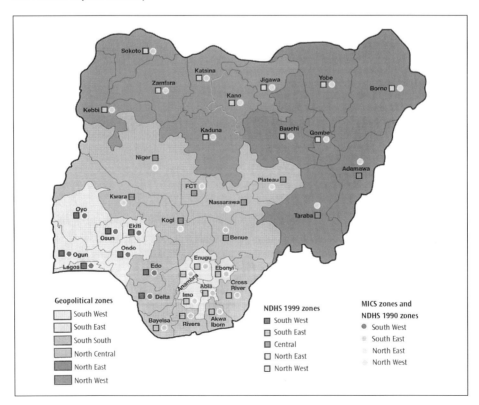

The notion of geopolitical zones pervades all tiers of government. Every State distributes its political and social amenities with due respect to equity among its three senatorial zones (each State is represented in the Nigerian senate by three senators). The local governments also have their own arrangements for ensuring geopolitical equity

Let us consider what the relationship between geopolitical zones, education in general and UPE in particular has been. First, one major objective of UPE programmes implemented over the years has been to bridge the zonal divides in access to schooling. Secondly, the northern section of the country has remained largely educationally disadvantaged. Since that status comes with increased federal financial aid to education, it is, ironically, to a State government's benefit to be classified as educationally disadvantaged.

How far the policy of evening out imbalances has succeeded is not yet entirely clear; but certain disparities within the system are still very noticeable. Participation rates continue to be lower in the three northern zones than in the three southern zones and gender imbalance is high in the former, whereas parity has almost been achieved in some of the States in the latter. Table 5.1 gives an indication of these phenomena.

The uneven education topography seems also to be correlated with poverty levels, which tend to be higher in the northern zones than in the coastal zones, as illustrated in Figure 5.2 below, sourced from Nigeria's 2005 MDG Report.

Figure 5.2. Nigerian regional variations in poverty levels

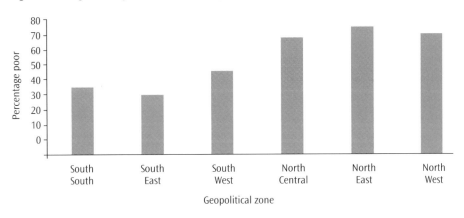

Nigeria's UPE adventures

The term adventures seems very appropriate here, for even though the initiators of UPE in Nigeria over the years meant well, and set out to address a serious educational problem, the programmes were not always well thought out. This is to say that the groundwork necessary for effective execution of UPE was not given the attention it needed. However, the efforts made were not all in vain. As the following review will show, progress was achieved as well as mistakes made, and there are useful lessons to be recorded for informing UPE in Nigeria (and perhaps elsewhere as well) and for suggesting ways of making the achievements more sustainable.

Table 5.1. Average participation rates and girls' participation in primary education in Nigeria

Geopolitical zone	State	% girls in primary education	Average participation rate %
North West	Sokoto	19	32.5
	Katsina	33	
	Kano	39	
	Kaduna	42	
	Jigawa	36	
	Kebbi	33	
	Zamfara	26	
North East	Yobe	31	37.5
	Borno	42	
	Bauchi	35	
	Gombe	39	
	Taraba	36	
	Adamawa	31	
North Central	Niger	35	43
	Kogi	49	
	Kwara	47	
	Benue	45	
	Plateau	42	
	Nassarawa	39	
South West	Oyo	50	48
	Oshun	46	
	Ogun	50	
	Lagos	50	
	Ondo	45	
	Ekiti	48	
South East	Enugu	50	51
	Ebonyi	50	
	Anambra	52	
	Imo	50	
	Abia	53	
South South	Cross River	49	49
	Akwa Ibom	51	
	Rivers	?	
	Delta	49	
	Edo	47	
	Bayelsa	?	
FCT	FCT	42	42

Source: UBE: 2001

UPE at Independence

Nigeria's first UPE programme came in the wake of internal self-government in 1955 (the pre-cursor to full political independence). This was also the era of resource control at the regional level and of competition in the three constituent regions and the elected governments of the two coastal regions both made a commitment to UPE. It was part of the election manifesto of the party in power in the then Western Region (the Action Group) that also wanted free medical services for all citizens under the age of 18.

The free, compulsory primary education scheme in Western Region took a pragmatic approach, reducing the normal eight years of education to six in an effort to keep a balance between financial constraints and maximising the number of children benefiting from the scheme. This led to criticism about lowering standards (Abernethy, 1969). Though some quality may have been sacrificed, a number of characteristics made it workable:

- As part of the ruling party manifesto, the electorate was aware of the scheme long before it became official government policy.
- The formal proposals came, as a bill, before a regional assembly that had a very strong opposition. It was therefore subjected to wide ranging debate.
- The citizenry had already embraced western-type education and saw its advantages, especially for the upward mobility of the younger generation. Support from the citizenry was assured.
- The scheme brought schools nearer to rural and urban slum communities.
- The Western region was the richest region in Nigeria at the time and therefore could fund the programme.
- There was some thought given to what would happen to the children after primary education, as there was an upsurge in the number of secondary grammar (5-year classical programmes) and secondary modern (3-year general education) schools. Local communities and voluntary agencies (mainly religious bodies) were fully mobilised for this purpose.
- There was also an upsurge in the number of teacher training institutions, to train teachers rapidly (mainly in 2-year post-junior secondary colleges) to cope with the envisaged increase in enrolment.

Despite the years of planning, however, enrolment projections were grossly under-estimated. It was said that while provisions were made for 170,000 children, 391,895 showed up on the first day of school in January 1955 (Abernethy, 1969, Okedara, 1979). One reason for this was that over-aged and under-aged children also turned up for registration. The other reason is that accurate population projection had been impossible due to the lack of reliable population data. The Western Region Government's response to the overcrowding was (without explicitly saying so) to remove the term compulsory from the scheme. This meant that, while primary education remained free, it was not legally obligatory for parents to enrol their children in school.

As well as being overcrowded, the schools were in a poor state, lacking equipment and enough trained teachers. In spite of such difficulties, enrolments in primary school in the region increased from 35 per cent in 1954 to 90 per cent in 1960 but, as numbers crept up, so did textbook fees, building levies and examination fees. Numbers fell again after 1960; disillusionment regarding work prospects is considered one of the reasons for this (Bray, 1981).

The Eastern Nigerian government, in keeping with the nationalist mood of the time, also embarked on a universal primary education scheme in 1956, but it encountered less success. It retained the eight-year education cycle with the intention of making the first four years universal. Local communities were expected to share in the cost. Unfortunately the scheme suffered from poor planning and the creation of government schools led to opposition from church schools and further rivalry between Catholic and Protestant (Abernethy, 1969). It neglected both the socio-political and the technical homework. Huge numbers of youngsters enrolled overwhelming the system and poor financial planning soon became apparent; fees were reintroduced and this led to demonstrations and riots, children were kept at home for the sake of safety or because they could not pay the fees, uneconomic schools were closed. The disappointing outcome was blamed on insufficient planning, religious and political rivalries, administrative inexperience and corruption (Bray, 1981). All the same, this region remained almost on a par with the West in the promotion of education, largely because community participation (in the form of cohesive town and village unions) was a strong feature of social organisation in the region.

In Lagos, at that time the Federal capital, a further push at UPE was established as politics had kept it out of the Western scheme. This small scheme was relatively successful though it required the introduction of double and even triple shifts to accommodate the youngsters. By 1964, however, nearly 88 per cent of primary school children were in school.

Primary education had always been free in the Northern Region, but participation had also always been limited. In the Middle Belt and in the areas with mixed populations like Kaduna and Jos, the spread of educational facilities (and the acceptance of 'western' schools by the people) was closely related to the level of Christian penetration.

After 1966, political instability prevented Nigeria from capitalising on the initial gains of UBE. Quality and efficiency issues did not receive due attention, but numbers in primary school remained high and continued to grow as illustrated in Figure 5.3.

UPE under military rule

In 1974, General Yakubu Gowon announced in a major speech in Sokoto, to the surprise of his officials, that his administration was intending to launch UPE. Planning was set under way but the launch was delayed. In 1976, Obasanjo, having usurped Gowon, launched UPE in the September. The promotion of UPE in 1976 was in the wider context of the National Policy on Education, as officially published in 1977. The policy saw education as a huge national enterprise, and an undertaking solely the responsibility of government. It came during Nigeria's oil boom years and was to be entirely funded by the federal government.

The primary education sector was projected to increase five-fold over a ten year period; 108,000 new primary school classrooms were planned for the northern states and 43,000 for the southern states, while teacher training places were set to increase five-fold

Figure 5.3. Total primary enrolment in Nigeria, 1970–2004

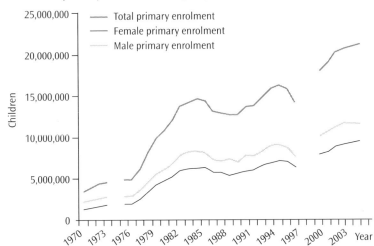

with the aim of having nearly 250,000 places by 1980. At the same time, the government planned expansion of the other sections of education in an effort to maintain the balance of flow through the system. This was a hugely ambitious and very expensive undertaking.

The scheme received a good deal of publicity generated by the government propaganda machinery, the entire country was geared up for mobilisation and funds were made available to State governments. The achievements, however, did not live up to expectations for a number of reasons:

- The plans seriously underestimated the numbers of youngsters enrolling, particularly the over-age children;
- They also underestimated the cost, having not included the recurrent burden on the budget;
- Social mobilisation by the military regime did not penetrate successfully to the lowest levels;
- The States had no systematic UPE development plans and the monitoring of needs and efforts of the States was poorly done. States tried to inflate figures based on needs (to attract more federal government funds) and at the same time inflated the figures on achievements to impress the same federal government.

The 1976 UPE created a boom in publishing. Books for UPE were written by government agencies and private companies who did brisk business capitalising on the programme. However, the books did not always get to the learners, leading to the loss of potential improvement in the quality of the education.

Another threat to quality at the time was the UPE teacher-training programme that saw tremendous expansion in the facilities in teacher training colleges. It was however an emergency type of training programme that recruited students who had not successfully completed secondary education, whose training was too short and considered too shallow. Even using distance education to train teachers quickly and without keeping them out of the classroom did not result in a sufficient supply of qualified teachers. A study in the 1980s in fact showed that UPE teachers were not warmly received in schools (Obanya, 1982). Nevertheless, it should be said that though the educational establishment often considered these teachers to be second rate, research in Nigeria (Ismaila et al. 2004) has indicated that the local communities where these teachers live recognise the effort it takes to study while working by assisting in the organisation and communication of the programmes being implemented (Binns and Wrightson, 2006).

The UPE programme of 1976 was introduced in haste and had had no clearly articulated policy and no clearly elaborated plan. It was a federal government initiative that did not fully carry the States and local governments with it. The oil boom period was also the time of big spending by the Nigerian government, a period dominated by emergency contractors, who collected mobilisation fees on government contracts that were later abandoned mid-stream. UPE classroom construction became a victim of the abandoned project syndrome, and many of these projects remain abandoned to this day.

Perhaps the most difficult challenge of the period was that there were no reliable data to aid planning. Once again the poor data from the population census left much to be desired and there remained low technical capacity for planning in the entire system.

The UPN version of UPE: 1979–83

The South-Western States carried a continuing memory of the free education policy of Awolowo's government and still favoured his party, the UPN. That policy was proclaimed again on 1st October, 1979 (Independence Day) by the governors, on their inauguration, in each of the five States controlled by the UPN.

As it had done in 1955, the 1979 thrust for UPE fell on fertile ground:

* It was part of a party manifesto that grassroots communities had bought into, and therefore it enjoyed popular support;
* It was implemented in a territory that had already benefited from free education; a society for which free education was already an accepted idea.

However, like many over-politicised education policies, UPE in 1979 was announced, and was being widely backed before its technical details had been worked out. Worse still, the programme was over-ambitious as its aim was to provide free education at all levels. In the process, examinations for selection into secondary schools were abolished and all 12-year-olds and above were free to walk into nearby secondary schools. In addition, schools were forbidden from collecting even a *kobo* (a penny) from parents, everything was to be free including books, stationery and uniforms. The effect of this manifested itself in a number of ways:

* There was much less emphasis on the primary education sub-sector;
* Hundreds of thousands of over-aged boys and girls (including apprentices, the unemployed and others) enrolled in secondary school;
* Secondary schools were quickly planned (though not established) to absorb the swollen demands for secondary education;
* Primary school teachers were drafted into teaching in secondary schools;

- Inexperienced secondary school teachers became founding principals of secondary schools that were randomly set up;
- Elementary/basic facilities (classrooms, desk/seats, chalk, textbooks) were in very short supply;
- As schools were government-owned and government propaganda advertised that education had become free at all levels communities were no longer motivated to contribute to the system;
- The contractor mentality that began in Nigeria during the civil war years (1967–1970) had become well-entrenched by 1979. Contracts for educational supplies went to party faithful, who regarded these as patronage and did very little to meet their contractual obligations.

By 1983, when the military took over political power once again, the 1979 version of UPE in the South-West had succeeded once again in expanding access, but quality had suffered tremendously.

Lessons from the UPE adventures

We see from the early attempts that successive Nigerian governments, Regional, Federal and State, have placed considerable importance on education and in particular primary education. We note that there was also public demand for an expansion of the education system and that there was some recognition of the political urge to address education at all levels. With the return of civilian rule, Nigeria is currently embarked once again on an expansion of its schooling system and it would be wise to learn from the lessons, the successes and failures, of the past. The country has succeeded in increasing the numbers of children in primary education (See Figure 5.3 on page 89) but it still has major difficulty in sustaining efforts on the large scale needed or at the huge cost required to deliver good quality education through well-trained teachers and well-equipped schools (see Figure 5.4 below).

Figure 5.4. Gross enrolment ratios (GER) in Nigeria, 1970–2004

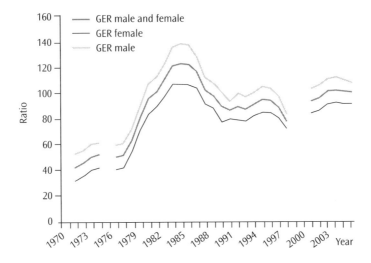

With the benefit of hindsight, the following appear to be the most important lessons:

1   **Development initiatives (in this case, UPE) require rigorous planning.** It is now a common saying in Nigeria that to fail to plan is to plan to fail. Planning for UPE in Nigeria requires a combination of socio-political awareness raising and technical research and analysis. Successful mobilisation of the citizenry was largely responsible for the widespread support accorded the first UPE experiments in the Western and Eastern Regions in 1955. UPE under the military regime might have been more sustainable had the public championed it; after all Nigeria was in a strong position to pay for educational expansion, since it was enjoying the oil boom revenue at the time.

2   **Technical research and analysis requires rigorous methodology and suitable tools.** Demographic data on the school age population and school enrolment, and geographical data on the distribution of populations and so on have been in short supply in Nigeria and when they have been available they have also been unreliable and this has turned planning into day-dreaming. With reliable data it becomes possible to make projections and do accurate forecasting thereby calculating trends and enabling planning in accordance with such trends.

3   **Enlightened forecasting helps in determining future needs and plans can be made in anticipation of such needs.** When we know how many children are due to enter primary school we can plan for the number of classrooms and teachers required to service those children. However, it will remain very difficult to estimate the number of over-age children who will try to enter school late if there is a sudden softening of the terms of attendance.

4   **Technical information enables us to take due account of the unexpected.** A variety of scenarios can be planned for and costed. For example, rapid population growth, decline in government revenue, unanticipated political events, changes in the international scene, impact of donor funding and the impact of such funding coming to an end. Thus it becomes possible to plan how to mitigate some of the problems that may arise and forestall UPE.

5   **Kicking with both legs at one and the same time does not pay.** It could be said that Nigeria took on too much when it started the pursuit of compulsory, free primary education for all. UPE might have benefited from addressing key strategic objectives in a staged or stepwise manner.

6   **Investment planning,** based on 1 to 5 above, might be a way of ensuring that estimates of the required funding (and of every other necessary input) are as accurate as possible and that resourcing strategies are carefully worked out and agreed in advance.

7   **Phased Implementation.** Tackling a number of problem areas at a time and progressively broadening the scope of UPE might ensure that specific goals are addressed by a given time and that implementation at each phase builds on upon lessons learned at an earlier phase.

8   **The nearer the policy pole is to the people the greater the impact.** UPE administered from the centre as a huge, federal initiative has proved difficult to manage, even under the strong influence of the military. In a federal Nigeria, diversity might be seen as an asset, enabling emphasis of different issues in different places and adjusting communication to local cultures. Also assigning key monitoring roles to local education authorities might ensure more intensive local involvement and community ownership of UPE; there is evidence of the influence of community involvement through the activities of the national advocacy organisation, Civil Society Advocacy Consortium for Education for All (Nigeria) CSACEFA, with its branches in the various States.

9   **Government should not aspire to fund UPE 100 per cent.** Despite Nigeria's oil wealth it has been unable to sustain the funding required to promote good quality primary education for all. The dependence on the oil and gas industries also leave it vulnerable to the volatility in oil prices. Nigeria's experience raises a question about how free is free, or better still, how free should free be? History shows that the Government underestimated the financial requirements of UPE but it has not acknowledged publicly its inability to fund 100 per cent. It was once said that *good politics is good for good education.* Good politics would dictate that government reaches agreement with the people on how free is free as a policy development strategy.

10 **Management capacity, above everything else.** For UPE to be successful there must be the capacity, at the respective government levels, to manage the policy development process, the technical planning process, the implementation process, the input of resources, the finances and so on. To date, this kind of management has been sadly lacking in Nigeria's UPE adventures.

The paradigm shift to UBE

In September 1999 Nigeria launched yet another attempt at UPE. This time it is part of an ambitious programme of UBE.

Nigeria is part of the EFA movement that came out of the Jomtien Conference on Education for All of 1990. That conference championed the concept of basic education as the foundation level of education that consolidates the acquisition of literacy and numeracy, life skills, and lifelong learning skills. As every nation of the world was expected to define its own basic education package, Nigeria, soon after Jomtien, designed a nine-year basic school policy. This concept directly and indirectly influenced the post-military return of UPE to Nigeria. Government commitment to UBE continues following the recent, 2007, elections though it seems likely that the new administration wishes to stamp its own authority on it. The donor community also remains committed to supporting Nigeria's initiatives in UBE.

UBE, in keeping with the requirements of the global EFA movement, is an enormous undertaking, judging by its objectives and scope (see Table 5.2). The paradigm shift here is clear to see:

- while UPE is concerned with primary education, UBE embraces all formal schooling from early childhood to junior secondary,
- UBE also embraces mass literacy programmes, as well as
- all forms of non-formal education, including
- non-formal apprenticeship programmes.

Table 5.2. Objectives and Scope of Nigeria's UBE

a Objectives	b Scope
• Developing in the entire citizenry a strong consciousness for Education and a commitment to its vigorous promotion.	• Programmes/initiatives for early childhood care and socialisation.
• The provision of free, universal basic education for every Nigerian child of school-going age.	• Educational programmes for the acquisition of functional literacy, numeracy, and life-skills, especially for adults (persons aged 15 and above).
• Reducing drastically the incidence of drop-out from the formal school system (through improved relevance, quality, and efficiency).	• Out of school, non-formal programmes for the up-dating of knowledge and skills for persons who left school before acquiring the basics needed for life-long learning.
• Catering for the learning needs of young persons, who for one reason or another, have had to interrupt their schooling, through appropriate approaches to the provision and promotion of basic education.	• Special programmes of encouragement to ALL marginalised groups: girls and women, nomadic populations, out-of-school youth.
• Ensuring the acquisition of the appropriate levels of literacy, numeracy, manipulative, communicative and life skills, as well as the ethical, moral and civic values needed for laying a solid foundation for lifelong learning.	• Non-formal skills and apprenticeship training for adolescents and youth, who have not had the benefit of formal education.
	• The formal school system from the beginning of primary education to the end of the junior secondary school.

Source: UBE Implementation Guidelines: 2000

Early thinking on UBE in federal government circles dwelt much on avoiding the mistakes of the past, and the implementation guidelines claim to be guided by this maxim. The chronology of UBE does not fully match this claim, as shown by the following sequence of key UBE events:

- 9th September 1999: Meeting between federal ministry of education and the States to discuss the re-launching of UPE (a presidential initiative). The meeting agreed to recommend a programme of UBE, an idea immediately accepted by President Obasanjo and approved by the federal executive council;
- 30th September 1999: Formal launching of UBE by the President;
- 29th October – 1st November: National Mini Summit on UBE.

Consultation and planning followed the announcement. A national coordinator for UBE was appointed in December 1999. He submitted a memo to the Minister of Education, entitled 'Ensuring the Success of the UBE Programme', relying heavily on government's desire not to repeat the mistakes of the past and this document was transformed into draft implementation guidelines and was then used for a series of stakeholder consultations between January and March 2000 with:

* agencies of the federal ministry of education;
* state primary education boards;
* development partners;
* Nigerian Union of Teachers;
* National Parents' Teachers' Association of Nigeria.

These consultations led to drastic revisions in the draft implementation guidelines. The revised version was then used for six zonal-level consultations in April 2000 and 31 (out of 36) State-level consultations in May. These led to more revisions of the guidelines, which were then further discussed at a national press briefing on 30 May 2000. Then followed a national pupils' registration exercise and monthly consultations with the States (expanded to include State mass literacy and nomadic education commissions).

By August 2000, the Governors of the 36 States had come together with the Presidency and formed the National Council on UBE which met regularly to consider matters arising from the UBE process. Two concerns were prominent on the list of the matters arising. The first was over the enrolment figures – a matter on which there was never agreement. The Council in fact eventually resolved to use 1991 figures, as these were considered the most politically acceptable. The second matter regarded the extent to which the federal government could remain the conductor of the UBE orchestra, with the States always insisting on the need for devolved responsibility.

Federalism at State level was put to the test when, early in 2001, the federal authorities decided to contribute 1548 blocks of six classrooms (two blocks equally distributed to each of the 774 local government areas (LGEAs) of the federation). The States had argued that it was not the business of the federal government to award contracts for the construction of these classrooms. In the end, a compromise was struck, and State authorities were allowed to award 50 per cent of the contracts.

Progress of the UBE initiative

UBE has been actively pursued in Nigeria now for nine years, even in a tumultuous political terrain. One reason for this is a series of Supreme Court rulings that seem to have properly delineated the constitutional powers of federal and state governments. For UBE, this has meant limiting the powers of the federal government to policy coordination and devolving financial and technical support to States, along with overall monitoring of implementation.

Achievement on the ground (mainly in terms of increased enrolments) has been captured in the 2005 Millennium Development Goals (MDG) report of the Nigerian government in the following words:

'Trends in enrolment from 1999 to 2003 show that on average, enrolment consistently increased over the years for both males and females from 7 per cent, 8 per cent, 11 per cent and 14 per cent in 2000, 2001, 2002 and 2003 respectively. Primary school enrolment rates were, however, consistently higher for boys than for girls. The general increase could be as a result of the launching of the Universal Basic Education (UBE) programme established in 1999 with the sensitisation, mobilisation and advocacy carried out by the federal government.

The efficiency of primary education has improved over the years. The Primary-six completion rate increased steadily from 65 per cent in 1998 to 83 per cent in 2001. It however declined in 2002 only to shoot up to 94 per cent in 2003.

Completion rate for boys has been higher than that of girls except in 2000 and 2001.'

Closely related to the above is the encouraging signal that Nigeria might be in the process of moving away from its recognised lack of data on education. Technical capacity for data collection and analysis is being progressively strengthened through concerted donor assistance. In fact, figures from the national school survey of 2003 (Table 5.3) are generally adjudged satisfactory by stakeholders.

Table 5.3 also shows, however, that the data problem is not over yet. Access cannot be determined from the table, as it does not give any clue on gross enrolment rates. There is also no indication of the extent to which UBE has helped to make the education topography more even, as State figures are not easily available.

Table 5.3. Nigeria primary school enrolment by Grade and gender (national): 2003

Grade	Total enrolment	Boys	Girls
Primary One	5,505,886	3,063,436	2,442,450 (44.36%)
Primary Two	4,960,968	2,797,272	2,163,696 (43.61%)
Primary Three	4,369,498	2,466,359	1,903,139 (43.56%)
Primary Four	3,746,721	2,103,585	1,643,136 (43.86%)
Primary Five	3,313,227	1,853,333	1,459,894 (44.06%)
Primary Six	2,876,788	1,607,310	1,269,478 (44.13%)
Total	**24,773,088**	**13,328,075**	**10,881,793 (43.93%)**

Source: UBE, Abuja, 2003 NSC (quoted from Nigeria – Federal Ministry of Education (2004) Education Sector Analysis – Diagnostic Report)

It is also not clear the extent to which the 'grade gradient' shown in Figure 5.5 – larger numbers in the lower grades – is due to UBE. These data plot enrolment in the Grades of 2003.

Once again large numbers of youngsters are enrolling in school, but improvement in terms of quality and efficiency is being hampered by a number of factors. These factors include policy challenges, dissipation of effort, unclear lines of authority, lack of involvement of local government and communities, poor management capacity and the lack of data.

Figure 5.5. Grade gradient in primary school enrolment in 2003

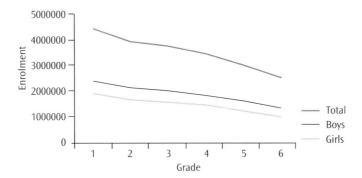

UBE policy challenges

The policy framework on UBE was enshrined in legislation by the Compulsory, Free Basic Education Act, passed by the National Assembly in 2004, which deals mainly with the governance and management structures and duties of UBE commissions at the federal and state levels, as well as punishments to be meted out on parents who fail to send their children to school and to persons collecting fees from pupils. Despite the policy and an implementation strategy, roll-out of the programme has been uneven and it is questionable whether or not the citizenry fully understands the changes going on around them.

As noted earlier, guidelines for implementation were drawn up and these included a possible sequential implementation as indicated in Box 5.2.

Box 5.2. A sequential implementation strategy for UBE

> Detailed, strategic planning is still needed to ensure the unqualified success of the UBE programme. One way of ensuring success would be a process of sequential implementation that starts by focusing on the primary I cohort of 2000/2001 and progressively introduces quality education for them over a nine-year (formal) education cycle. The progressive (and cumulative) nature of this strategy might be as follows:
>
> UBE year I   Primary I of 2000/2001
> UBE year II   Primaries I and II of 2001/2002
> UBE year III   Primaries I, II, III of 2002/2003
> UBE year IV   Primaries I–IV of 2003/2004
> UBE year V   Primaries I–V of 2004/2005
> UBE year VI   Primaries I–VI of 2005/2006
> UBE year VII   Primaries I–VI and JSS I of 2006/2007
> UBE year VIII   Primaries I–VI and JSS I and II of 2007/2008
> UBE Year IX   Primaries I–VI and JSS I–III of 2008/2009

Source: Implementation guidelines for UBE

The formal launch of the programme was made much of by the government, a priority undertaking coming soon after the then administration came into office in 1999. It took off quickly and by August 2000, some 11.5 million children had been registered (as claimed by the States during a field verification exercise by federal authorities). These youngsters were expected to be the first batch of UBE pupils to benefit from nine years of compulsory and free basic education. Annual registration exercises have continued since then, but these are no longer coordinated at the federal level.

Implementation across the States has been uneven; by the year 2006, when UBE was supposed to be in its sixth year (see Box 5.2), the authorities were talking of preparations for the take-off of UBE and some states were being scolded for not being prepared. Some of them are in fact (as at August 2006) yet to establish basic education commissions and work out implementation plans. The donor community is assisting in the development of ten-year educational plans which will help these states to move forward in UBE.

The authorities have also been talking of a change in educational structure from 6-3-3-4 to 9-3-4, to reflect the 9-year basic school concept of UBE, but this has not gone down well with the populace.

Dissipation of effort

The paradigm shift from UPE to UBE was made in the overall context of EFA. UBE is a significant part of EFA and yet UBE and EFA in Nigeria seem to coexist rather than be part of a whole. The institutional structures for both are separate. EFA has engaged in data collection and consultations at all levels since it became operational in mid-2001. A draft state and national EFA plan with the 2015 deadline for achievement has been drawn up. What is not clear is whether EFA will now be integrated into UBE or UBE into EFA and there is a lack of clarity about the roles of each and how they should relate to each other.

The same dissipation of effort is seen in the continuing existence of commissions for nomadic education and mass literacy alongside the universal basic education commission. As shown in Table 5.3, mass literacy and nomadic education fall within the scope of UBE, but programme activities in these areas are carried out outside the ambit of UBE. The lack of rationalisation of administrative structures and consequent tendency for inefficient use of resources has potential to hold back development of UBE.

Unclear lines of authority and vague distribution of responsibilities

The lines of authority and the distribution of responsibilities are not clear, particularly in the States, where there is a permanent conflict between ministries of education and State Primary Education Boards (SPEB) which were set up in the early nineties in response to the shambles created when, in 1991, the federal government transferred full responsibility for primary education to the local governments. Following serious strike action by teachers, the federal ministry re-established the National Primary Education Commission and required states to establish SPEBs. In each of the 36 states the Commissioner (minister) for education should, in principle, be in-charge of the entire education sector, but the prevailing situation is one in which a SPEB is headed by an executive chairman, who reports directly to the State Governor. With the transformation of SPEBs into State Universal Basic Education Boards (SUBEBs), much of the school system is liable to escape the direct control of the ministries of education in the States.

Edging out local governments and beneficiary communities

In the days of true federalism, all types of primary social services (for example, primary health care, primary education and primary (rural) roads) were the responsibility of local government. Over the years, this has become a responsibility in name only. The 774 local governments still have their supervisory councillors for education and their local government education authorities (LGEAs), but they are nearly all poorly funded. Meanwhile, the relatively better funded State governments have been progressively usurping the roles of LGEAs in the management of education.

The effect of this unconstitutional trend on UBE is that the initiative is in danger of becoming removed from the grassroots communities that it is intended to benefit. Since all major decisions are made from far away (geographically and politically), there is little commitment from some members of local communities, particularly as the better-off take advantage of the parallel, strong, and ever-growing private primary education sector.

Poor management capacity at all levels

The low level of capacity to manage the planning and implementation of UBE has been the major focus of external assistance to the programme. The need to address this issue was raised in the publication of a World Bank study (Orbach, 2004). The report highlighted a number of issues:

* Heavy and clumsy bureaucratic structures both in the ministries of education and in the education sector parastatals;
* Over-staffing of existing bureaucracies with non-professionals – a heavy preponderance of 'junior' staff, most of whom have no modern skills;
* Poor decision-making tools, in the absence of reliable statistics;
* Outdated working tools, in an atmosphere in which computers are a luxury;
* Near-absence of training facilities in management, accounting, planning and project monitoring.

Most of the on-going donor-funded technical assistance focuses on institutional capacity strengthening. However, technical assistance can best operate in a situation of strong political will to effect civil service reforms, as well as profound reforms in governance practices.

The data problem

The issues around data collection, analysis and use of the reports generated have both political and technical dimensions. Population censuses have always been a politically charged issue. For this reason, projections based on population figures (such as net and gross enrolments) have remained in the realm of conjecture. At the technical level, the human capacity is still seriously deficient. There is even an attitudinal/behavioural dimension to the problem, arising from a general apathy towards record keeping and to using facts and figures for planning and decision-making.

There is no doubt that some progress has been made in recent years. In 1988, Civil Service reforms led to the creation of the Education Data Bank (EDB). EDB started by undertaking a school census every year from 1988 to 1992. The project ended in 1993 and there are no data for 1993 to 2001. World Bank loan support enabled a baseline 1999 to 2001 census and 2002 and 2003 school censuses to be completed but ownership of, and access to, the data was fragmented. The current strategy is to decentralise the education management information system and this is showing some promise.

A sustainability path for UPE/UBE

A 2005 study of Anglophone African countries identified the following enabling factors to explain the relatively fast move of a number of African countries towards the attainment of EFA goals (Obanya, 2005):

- Political stability – a pre-condition for everything else;
- Long-term strategic planning – UPE/EFA as an integral part of an over-arching national vision;
- Developing UPE/EFA in a systemic context – along with the post-primary sector of education;
- Paying special attention to the out-of-school population – thus the need to carry UPE/EFA along with non-formal basic education and literacy;
- Adopting an inclusive approach – access, equity, relevance, quality and efficiency promoted from the very beginning;
- Strong civil society involvement;
- Broad growth strategy – expansion of educational opportunities along with expansion of other socio-economic services;
- Building national capacity for planning and execution.

These points echo what was said in the early days of promoting UBE in Nigeria (Obanya, 2006).

The sustainability path for UPE/UBE in Nigeria must lie in the country genuinely taking steps to avoid the mistakes of the past and drawing on the experience of its own UPE/UBE history. Borrowing from the promising experience of the African top scorers on the EFA league table (see EFA Monitoring Reports) would be one way of building sustainability safeguards into its on-going efforts to bring basic education to all and, through education, contribute to the attainment of the MDG goals.

Conclusions

The discussion in this chapter should be understood in the context of the geographical, political, and socio-economic complexity of Nigeria. It should also be seen in the context of the huge development burden that Africa's most populous country has had to carry.

Even with these harsh political and socio-economic and even demographic realities, the country has made some bold steps over the years and undertaken a series of UPE adventures. Political instability has been a major drawback to the country's development over the years, and experience elsewhere in Africa shows that stability is the number one condition for sustainability of UPE/EFA initiatives. Given Nigeria's oil wealth (and now that indebtedness is not a hindrance), lack of funds is not likely to be a disenabling factor; while there are at present great fluctuations in the oil market, past history seems to indicate that the trend is upwards over the long term.

Nigeria is slowly and steadily returning to political stability. Its debt burden has been considerably reduced, while recent increases in petroleum prices have enhanced its income. Reforms are going on in many aspects of national life. There is now a national development blueprint, the National Empowerment and Economic Development Strategy (NEEDS). Donor interest is high. The country may benefit from a re-think of UBE. This could be undertaken in the following manner:

- Through a process of enlarged policy dialogue for wide-scale consensus building;
- Placed in the overall national development framework, NEEDS;
- Closely knit with the national and state EFA action plans;
- Implemented in the spirit of true federalism, with State and local governments at the helm;
- With the support of a technically strong, less bureaucratic administrative structure;
- With a functional EMIS, linked to an improved population census and other national statistical data bases; and
- With improved financial management.

These steps might require going back to the drawing board on a number of issues, but since a few months spent on this kind of planning might enhance sustainability considerably, it would be worth investing time, energy, political and social engineering to put UPE/UBE squarely on course for success.

Peter Williams

Sustaining UPE against the odds in Tanzania

Chapter 6

Introductory note

This study refers basically to experience in Mainland Tanzania. The Zanzibar education system is separately administered from education on the Mainland, where 97 per cent of the population resides. UNESCO data aggregates information for the two constituent parts of the Union but most of the reports and monographs on education in Tanzania confine their discussion to the situation on the Mainland. In the present study, wherever it is known that observations and data apply to Zanzibar as well as the Mainland, that fact is made known.

Background data

National data

The United Republic of Tanzania is situated on the coast of East Africa and has a land area of 883,000 km^2 (of which Zanzibar accounts for just 2,000). Projections from the National Bureau of Statistics give a population of 38.7m for 2006 (Mainland 37.5m and Zanzibar 1.1m), the annual growth rate is estimated to be 2.9 per cent and the average density of population is about 44 per sq. km. for the whole country. Expectation of life at birth is 54 years. The political capital (seat of Parliament) is Dodoma in the centre of the country, but Dar es Salaam (population 2.3m) is the commercial and administrative capital where most Ministries are housed. The official language, used widely in commerce and in international dealings, is English: but the most widely spoken national language is Swahili and that is the language of instruction in primary school.

The United Republic was formed in 1964 by the union of mainland Tanganyika, a UN Trusteeship Territory, that became independent from Britain in December 1961, and the islands of Zanzibar a former British Protectorate that became independent in December 1963. It is a multi-parliamentary democracy. The Executive Head of State is the President: the current incumbent is Jakaya Mrisho Kikwete, the fourth President, succeeding Benjamin William Mkapa (1996–2006) Ali Hassan Mwinyi (1986–1996) and Mwalimu Julius Nyerere (1961–1986). Successive governments have all been formed by the TANU party, which changed its name to CCM in 1977.

Tanzania is a member of the UN, the African Union, the Southern African Development Community (SADC) and the Commonwealth of Nations.

Tanzania's GDP has recently been growing at over 6 per cent p.a. and was approximately $US120 billion at factor cost in 2005 giving a GDP per capita of roughly $320. The country is largely agricultural and the agriculture sector accounts for half of GDP. The next most important productive sector is manufacturing with about 7 per cent of GDP in

1999. Minerals (gold in particular, diamonds, gemstones) account for a high proportion of foreign exchange earnings. The national currency is the Tanzanian shilling (£1 = Tshs. 2,500, $US1 = Tshs. 1,280 as at August 2007).

Education

Education in Zanzibar and education on the Mainland are separately administered, each of the two constituent parts of the Union having its own Ministry responsible for Education. On the Mainland this is the Ministry of Education and Vocational Training for school-level education and the Ministry of Higher Education, Science and Technology for post-secondary education, each headed by its own minister. As said in the introductory note to this chapter, reflecting the separately administered education systems, the most commonly used, quoted and published statistics from the Ministry in Dar es Salaam are for Mainland Tanzania only, and exclude Zanzibar. Unless otherwise stated, therefore, the discussion and analysis in this study applies only to the Mainland.

The formal education system in each of the two parts of the United Republic has a 7-4-2-4 (3-5) structure for general studies: seven grades of primary school, followed by four years of secondary, two years of upper secondary ('sixth form') and then three to five years' university. Pre-primary education for two years, mainly in the voluntary sector, precedes this and has a 29 per cent coverage. The primary school system was reduced to seven grades from eight in the 1960s, when the two-stage system (Standards I–IV lower primary school and Standards V–VIII upper primary) had the selection bar at the end of Grade IV removed. The overwhelming majority (99.8 per cent) of primary schools are in the public sector, but at secondary level the non-government sector is more important and in 2006 accounted for 30 per cent of students.

Table 6.1. Tanzania: enrolments, enrolment rates and teacher situation by level of education, 2006 (Mainland Tanganyika and Zanzibar combined)

Education level	Pupils '000		GER	NER	Teachers '000		% trained	PTR
	T	(%F)			T	(%F)		
Pre-primary	638	(50)	29	29	11	(58)	22	57
Primary	7 960	(49)	110	98	152	(48)	100	56
Secondary	676	(47)	n.a.	n.a.	23	n.a.	n.a.	n.a.
Tertiary (2005)	43	(29)	1	3				

Source: UIS Global Education Digest 2006

The number of primary pupils recorded by UIS represents the third highest for any country in Sub-Saharan Africa, exceeded only by Nigeria (21m. in 2005) and Ethiopia (8m.).

The official age of entry to school in Tanzania is 7 years, so that the primary school age-range is ostensibly 7–13, and secondary school 14–17/19. National examinations at Grade 7, 11 and 13 are set and marked by the National Examinations Council of Tanzania.

Tanzania and Universal Primary Education

This study focuses on Tanzania's efforts since Independence in 1961 to attain universal primary education. There have been two main thrusts: the first was in the decade following the 1974 Musoma Resolution and included the UPE declaration of 1977, and the second was ushered in by the abolition of primary school fees in 2002 and is still on-going. The first drive for UPE peaked in enrolment terms in 1983. The *UNESCO Statistical Yearbooks* for 1983 and 1984 showed gross enrolment ratios in primary education of over 100 for the period 1980–1982, but later estimates made in the light of more accurate population data suggest that the highest GER reached at that time was 96.3 in 1981 (a composite of male GER at 100.7 and female at 91.9). The numerical enrolment peak (most children enrolled) in those years was actually two years later, in 1983, when 3.56m children were in primary school. That was 23,000 more than in 1981 but the GER had dropped sharply to 90.5 by 1983. This illustrates how a rapid increase in school-age population (3 per cent p.a. in Tanzania in the early 1980s) can cause GER to drop sharply even if enrolments are stable or on a slight upward trend. An important supplementary feature of this first quest for 'education for all' was that Tanzania also claimed to have achieved universal adult literacy at the same time.

Tanzanians were well aware that the recorded GER of close to 100 at the start of the 1980s did not mean that all children of school age were actually in school. Many school places were occupied by learners over the official primary-school age and in 1981, when GER is now estimated to have been 96.3, the net enrolment rate (NER) was only 68.1. (In those years NER peaked in 1980 at 69.4).

These UPE peaks in the early 1980s were followed by a slump in enrolment rates between the mid-1980s and late 1990s. Actual primary-school enrolments only fell 11–12 per cent, by 400,000, from 3.56m in 1983 to 3.16m in 1988: and by 1992 were back at record levels of 3.60m, rising to 4.04m in 1998. Because of substantial population growth, however, both GER and NER steadily declined and in 1998 stood at 63.6 and 47.1 respectively, far below the levels attained in the early 1980s. Half a million more children were in school in 1998 than in 1981, but enrolment *ratios* were 20 points down for NER and 30 points down for GER.

The situation has been turned round dramatically since 2000, and especially after tuition fees were abolished in time for the 2002 school year. Enrolments have risen from 4.38m in 2000 to 7.96m in 2006 which is well over twice as many pupils as in the peak year (1981) of the first thrust. The GER is estimated at 110 in 2006 and exceeds 100 for both boys (112) and girls (109), while the NER at 98 is far above its former peak level in 1980.

The remainder of this brief study:

- summarises Tanzania's efforts to achieve UPE in the 1970s and 1980s (part 3);
- describes the period of regression from the early 1980s to the turn of the century (part 4);
- provides some glimpses of the 'second wave' starting in 2001 and now ongoing (part 5);
- sets out summary conclusions (part 6);

- comments finally on the terms of reference of this project as they apply to the Tanzanian case (part 7).

Tanzania's first thrust to UPE

The Addis Ababa Conference on African Education in 1961 had set a target date of 1980 for the achievement of UPE in sub-Saharan African countries. But even though both Gold Coast/Ghana (Nkrumah) and the Western and Eastern Regions of Nigeria (Awolowo, Azikiwe) among British dependencies had already embraced the aim of universal primary education as a means of mobilising public opinion behind the 'Independence project', Tanzania did not attempt to follow suit. This was certainly not because of any lack of sympathy on Tanzania's part with the goal of UPE. It simply reflected economic and political realities. For the stock of skills inherited at Independence was pitifully small and the education system was hopelessly underdeveloped – in 1961 at Independence there were only 1,603 students in Form 4, and 176 form 6 students, of whom 14 per cent were females. Higher education was in the very first stages of development.

Economic resources were short – unlike its West African cousins Tanzania did not go into independence with substantial financial reserves – and so the Government of Julius Nyerere had to choose priorities carefully. With some reluctance, given the socialist philosophy of the regime, the decision was made to focus initially on developing the human resources that would enable Tanzania to localise key positions in Government and the public services. Secondary and higher education consequently received the bulk of the investment resources in the 1960s. It was not a comfortable situation to be constrained to invest heavily in the education of a few, as Nyerere frequently insisted:

> 'In a socialist country universal primary education would be provided for all children, and post-primary education would be available to all who could benefit from it, however old they may be ... . The poverty of Tanzania does not allow for the kind of expenditure which would be necessary for such universal services, however much we would like them'.

> (Nyerere in a 1971 speech, quoted in Omari et al. p. 37)

Nyerere repeatedly exhorted the recipients of secondary and higher education to remember their obligations to Tanzania's poor rural masses on whose behalf (and from whose taxes) investment in their education was being made. It was always clear that as soon as circumstances allowed the emphasis would switch to extending primary education and adult literacy, in accordance with the philosophy of *ujamaa* as expounded in the *Arusha Declaration* and in its education counterpart, *Education for Self-reliance* (1967).

The Government did not neglect primary education in this period. The 1961 Education Act removed racial and other discrimination from the education system. The eight-grade primary education system with a selection exam at Standard IV was converted to an all-through seven-grade system so that by 1968 entrants to all primary schools would have the possibility of continuing through to Standard VII. From 1969, by circulars issued in 1967, Kiswahili was made the medium of instruction in all grant-aided primary schools.

But it was only in 1969, in its Second Five-Year Plan, that the Government felt able to set a target for achievement of UPE. Conservatively, its proposal was to increase the enrolment rate steadily to reach 95 per cent by 1989, and this obviously had to involve expansion of primary education at a rate exceeding expected population growth. The Plan still put most emphasis on consolidating the development of those parts of the system that produced high-level manpower, and emphasised that the expansion of primary education would have to involve a great measure of self-help in order to keep down the budgetary costs. In the event, partly no doubt as a result of improved transition rates to upper primary grades under the new seven-year primary system, a period of substantial growth of primary-school enrolment took place in the Second Five-Year Plan – 6 per cent in 1971, 9 per cent in 1972 and over 10 per cent in 1973. The planned increase in Standard I enrolments over the Plan period was 203,000, but the actual figure was 247,000 (Omari et al. p. 36).

In 1971 primary school fees were abolished in Maasailand (Mosha, 1995) and in 1973 across the whole country. In 1974 at the ruling party meeting in Musoma, the National Executive Committee passed a resolution directing the Government to make plans that would enable every school-age child to go to primary school by 1977, twelve years sooner than had previously been planned. Omari et al. (p. 38) point out that this decision could hardly have been predicted from previous events: the planners had long been emphasising the need for caution calculation of logistics and costs and Nyerere himself had stated in 1971 that:

> 'We have provided school places for only about 52 per cent of the children of primary school age – that is how far we are from our objective of universal primary education! And it is absurd to think that passing resolutions at TANU Conferences, or asking questions in Parliament, can solve this problem.'

Yet that is exactly what took place three years later at the Party Conference in Musoma in November 1974, all the more unexpected given that the country was suffering from drought conditions.

According to the Government's own review of the implementation of UPE (1989, pp. 4 and 5), the reasons for deciding to advance the date of UPE were that villagisation (the creation of central *ujamaa* villages) had been proceeding apace and government had justified this in terms of the possibility it afforded to make available to the public essential services, including schools:

* the process of villagisation itself created demand for school places;
* the TANU Congress in 1973 had learned that schools had capacity for more children than were actually in school;
* UPE was seen as a means to promote universal literacy, another key aim of the Party and Government's programme. It was realised that almost as fast as the ranks of adult illiterates were reduced by the campaigns, their number was replenished by illiterate youths reaching adult age (Omari et al. pp. 37 and 39).

A further consideration may have been consciousness that serious disparities were developing in primary education enrolment, reflecting the emphasis on self-reliance and differential resource availability between districts (Omari et al. p. 36). A policy of universalisation represented a promise of 'catch-up' for poorer districts.

The decision to abolish school fees and the Musoma Resolution set in train an explosion of enrolments, amounting to a tripling of the numbers in primary school between 1973 and 1981 and a big jump in the enrolment ratios (compare 1973 – enrolment 1.13m, GER 40.1, NER n.a. with 1981 – enrolment 3.54m, GER 96.3, NER 68.1).

What do we know about how this was achieved in logistical terms? It seems to be generally agreed that there was rather little by way of feasibility studies and careful forward planning before the UPE policy decision was announced. Thereafter, however, a period of intensive activity took place to ensure implementation of the Musoma decisions that 'within three years ... by November 1977 arrangements must be completed which will enable every child of school age to obtain a place in a primary school'.

Preparations and policies

The preparatory work was both political and technical. In fact, the Ministry of Education's account of the preparatory phase lists 'campaigns for mass education' as its first item. Tanzania used the press and radio to get messages across to the people about the need to send their children to school and the part they should play through community effort. Government and party leaders toured the country to provide motivation.

It was recognised that resources were short and that resort must be had to self-reliance and radical alternatives in education delivery. The latter would include, for example, community construction of classrooms and teachers' houses, slates instead of pencils and paper for pupils' use, resort to double sessions, older students teaching younger ones in the same school, and secondary school pupils teaching in primary schools.

A series of three implementation guidelines was issued in 1974 and 1975 dealing with classrooms, teachers and equipment preparations. There were to be volunteer teachers given a monthly allowance of 150 shillings, and short term courses[1] were to be provided for them. Half-day schooling was to be introduced to make possible the admission of more children to Standard I. A maximum age of entry to primary school of 12 years was laid down. A census was carried out by regional education officers in 1975 which showed that there were 1.8m school-age children, and these data were used as the basis for ordering supplies.

Construction of classrooms and teachers' houses etc was to be by community effort, but Government offered help of Tshs. 5,000 for every teachers' quarters (later raised to Tshs. 12,000) and Tshs. 7,000 for classrooms (raised to Tshs. 10,000 later). Villagers were supposed to build latrines using their own resources.

Teacher supply was a crucial concern. It was estimated in 1975 that 68,900 teachers would be needed compared with the availability of 28,900, a shortage of 40,000. The annual output from training colleges was only 4,000 a year. To deal with this:

- Efforts were made to draw retired trained teachers back into service;
- Existing training colleges were expanded and new ones built;

- The grade A course was restructured to provide just one year in college followed by a second year in the schools on teaching practice;
- A programme to train Grade C teachers outside colleges was introduced. This new programme, to train P7 students in a three-year course leading to a Grade C certificate, had the following elements:
  1 class training in special centres 2 or 3 times a week for three years given by ward education co-ordinators who were trained for the purpose;
  2 training by radio and cassettes;
  3 education by correspondence (materials provided by the Institute of Adult Education);
  4 practice class teaching for 10–15 periods in the first year and 24–30 periods in the third year;
  5 this was followed by a six-week training course in college.
- Education was introduced as a subject in secondary schools and technical schools with a view to using graduates of these institutions as teachers (however this plan was actually abandoned before implementation).

Achievements

Pupil enrolments
There was a marked increase in intake in 1975, the year after the Musoma Resolution, perhaps by as much as 60 per cent and there were further big increases in Standard I intake in 1977 and 1978. Standard I enrolment appears to have peaked at 878,000 in 1978 (compared with only 248,000 in 1974). To judge from the data in the *Implementation Report* (p. 71) and *Basic Statistics in Education (BEST) 1999* (Table 4 1h), the swollen 1978 intake passed through the system in a tsunami-like surge, almost 200,000 larger than the cohorts either side of it, which finally reached Standard VII in 1984. Total enrolments expanded cumulatively by 26 per cent in 1975, a further 23 per cent in 1976, 16 per cent in 1977, and a staggering 32 per cent (representing an extra 720,000 pupils) in 1978. By 1978, indeed, total primary school enrolment had doubled in just three years since 1975; and between 1973 and 1981 there was a tripling of enrolment.

Particular success was achieved in the gender ratio which, for all primary classes taken together, rose from 42 per cent females in 1974, to 46 per cent in 1978 and 50 per cent in 1985. To have achieved gender parity at that time was very remarkable and far ahead of other African countries.

In spite of these successes, the best information currently available from the UNESCO Institute for Statistics suggests that Tanzania never did better in this period than about 70 per cent in terms of NER and 96 per cent GER. Ministers at the time claimed to have very nearly achieved their UPE objective, but it seems they in fact fell quite far short of it. The Ministry's own 1989 report on UPE confirms this in its analysis of regional variation of GERs and NERs for 1986, showing that GER varied from 93 per cent in Iringa to only 66 per cent in Dar es Salaam, and NER from 78 per cent in Coast Region to 56 per cent in Dar (Table 2, page 18). With reference to this rather unexpected data for Dar es Salaam, Sumra (1995) states:

'... nowhere is the problem as big as in Dar es Salaam. In Temeke district, Dar es Salaam, there were 57,594 children between the ages of 7 and 13 not in school, that is nearly 60 per cent of the age group in the district. Out of these 63.38 per cent were boys and 52.39 per cent were girls. In urban areas, one of the reasons for not enrolling could be lack of space in schools. In all three districts in Dar es Salaam, and that is true for all the urban districts in the country, there are more males who are not enrolled than girls. The lure for making quick money through petty trade and in some cases desperate needs of the family push children to engage in economic activities instead of attending school. In Dar es Salaam the problem is made worse by a large number of street children.'

The recorded enrolment figures also overstate actual achievement in another major way: the Ministry's data suggests that average actual *attendance* was only 83 per cent of those nominally registered. (MoE 1989, p. 22).

The Ministry itself explains the shortfall in enrolment in the following terms, (some of them somewhat implausible):

* some parents didn't know the age of their children and were late in sending them to school for that reason;
* children were engaged in income-earning for the family, e.g. cattle and goat herding, or in child caring;
* some deliberately left education to get wage employment;
* some communities married their children after puberty (age 13–15) and hence they couldn't continue with schooling;
* disruptions to schooling caused by disturbances like cattle raiding;
* witchcraft (fear of witchcraft deterring teachers and supervisory staff enforcing attendance in communities where witchcraft practices existed);
* Koranic classes took priority over formal school for some Muslim parents.

One might have expected that with the passage of time the age range of children in Standard I would get closer to the official entry age of 7, but the fragmentary evidence provided for the years 1982–86 in the Ministry's report suggests that this was not the case. In Table 6.2 1999 data taken from BEST 2000 are given for comparison.

Table 6.2. Age distribution of children enrolled in Standard I in Tanzania 1982, 1986, 1999

	1982	1986	(1999)
7 years	24.2	17.4	(19.0)
8 years	29.1	25.0	(26.5)
9 years	22.7	24.2	(23.3)
10 years	13.8	18.2	(17.1)
11 years and above	5.9	9.5	(8.3)
Other ages	4.1	5.4	(5.9)

Sources: for 1982 and 1986: Ministry of Education (1989) Table 3 p. 18. For 1999: *Basic Statistics in Education 1999*, Regional Data: Table 1(d). Ministry of Education and Culture (2000).

Repetition and drop-out

Omari 1994 p. 27 gives crude wastage rates of 28 per cent for the 1978 Standard I cohort, as it progressed over the period 1978–84 and 47 per cent for the 1983 cohort over the period 1983–89. The Ministry report on UPE implementation shows 102,000 drop-outs in 1980, with drop-out between Grades III and IV accounting for 32 per cent of this and drop-out between Grades VI and VII 18 per cent. Repetition rates are not readily available for the bulk of this period but in 1991, according to Omari (1994), repeaters accounted for 124,000 out of 3.51m enrolled, i.e. just under 3 per cent of the total.

School buildings

The number of primary schools in Tanzania grew by 27 per cent in the decade after 1976. In 1983 when the condition of classrooms was assessed, there were only 57,000 classrooms, a third of which (17,000) were temporary. The absolute shortage was reported to be 20,000.

The Ministry of Education reported a 59 per cent increase in the number of teachers' houses (1978 to 1982). Nevertheless, out of about 90,000 teachers only 15,600 (17 per cent) had permanent housing and a further 12 per cent had temporary housing.

Equipment

As at 1983 there was a serious shortfall in available equipment, with only 56 per cent of the number of desks, 27 per cent and 12 per cent of teacher's tables and chairs, and 13 per cent of cupboards required. In 1983 only a third of the pupil exercise book requirements were met and books, pens and pencils were in very short supply.

The reasons given by the Ministry of Education (1989) were:

- shortage of funds, equipment and personnel at the Institute of Curriculum Development;
- shortage of foreign exchange and devaluation of the Tanzania shilling making it hard to obtain equipment made abroad;
- lack of transport for distribution;
- inadequate budgetary allocations for equipment, and failure to collect more than 38 per cent of the required parental contribution of 20 shillings per pupil.

Teachers and teacher education

Primary teacher numbers rose sharply to reach 94,000 in 1986, compared with only 39,000 ten years earlier. Understandably teacher supply could not keep pace with enrolment growth so that in the early years of the UPE project the teacher-pupil-teacher ratio rose sharply to 50 in 1976. But as the supply of new trainees, especially the out-of-college Grade C teachers, 'kicked in' the ratio fell back to 33 in 1986. In fact the teacher supply situation improved fast enough for Grade A teacher education to revert to two years in college in 1980 (as distinct from the truncated one-year-in-college course introduced in 1977) and for the Grade C college course to be lengthened from two years to three years at the same time.

Evidently, the composition of the teacher force changed quite substantially. Over the whole period 1975 to 1983, 82,000 new teachers were produced but less than 30 per cent of these were Grade A. Over 40 per cent were Grade C teachers produced by the distance-education route, and the remainder were college-trained Grade C teachers. Even as late as 2000, there were 62,000 teachers of this cohort remaining in schools, most with poor qualifications and hardly retrainable.

Recoil: the Eighties and Nineties

Almost as soon as UPE had been launched, the situation of the country changed for the worse, with a serious economic crisis reflecting the downturn in the world economy, exacerbated in Tanzania's case by the strain of the Uganda war.

An early response to the economic difficulties was the decision to ask parents to contribute 20 shillings per school child – this was not easy to collect and the Ministry of Education reported (MoE 1989, Table 20) that only 34 per cent of the levies could be collected in 1980 and 39.5 per cent in 1984. Some regions were only able to collect between 10 per cent and 20 per cent of what was due. Despite the rate of non-payment when the fee was only TSh20/=, it was increased to TSh100/= in 1985. Later, in 1995, primary school tuition fees were formally reintroduced and a rate of about TSh2000/= per pupil was being charged by the end of the century. According to the Education Sector Review, only 51 per cent of fee income due was being collected in 2000.

Economic difficulties persisted throughout the 1980s despite the introduction of an economic reform package under the Structural Adjustment and Economic Recovery Programmes, and foreign indebtedness considerably increased. Consequently, the resources invested in the education system diminished and there were serious shortages of key inputs to the schools. A drastic drop in the quality of education was experienced in the three dimensions of inputs, process and outputs.

Inputs: In the decade after the Musoma Resolution expenditure on education increased markedly in current price terms, but in constant prices it fell; and the share of the budget set aside for education diminished dramatically from 14 per cent in 1975/76 to only 6 per cent in 1985/86. Donor contributions to education development were minimal over much of the period of greatest expansion. Although Government subventions to the schools were supplemented by parental financial contributions, by self-reliance efforts in construction, and by schools' own productive activities, there was a serious shortfall of resources. The impact was particularly severe on books, materials and equipment where provision was totally inadequate – the number of textbooks per pupil was only 1:10.

One area where inputs per pupil did not decline was in the supply of teachers. The large investment in teacher production in the late 1970s yielded its dividend in subsequent years. The size of the teaching force grew strongly right up to 1986 and the teacher-pupil ratio improved from 1:50 in 1977 to 1:33 in 1986. It was only later, when budgetary cuts began to bite more severely, that newly trained teachers lacked jobs and a pool of unemployed qualified teachers developed.[2]

Process: The situation in the schools is described by Omari et al. (p. 45) in the following terms:

'By January 1978 the program of universalization of primary education started to show signs of stress. Classrooms designed for 45 pupils were serving 80. Children were attending classes under trees and sitting on the ground; newly constructed classrooms were falling apart; and some classrooms were small and hazardous. The classes and teachers that were produced for the universalization program were considered second-rate. The trainee teachers had no offices, and the established teachers began to feel threatened by the para-professionals. Discipline problems increased with rumours about the para-professionals having sexual relations with their students, coming to school drunk, being given too heavy a work load, and being expected to teach the difficult classes. There was an aura of chaos mixed with the enthusiasm. Parents were complaining about 'universalization of illiteracy' rather than universalization of literacy and newspapers carried articles about the falling standards and chaos in primary schools.'

There seems little doubt that the quality of education did suffer badly as a result of resource shortage, overcrowding and the pace of expansion. No doubt the quality of management and supervision also left a lot to be desired, and this was exacerbated by poor communications and lack of transport to visit schools.

Outputs: Wastage (drop-out) was serious, but not exceptional by comparison with other countries. The Ministry of Education reports an average rate per grade in 1980 of 3.5 per cent which when compounded would yield about 23 per cent over the cycle. Nor was repetition a major problem overall during most of the period, given that regulations were in place to limit it. However when the Standard IV exam was re-introduced in 1986, it resulted in 190,000 out of the 1986 Standard IV class repeating the grade in 1987 (MoE 1989, p. 35). Some 36 per cent of pupils had failed the exam. An analysis of the Primary School Leaving Exam (Standard VII) results in 1986 showed that only 17 per cent of pupils scored 50 per cent or more on the exam: the regional variation was from 37 per cent in Dar es Salaam to 8 per cent in Coast Province.

For a time, the turn-around in the progress of UPE was masked by the progression through the system of the cohorts already enrolled. Numbers in school continued to increase right up to 1983 and it was only after 1984, when the bulge intake from 1978 had passed through the system, that overall enrolment started to contract. The 1978 intake to Primary 1 represented the peak during the first UPE thrust. Thereafter, there was stagnation in primary-school entrants, but no complete collapse in numbers. Only when the enrolments are matched against 3 per cent population growth, does the serious decline in the coverage of the system become apparent.

Total enrolments were on a rising trend after 1985 and reached 4 million at the end of the 1990s. However they failed to keep pace with population growth and the net enrolment

Table 6.3. Enrolment in Standard I and all grades of primary school, 1974–85

| Year | Standard I (000s) | | | All Enrolments | | |
	Boys	Girls	Total	Boys	Girls	Total
1974	139.6	108.0	**247.6**	727.2	501.7	**1 228.8**
1975	239.1	194.1	**433.2**	888.9	644.0	**1 533.0**
1976	270.4	236.1	**506.5**	1 064.3	810.0	**1 874.4**
1977	287.5	255.7	**543.2**	1 221.7	972.5	**2 194.2**
1978	461.0	417 3	**878.3**	1 582.9	1 330.1	**2 913.0**
1979	276.6	264.0	**540.6**	1 713.1	1 484.3	**3 197.4**
1980	246.8	240.0	**486.9**	1 779.1	1 582.1	**3 361.2**
1981	249.8	248.2	**498.0**	1 846.9	1 683.7	**3 530.6**
1982	248.3	249.2	**497.5**	1 810.5	1 693.2	**3 503.7**
1983	271.4	271.2	**542.6**	1 816.6	1 736.6	**3 553.1**
1984	264.5	268.9	**533.4**	1 762.8	1 721.1	**3 483.9**
1985	265.0	260.0	**525.0**	1 584.5	1 575.6	**3 160.1**

Source: Ministry of Education (1989) Appendix '0', p. 80.

rate of only 47 per cent at its nadir meant in effect that in a 20-year period coverage of the system had declined by a third (from a NER of 70 per cent) in 1980. This seems to have represented the combined effect of falling supply of primary education on the part of Government and falling demand from parents. Tanzania may have signed up to the global Education for All campaign launched at Jomtien in 1990, but it had not progressed towards the goal by the time of the successor Dakar Conference in April 2000.

The leadership of the country remained with the TANU/CCM party throughout the 1980s and 1990s, but the phase of enthusiasm and exhortation that had driven the UPE campaign in the 1970s was over. This may have been partly due to the perception initially that UPE and universal adult literacy had in fact been achieved soon after 1980: it took some time for the realisation to sink in that progress had been halted. But there was also a change of mood, with access and equality no longer being the drivers of policy. Economic efficiency and productivity were the new watchwords, and Government stressed cost-sharing and encouraged voluntary and private sector schools to establish themselves. 'Expert' advice, supplied mostly by the donor countries and creditor agencies, was that UPE could not be afforded and that the search for cost savings should take priority in education policy. Lawson (1995 p.19) cites the World Bank's Public Expenditure Review as calculating that, in 1993/94, the education budget would have to be increased by 25 per cent if UPE was to be attained at then-existing standards of school provision: but additional funding equal to 176 per cent of the entire education-sector budget would have been required if UPE was to be attained at what were considered to be 'acceptable standards' of school provision!

It is hardly surprising that Galabawa in his paper on Tanzania for the ADEA Biennial Meeting in Arusha in 2001 should give such a gloomy prognosis for UPE prospects:

In spite the very impressive expansionary education policies and reforms in the

1970s, the goal to achieve UPE which was once targeted for achievement in 1980, is way out of reach. Similarly, the Jomtien objective to achieve Basic Education for All in 2000 is on the part of Tanzania unrealistic. The participation and access levels (as shown by enrolment and intake rates) have declined to the point that attainment of UPE is once again an issue in itself.

A new attempt in a new century

In his re-election campaign in 2001, President Mkapa promised to abolish primary school fees. Meanwhile, agreements were reached with the main donors to reschedule Tanzania's external debt and that the funds released should be devoted to universalising primary education. The World Bank agreed to make a loan to Tanzania of $US150m in support of a new programme to expand and reform primary education. A Primary Education Development Programme (PEDP), to run from July 2002 to June 2007, was launched with the aim of expanding enrolment, improving quality, building capacity and instituting more efficient resource use. A key aim was to achieve UPE by 2005, and, in quality terms, to reduce pupil-teacher ratios to 40:1, expand in-service training of teachers and make available a per capita grant per student of $US10 to be allocated directly to schools and be spent on teaching-learning materials, including one textbook for every three students in each subject.

As a result of external inputs and the greater commitment of Tanzania's domestic funds, substantially more resources went into primary education. Mushi (2006) shows that as against 11 per cent of the Government budget devoted to education in 1997/98 (and 13 per cent in 1999/2000) the proportion rose to over 19 per cent in 2003/2004. Basic education gained at the expense of other levels, the share of the education budget increasing from 64 per cent in 1997/78 to 73 per cent in 2003/04. Secondary education (1 per cent lower share) and tertiary education (4 per cent lower share) were the main losers.

The effects of the new policy on enrolment was immediate. Enrolment has climbed steeply from 4.4m in 2000 to almost 8m in 2006 when the NER reached 98 and the GER 110. Wedgwood points out that, as well as the abolition of tuition fees, the PEDP's restrictions on all other kinds of charges previously made by schools have also been a positive factor. Most likely, too, the inputs aimed at improving quality, and the system of direct grants to primary schools, have had their effect. For example, in 2003 the book/pupil ratio had improved to 1:4 from 1:8 previously. Between 2001 and 2002, the number of teachers rose by 6 per cent, the number of primary schools increased by 5 per cent, and a total of 29,922 new classrooms were built during 2002–2004. Dropout rates between Grades 4 and 5 declined from 6.8 per cent in 2000 to 5 per cent in 2004. Pass rates on the Primary School Leaving Exam have improved to 40.1 per cent in 2003 compared with 27.1 per cent in 2002 and 19.9 per cent in 1999, but Wedgwood attributes this in part to the incorporation in the exam of Kiswahili on which students tend to do well, and consequently according less weight to mathematics and English where they perform less strongly.

The record on quality is, however, still ambivalent. Wedgwood quotes Sumra as claiming that 'At the community level key stakeholders have seen no evidence of efforts to improve quality', with the pupil-teacher ratio worsening from 46:1 to 57:1, and being as high as 71:1 in some regions. In individual schools there are classes of up to 200 or more (Sumra 2003). Wedgwood goes on to say:

'Many schools have adopted double shift teaching to cope with the increased enrolment. This has led to a reduction of teaching hours from 6 to 3.5. Little in-service training has taken place and many schools are still lacking textbooks. District spending on learning resources has mainly gone on expensive science kits but few teachers have the skills to use these. There has been a great deal of construction but most of this has been classrooms. Far fewer teachers' houses or latrines have been built. Teachers' houses are important for staff retention, especially in remote areas, whilst latrines are important for maintaining attendance, especially for girls. In some areas the quality of construction has been low.'

Wedgwood reports that more students have been dropping out and more repeating. Because of the large numbers passing through the primary system, transition rates to secondary school will fall sharply, despite the recent launch of a Secondary Education Development Programme (SEDP), and act as a disincentive to enrolment of primary pupils.

The improved provision of books and materials for the schools is contributing to create a better image of primary education, though a recent research report for CODESRIA (Mushi, 2006) details a number of problems that can arise. Mushi's basic conclusion on the direct support programme is guardedly positive:

'Although a number of significant quantitative achievements have been identified under PEDP, we cannot attribute them entirely to the direct support component; in fact the massive flow of funds is more associated with the achievements than anything else. However, there are other achievements which are purely qualitative and are attributable to the direct support.

PEDP is too much dependent on external financing; its sustainability is susceptible to donor politics and their domestic policy environment. And as thus, sustainability of the achievements is not guaranteed. It is not the right time to declare that the direct support to schools in Tanzania is a success, there are many issues that remain unstudied and unresolved, but the lessons so far are mainly in support of the mechanism.'

Never has it been so important for Tanzania to recruit good quality teachers given that, far from achieving the 1:40 teacher-pupil ratio aimed at under PEDP, the actual ratio declined to 1:58 in 2005 (Mushi 2006 table 4), and the UNESCO Institute for Statistics still records 1:52 in 2006. A PTR of 1:52 may well imply an average size of the taught group of 65 or more, because many teachers are absent for reasons of sickness or in-service training, or have to devote some of their time to administrative and other duties. The reality is many classes with 100 or more children.

Unfortunately, teacher supply is under huge strain, as Wedgwood has shown. She demonstrates that teacher education in Tanzania is still beset by severe problems that impact on the quality of teachers. Just as happened thirty years ago, the Grade A course has been temporarily restructured to replace a two-year college course with one year in college and one year under supervision in schools. Arrangements for this supervision have so far been far from adequate. The qualifications of those going into the Grade A course are well below the Grade III secondary certificate that regulations stipulate – Wedgwood demonstrates that once the intake to Form V has been catered for, there are far too few Grade III and better certificate holders left over to fill the Grade A teacher training places, even if it were heroically (and wrongly) assumed that Form V and teacher training are the sole destinations of good Certificate holders. And it has been found that one in six of newly graduating teachers assigned to posts fails to take them up – partly because of the tendency to assign new teachers to rural areas where supply is most deficient, but by the same token conditions of work, professionally and domestically, are known to be unfavourable.

There has also been something of a continuing crisis in respect of the under-qualified teachers from the previous UPE drive, who were taken on without secondary school qualifications. They have been required under recent directives to 'upgrade' to grade A by studying and sitting for O' levels. But Wedgwood reports that 'results released in 2001 showed that over 90 per cent of teachers sitting O' levels failed (Rajani, 2001)'. Although the teacher upgrading programme has been reformed, Tanzania has still not emerged from the serious problems of quality in the teaching force resulting from the emergency recruitment programmes in the 1970s. There is still a large residue of poorly qualified teachers from that earlier period.

General conclusion

The Tanzania experience of attempts to reach UPE is one of the most fascinating in Commonwealth Africa. A very poor country with a rapidly growing population managed, largely by its own Herculean efforts, to enrol a very high proportion of its children in school in the 1970s and 1980s. It did this at the same time as implementing a universal adult literacy campaign.

To the extent that the first UPE campaign was successful, this was apparently due to two main factors. Most important was the political and social mobilisation that took place under a committed leadership, engendering a level of enthusiasm and energy among the people that carried the programme forward so far. Second was the programme of emergency measures and 'short cuts' that produced spectacular short-term results in terms of new teachers and new classrooms.

Unfortunately the roots of success were shallow and the project was not sturdy enough to withstand entirely the effects of international and domestic economic crisis in the late 1970s and the 1980s, and the simultaneous inexorable population increase. The level of enrolments dipped, though it should be recognised that even at the lowest point in 1986 the number of Tanzanian children in primary school was three times the 1971 figure – an enormous achievement. But measured by net enrolment ratios, the 'regression' was serious, because at the end of the 20th century Tanzania was only half way to having all children of primary-school age enrolled compared with 70 per cent in 1980.

This regression was no doubt rooted in poverty and the wretched economic situation in which Tanzania found itself due to a combination of circumstances, some of the country's own making and some imposed on it by the international creditors working through the Bretton Woods institutions. But there is little doubt, too, that the very low quality of education – partly the direct result of the pace at which UPE had been introduced – depressed enrolment.

Tanzania is now embarked on a second attempt at UPE. In many respects the prospect is more hopeful than with the first attempt, largely because of massive donor support translated into more plentiful physical resources in the schools. The numbers in school and the enrolment ratios far surpass what was achieved thirty years ago and there is a more concerted attempt to get materials and equipment into the schools.

Yet this 'second time round' attempt has some of the characteristics of the first. In 1974 UPE was sprung on the country by the political leadership 'out of the blue', not very different from what happened in 2001–02. The risk involved in this top-down campaign is all the greater in that this second attempt at UPE is so dependent on donor support and donor whims. Moreover, this time round, as before, the structural imbalance in the education system reflected in the limited availability of secondary schooling threatens to depress the supply of competent teachers and the enthusiasm of parents for enrolling their children in primary school. Third, the quality of teachers remains a problem. The hastily recruited and inadequately trained Grade C teachers from twenty five years ago, having not yet reached retirement age, are still a drag on quality.[3] The average pupil-teacher ratio of 52 or more is incompatible with quality primary education. Tanzania still has very much to do.

Summary assessment of the Tanzanian experience in relation to the terms of reference of the study

To expand and supplement the general conclusions above, here the Tanzanian education story is related to the basic questions asked in the terms of reference for the study.

The educational system

Features of the education system itself that have influenced success or failure in UPE
One can look at this in two ways. On the one hand, Tanzania was ready to be radical in its approach to UPE and adopt emergency measures to save expense and to move things along quickly. These measures made possible a very rapid increase in enrolment in the second half of the 1970s. On the other hand, these same devices were not such as to command the confidence of parents in the quality of education, and insufficient funding was allocated to efficient management of the system and to provision of necessary support materials.

There was a divorce in Tanzania at critical junctures between the political perspective and the professional perspective. Decisions were made on purely political grounds and the bureaucrats were told to find ways to implement the political decisions. Without this sense of urgency and direction, however, UPE in the 1970s would not have happened at all, for good or ill.

In spite of the attention paid to secondary education development in the first decade of Independence, the rate of increase could not keep pace with the growth of primary enrolments and the transition ration declined from 36 per cent in 1961/62 to 11 per cent in 1971/72 and only 6 per cent in 1980/81 (Omari et al. Table 33). The contrast with neighbouring countries was stark and even in 2005 when fresh attention had been paid by Government to secondary school development, the transition rate from primary to secondary school in Tanzania was the lowest shown for all 33 Sub-Saharan African countries for which the UNESCO Institute for Statistics provides the data in its 2006 *Global Education Digest* (Table 4, pp. 93–94).

It seems likely that the failure to allow secondary education to develop – even community secondary schools were discouraged for a long period – had two adverse effects. First, it led to intense competition for secondary school places and was discouraging in terms of parents' aspirations and expectations that their children might continue their education after primary school, thus encouraging drop-out. Second, the shortage of people with secondary education delayed the upgrading of the primary-school teaching force and probably served to maintain higher pay differentials between secondary-educated teachers and primary-educated teachers than would otherwise have been the case.

The nature and impact of crash programmes, particularly in the training of teachers?
There is no doubt that Tanzania was only able to achieve what it did through the use of emergency measures which included a good deal of improvisation in classroom accommodation, organising of schooling by half day schooling/double shifts, and the massive resort to special teacher training programmes. In this regard, the out-of-college training of Grade C teachers deserves special mention given that in the period 1976/77 to 1980/81 it supplied nearly 88 per cent of the teachers required (MoE 1989, p. 33). Wastage on the distance education course was about 10 per cent. An evaluation conducted by Omari et al. in 1983 suggests that there were many deficiencies in the programme, with a failure to provide the back-up support planned in many cases: even so, the majority (60 per cent) of trainees in their sample were basically satisfied with the programme.

Importance of the base-line and scale of the prior 'backlog'
The baseline provision in Tanzania was rather low with a GER of only 34 in 1970 (41 for males and 27 for females). This gave plentiful scope for rapid enrolment expansion in the sense that there was a very large pool of correct-age and over-age potential students ready to enter school. This is reflected in the fact that the GER in the early 1980s was a full 25–27 points higher than the NER, implying that a high proportion of pupils enrolled was outside the official age-group.

On the other hand, when it came to teacher supply, Tanzania was compelled to recruit many persons to its out-of-college courses who had no more than a completed primary schooling as their basic education qualification. Although Tanzania insisted that all teachers should be formally trained (by a sleight of hand in a sense, because those on the distance course were teaching while they underwent training, and so were effectively untrained during much of their student-teacher period), there was no doubt that the quality of teachers was below what education administrators and parents would have liked.

Demographic issues

Effect of population growth or mobility in disrupting UPE plans
In Tanzania population growth was a hugely important factor in constraining the coverage of primary education in terms of GERs and NERs at times when enrolments were growing rapidly. The estimates of population growth being made on the eve of the UPE launch do not seem to have been wildly wrong. It does seem now, however, that the size of the baseline population on which projections were based was actually somewhat greater than thought at the time, and, for that reason, the estimates of GERs and NERs for that period have later had to be revised downwards by UIS.

Accuracy of population projections and adequacy of arrangements for monitoring population migration
Tanzania did its best by arranging a special census of school-age children in 1975. Nevertheless, the reported experience of regional and district education officers was that many more children enlisted for school than the plans and projections had provided for, and this may, in part, have been because more over-age children than anticipated turned up. The surprising fact that actual enrolment rates cited for Dar es Salaam in 1986 were reported to be the lowest in the country, suggests that urban provision of primary schools in particular did not keep up with the demographic situation on the ground, though other factors were at work too as Sumra has shown. Reliance on community self-help rather than tax revenues for the construction of schools may not have been beneficial in the cities, where self-help is more difficult to organise.

Societal factors

Relative impact of different factors on growth of enrolment
There was a strong pent-up demand in Tanzania for education, and this was fuelled by the good salaries earned in the post-Independence period by any Tanzanian possessing formal education qualifications. Exhortation by political leaders and the commitment to the ideas of *ujamaa* served to reinforce this sense that enrolment in school was not just an individual, but also a community endeavour. A compulsory-attendance law was passed by Parliament in 1978 (Omari et al. p. 45).

Considerations affecting demand for education by parents, guardians and communities
This has been a major problem in Tanzania, particularly because of poverty and the perception of parents that the quality of education is low. The decision to re-impose parental contributions of 20 shillings per child for school materials, only five years after school fees were abolished, hit many parents hard and indeed it was not possible to collect more than about a third of the levies due.

The survey undertaken by Omari et al in 1983 found education officers reporting 'rural populations, and especially parents, were mainly concerned about what their children would do after seven years of primary education. Would they have a life similar to their parents, join the labour force, or get secondary-school places? In addition, the parents were concerned about whether their children would actually learn to read and write and acquire skills for later life. The views suggested that many parents in the rural areas could not afford the annual 20 shillings per child along with purchasing uniforms and that many were sceptical and suspicious about the use of the accumulated subscriptions'. The response of urban middle class parents has been to put their children into private schools and this has contributed to the creation of a more stratified society, affecting even the composition of tertiary and higher education. There is a tendency for the UPE schools to cater for the poor while the rich and better-placed pay to obtain better-quality primary and secondary education.

Involvement of civil society organisations, private sector and local government bodies
The community was extremely important in getting facilities built and the whole construction programme was based on community self-reliance efforts. Religious organisations were no longer school managers after the nationalisation of schools under the Education Act of 1969, but were doubtless still influential in community leadership in many areas. As Masudi has pointed out, this 'meant that the NGOs' contribution to public education in terms of financial, material and human resources was put to an end. The Government had thus to spend more resources in education than had been the case before ... . The move to control education underscores a situation where ideological considerations took precedence over economic realities'.

The private commercial sector in Tanzania was small and no mention is made in the literature of it having been involved in support for UPE. The number of private primary schools shrunk from 561 in 1976 to only 21 in 1986, the political climate post-Musoma being distinctly unfavourable to them

It is understood that in the current UPE thrust, more attention is given to the role of the school committee which is now a budget-holding entity to which government funding is passed direct, but the extent of its democratic representativeness requires further research.

Reasons why communities do not send girls to school
Tanzania was outstandingly successful in closing the gap between boys and girls in primary school enrolment rates during its first UPE campaigns. This is not to deny that there were special factors affecting girls' enrolment and the willingness of parents in some areas to send girls to schools. Osaki and Agu (2005) have drawn attention to the effect of early marriage following girls' initiation ceremonies in Maasai and coastal areas of Tanzania, for example.

'Hard-to-reach' minorities
Omari et al. suggest that that the Maasai and some other nomadic groups are only likely to embrace education if its form is consistent with the demands of their herding culture. They also refer to 'cultural resistance because of religious and traditional beliefs' (pp. 68

and 69). The Ministry of Education alludes to the difficulties of providing education for the 20,000 or more handicapped children (this was even before the era of HIV/AIDS). The Ministry also refers (1989, pp. 19 and 20) to various social, economic and cultural factors underlying non-attendance at schools including nomadism and pastoralism, absence for circumcision ceremonies, cattle raiding, fear of witchcraft deterring officers from implementing the compulsory education directives, the competition from Koranic schools and so on.

Economic factors

Adequacy of UPE financing and the problems of sustainability
The main economic reason why UPE was hard to sustain was the high cost in relation to a constrained budget. Tanzania deliberately chose to launch UPE at a time when it acknowledged it could not afford it, and it managed to accommodate UPE by doing it 'on the cheap', using self-reliance, low-cost improvisations, and imposing resource starvation on schools and pupils. The tripling of school enrolment was bound to cause economic difficulty and once student teachers on emergency training programmes became qualified this had serious financial consequences.

A series of factors combined in the 1980s to create an economic crisis in Tanzania. They included the oil shocks to the world economy, the collapse in commodity prices, drought and consequent poor harvests, and the 'War to topple Idi Amin' in Uganda. These economic shocks meant that the necessary investments in quality of primary education could not be made and the share of education in the national budget fell quite steeply.

Primary education development in face of increasing demands for secondary and tertiary education
In the first fifteen years of Independence primary education expansion was undoubtedly held back by the political need to produce high-level manpower. The ratio of costs per student was fairly extreme in Tanzania with relative salaries and costs representing scarcities in the modern sector. In 1981/82 for example the unit cost ratios between primary, secondary and university were 1:26:298. Costs in secondary and tertiary education were high partly because provision was restricted: not only were economies of scale more difficult to achieve but, in a largely rural country, it was necessary to have a large element of boarding. For this reason, even though Tanzania was extremely restrictive in the provision of secondary education after the mid seventies – so much so that it had among the lowest secondary education enrolment rates in the world – secondary and higher education still consumed a high proportion of education expenditure. In 1982/83 the share of primary education was only 47 per cent even though the overwhelming proportion of students was then in primary schools – 3.5m against less than 100,000 at all other levels.

By the time of the launch of the second UPE drive, the unit cost of primary education had risen, and the unit cost ratio between the three levels in 1998 had narrowed to 1:4:62 (Galabawa 2000, Chapter 4). Reflecting this and because secondary and tertiary education had been held back, the shares of education expenditure in 1999 were primary 66 per cent, secondary 9 per cent and tertiary (including teacher education) 20 per cent.

The Government of Tanzania has more recently launched programmes of expansion of secondary and tertiary education recognising the need for a more balanced education development and it therefore seems likely that the proportionate share of primary schooling in the education budget will begin to fall.

Political factors

The commitment to UPE of the political leadership
Government and ruling party leaders in Tanzania showed strong commitment to UPE and campaigned vigorously for it during both of the main UPE thrusts. The Government was very single-minded in its selection of priorities, in the face of economic and other constraints.

Political disruptions and their impact on education
The war in Uganda to topple Idi Amin in 1978 occurred at the very moment when the main enrolment surge was taking place during the first drive for UPE, and had a serious effect on the economy, which was already under strain from the 1970s oil-price shocks. The main effect on primary education seems to have been qualitative: supply of materials and professional services to schools (inspection and advisory support) suffered, and teachers' salaries fell sharply in real terms. Later, Tanzania was affected strongly by the Rwanda/Burundi conflicts on its borders. Very many refugees crossed Tanzania's western borders to the Kigoma/Kagera regions and massive education provision for refugee children was made in camps established and funded by refugee agencies. This had some knock-on effect on the domestic system of education in those regions. Some resentment was felt among local people that the refugee schools often seemed better provided for than the Government's own system; and some local teachers may have been tempted by more favourable terms of service in the refugee schools.

International

International intervention and inaction by international partners
Tanzania's leadership was clearly heavily influenced by models from Cuba, China and other socialist countries in its radical approaches to education development, and was influenced by the continent-wide aspirations in Africa for UPE. More recently, as a participant in the Education for All conferences, it has been influenced to resume efforts at achievement of UPE – though it has to be said that in the decade following the Jomtien Conference Tanzania regressed rather than progressed.

In the first quarter of a century of Independence Tanzania was proud of its ownership of policy and in the education sector was not very dependent on foreign assistance at the time of its first UPE thrust. Some external funding was made available particularly by Sweden which through SIDA supported the Distance Teacher Training Programme in the late 1970s.

Following the economic crises in the early 1980s and the adoption of first a Structural adjustment Programme (1982) and then an Economic Recovery Programme (1986), Tanzania has been very much at the mercy of the international economic community which 'forced' on the country a package of liberal economic reforms, retrenchment of public sector expenditure including denationalisation of some state enterprises and cutting of the public work force. Overshadowing everything in this period has been the weight of external debt: servicing and repaying the debt has required annual outlays equivalent to about one third of the annual government budget. Debt servicing has been larger in magnitude than expenditure on education.

In the early years of the 21st century a shift in policy was made possible by the decision of Tanzania's international creditors, led by the World Bank, to cancel/reschedule the debt and earmark the released resources for expansion of education and other services. The current Primary Education Development Programme 2002–2007, focussing on UPE, is largely externally financed. This poses a serious potential challenge to the sustainability of UPE which is even more at risk than when Masudi wrote (University of Dar es Salaam 1995, p. 113):

> The country's dependence on external donor assistance puts it in a rather precarious situation. Should the donor-groups withdraw their assistance it is obvious that the government's capacity to provide primary education will be seriously affected.

The dangers of dependence on donors are well illustrated by the somersaults in donor policies in recent years. In the late 1990s, several influential donors, including DFID, were pressing the Tanzanian Government extremely hard to close teacher training colleges and lay off 'surplus' teachers. Their projections conveyed the message that this was incontestably necessary. Only three years later, with the renewed drive for UPE, Tanzania's supposed teacher surplus had evaporated and a severe shortage of teachers was being experienced.

Notes

1 A three month course at a teachers college followed by supervision in the school by an itinerant coordinator.
2 Better qualified teachers – Grade A – were without jobs while the UPE trained ex-primary school leavers were in schools.
3 A proposal by the Teacher Education Master plan (MOEC, 2000) to phase them out by 2003–4 has not been implemented, despite their professional incapability. Many are due to retire soon, but the damage will stay on for years to come. This time round, with Secondary Education development, a similar program for training secondary school teachers seems to have been adopted since 2005: this takes in form 6 leavers and after a one-month course, releases them into schools.

Lalage Bown

Chapter 7

Lessons for the future

Preliminary note: The substance of this chapter is from the research report prepared for the 16th Conference of Commonwealth Education Ministers, held in Cape Town in December, 2006. Some amplifications and additions have been made.

'The person who asks question doesn't lose their way.'

Nigerian proverb

The question and the context

UPE in question

In this book we have asked and tried to answer one question: *How can Commonwealth developing countries, once having attained Universal Primary Education (UPE) – assuming they will be successful – maintain it?* Some have come near to it before, but have had setbacks and have not been able to sustain it. Their experience can be useful in suggesting guidelines for political leaders and educational policy-makers on what directions to take and what pit-falls to anticipate and, preferably, avoid. Such guidelines should obviously be useful in informing strategies for *reaching* UPE as well.

All Commonwealth countries have committed themselves to the establishment (or re-establishment) of UPE by the year 2015; but as mentioned in Chapter 1, the 2006 Global Monitoring Report has raised serious doubts as to whether a number of countries, partic-ularly in Africa, can reach that goal. Yet some of the nations now apparently struggling have in the recent past come near to UPE, at least in terms of Gross Enrolment Ratios (GERs). Moreover, there has been important progress since the meeting of the World Education Forum at Dakar in 2000. Kenya has moved up 13 points on UPE, Tanzania 40 points and Ghana 8.

Our enquiry into the vicissitudes of primary education (or 'adventures', as the authors of Chapter 5 have put it) in five Commonwealth African countries was undertaken to learn from collective experience, for the benefit of Commonwealth policy-makers. Every country has specific political, socio-economic and cultural circumstances, which will affect educa-tional demand and colour educational provision; so no one would claim that there is a uni-versal magic formula for arriving at UPE and staying there. But from the experience of five very different countries it has been possible to draw out some generally applicable lessons and basic principles. Their validity derives from the concrete examples studied.

The choice of the five countries – Ghana, Kenya, Zambia, Nigeria and Tanzania – was explained in Chapter 1. The cases, as presented in Chapters 2 to 6, have been studied and described as objectively as possible and, in presenting a picture, which for every country includes mistakes and problems, as well as successes, do not in any way impute blame or criticism. The point of the enquiry is to seek positive lessons.

This chapter looks first at some major contextual issues, then describes some of the common aspects of past UPE efforts, and goes on to a detailed look at factors likely to help or hinder the sustainability of UPE – that is, what plans and strategies seem likely to work. It also mentions specific examples of instructive experiences in individual countries.

UPE in International and Commonwealth context

In the 1960s, the drive towards UPE was fuelled by visions of nation-building. There was *determined political leadership and social will.* These two factors remain crucial. Sustaining UPE will always depend on committed political leadership more likely to persist, where there are stable political regimes – and also on active community participation and support. Such stories as those of the early days of *harambee* in Kenya and *ujamaa* in Tanzania can still teach us this.

The wider context is now very different. There is much greater international commitment through agreement on Education for All and the Millennium Development Goals. This has provided the momentum for a renewed drive to UPE (a 'resurgence' as the authors of Chapter 4 have put it) and prompted the devotion of substantial new external resources to it. Paralleled with debt relief, African countries have therefore more financial resources to achieve their aims. There is still, however, a serious question as to whether, in the enthusiasm of international gatherings, Commonwealth African countries have entered into unrealistic undertakings.

The great progress achieved by some countries and the optimism it has engendered may perhaps now be at risk, with the economic recession likely to tighten budgets. Countries reliant to any extent on international aid may begin to fear that international pledges will not be kept. Here is a role for Commonwealth educational leaders: to campaign for the carrying through of all such pledges.

At the same time, there is another issue for Commonwealth educational leaders to reflect upon. Given the greatly increased awareness that UPE programmes require very long lead-times – demonstrated amply in the case-histories in this book – perhaps African countries have been tied to the reins of an international juggernaut and need to reflect on the ownership of their UPE programmes, setting up their own time-frames and pacing themselves on what actually looks doable. This is not to suggest that an international collaborative initiative isn't helpful. The EFA programme has rekindled interest and provided inspiration, but unrealistic targets can foster unrealistic planning and a constant lagging behind targets can be discouraging.

It is suggested that Commonwealth countries could work together to ensure continued international support for EFA and also to revise lead-times and targets for achieving and consolidating UPE.

UPE in the 21st century: The Big Picture

The last half-century witnessed many fluctuations in primary enrolments, for reasons which we will consider later. They include failure of political commitment, economic or political instability, planning deficiencies, civil war, natural disasters and the arrival of HIV/AIDS. The picture, though, in almost all Commonwealth African countries is one of expanded school populations and of an upward movement of Net Enrolment Ratios (NERs) – which indicate how far school provision has kept pace with population overall. Since the late 1990s, when the world community took up the banner of Education For All, most Commonwealth African countries have crept forward in net enrolment. Our research has shown that Tanzania, for one, has made outstanding progress.

This is modestly encouraging, though there are three *caveats* to enter into the picture. *One* is that most countries have populations which are left out or 'hard to reach'. Enrolments are low, for instance, among the pastoral Fulani and other nomads in Nigeria (estimated at some nine million people) and among the Maasai in Tanzania, as well as the people of Kenya's North Eastern Province. In Zambia, the very scattered low-density rural population has less opportunity for education than easy-to-reach urban children. In contrast, in Tanzania, urban children may be left out because there are not enough schools to cope with the numbers. Countries setting their sights on UPE come to realise that 'the last ten percent' will be the hardest to involve. This is already a major challenge for South Africa and is becoming so in other countries as they approach UPE.

The *second caveat* is about figures. Children who arrive in school may not necessarily stay there and it is incumbent on education ministries to look also at attendance statistics and at transition from one level to another. Dropouts (or pushouts) and repeaters must also be monitored. This is not just a matter of understanding the real dimensions of primary education – and not being lulled into false complacency by the enrolment figures – but also of studying the reasons for dropout and repetition, in order to reflect on ways of overcoming these problems. Where such monitoring has been undertaken, it has produced quite worrying information. In Kenya, cumulative dropout in the decade to 2005 was 37 per cent. Overall, it seems that nearly a quarter of children in Commonwealth Africa do not stay in school long enough to acquire permanent literacy and numeracy skills – a tragedy for them and a poor use of public resources. *Any claims to have reached UPE based on figures for initial enrolment will be bogus.*

The *third caveat* is that numbers don't tell anything about quality. Education policy-makers are concerned to ensure that the education to which their nation's children are exposed will be worthwhile. This is partly about a suitable physical environment, partly about appropriate curricula and learning materials and also quite largely about teachers. It is taken for granted that successful and good quality UPE requires an adequate number of well-trained teachers; but it isn't always appreciated that those teachers need reasonable pay and conditions and also opportunities for continuing professional development. Teachers who don't have the chance to keep up with curricular change and with younger, more highly trained entrants to the profession, will not only lose morale and interest in their work, they will be unable to deliver quality. One of the CEC research team suggests that to enlist teachers fully in any drive for UPE, their unions should also be fully consulted and enlisted in any campaign. They should have a stake in UPE and understand that its achievement is their success.

The picture, then, is of real progress, but of a need to move beyond basic enrolment to stable school populations, increasing at a more regular rate of growth, beyond the mainstream children to those who are harder to reach, and beyond simple numbers to good quality learning, nurtured by good committed teaching.

'Near-UPE': How it was reached and how it changed to 'Further- from-UPE?

Political decisions and public reaction

In all the cases studied, there was a political impetus to UPE. Political leaders around the time of independence regarded education as hugely important and it featured more strongly in declared policies than such other social provision as health. Some politicians made sustained campaigns, as in Western Nigeria on the cusp of independence, where UPE proposals were in the manifesto on which the Action Group government was elected and where there was extensive and widely-reported debate among elected members before the legislation was passed. Later, in other cases, the policy was simply announced by the Head of State, as in the Federation of Nigeria in 1972, when General Gowon promulgated universal free and compulsory education – inevitably it did not happen, but his successors pushed it forward as the case-study shows. Similarly, in 2003, the newly elected President Kibaki announced the revival of free education within days of the opening of the new school year. The ministry had to go into crisis mode.

The story in all the countries is one of successive jolts towards UPE. Changes of regime tended to bring about a renewed commitment, as the Ghana case illustrates. The Nkrumah government's Education Act of 1961 established the legal basis for compulsory primary and middle school education; the NLC regime in the late 1960s, Colonel Acheampong's government in 1972, the Rawlings government of 1981–91, the NPP elected in 2000, all in turn undertook educational reforms with some relation to primary education. Such constant new starts were partly because education was high on the political agenda and partly because of setbacks or loss of momentum in previous programmes.

The reasons for the various moves to promote UPE varied in different countries and at different times. In early days, it was, as already seen, associated with nation-building and in Nigeria some programmes were prompted by the desire for national integration. In Kenya, it was seen as an ingredient in development; in Zambia, as a pre-requisite for human capital development. The Ghana government recently announced that it wanted 'an efficient, credible and sustainable education system that will make the nation competitive in today's globalised economy, which is becoming increasingly knowledge-driven'. How far these views of political leaders and policy-makers have been shared by the ordinary citizen is a matter of guesswork.

One feature of all these sudden policies and new starts was that they somehow were implemented because the civil servants managed to get them on the road, in spite of short notice and absence of planning. Their work is not usually acknowledged, but it deserves to be.

Political leaders and public officials both had a head start because of sympathetic public response. Where there have been no inhibiting demographic, cultural or religious forces, people seem to have an urge for education. Even when the quality is not very good, even in times of disruption, they have continued to send at least some children to school. (This does not mean they have not been critical; the evidence shows that they have become disillusioned when the education is low-grade). Both in Tanzania and in Zambia, the story was one of pent-up demand, demonstrated by popular involvement, through *ujamaa* in the former in the 1960s and, in the present day, through the Community Schools movement in the latter. In Zambia, it was noted by the researchers as striking that though 70 per cent of the population live below the absolute poverty line of $1 a day, the schools are full and rates of attendance and transition high. This does not, of course, mean that poverty is not an inhibiting factor – see later in the chapter.

Trends in UPE

Political will and public support were factors in the general increase in primary school populations through the decades between 1960 and 2000. The following figures show the increase in three of the countries studied:

Table 7.1. Primary school enrolment in three countries

	1970	2000
Kenya	1,427,589	5,730,669
Tanzania	856,213	4,042,568
Zambia	694,670	1,590,000

Bearing in mind the earlier *caveat* about raw enrolment data, these figures show that the trend was substantially upward. It was not smooth and as the Tanzanian case-study explains, an upward trend may still equate to a hidden decline in coverage, when set against population increases. All the countries studied reached a point where population growth out-stripped educational provision.

Some countries had severe difficulties owing to miscalculation in planning of the actual size of the population. In Ghana, for instance, on the eve of independence, Dr Kwame Nkrumah spoke of Ghana's population as five million; in the event, the 1960 census showed that the number was seven million, so that the goal of UPE was further away than had been thought or hoped.

Population increases still offer a critical challenge for most developing countries and demographic trends will need careful scrutiny by educational planners if they are not to defeat them. Table 7.2 gives some data for the five countries studied here.

In common with most developing countries, these five have a demographic profile in which the under-15 cohort is a very significant proportion; in three out of these five, over 2/5 of the population is under 15. Overall growth rates have slowed down since the 1975–2003 period, but they still pose sizeable problems to governments of keeping pace in educational provision.

Table 7.2. Demographic trends in five countries

	Population (millions)			Annual growth rate % from 2003	Population under 15 as % of total
	1975	2003	2015		
Ghana	10.2	21.2	26.6	1.9	35.2
Kenya	13.5	32.6	44.2	2.5	26.0
Nigeria	58.9	125.9	160.9	2.0	41.3
Tanzania	16.0	36.9	45.6	1.8	38.9
Zambia	5.2	11.3	13.8	1.7	43.7

Source: UNDP Human Development Report, 2005

Policies and plans

Some underlying motivations for UPE have been given above. Whatever the original drivers for universalisation, policies have been framed by education authorities with reference to a mainly economic purpose, with an emphasis on basic and technical skills. For parents and guardians, schooling gave hope of leading to paid employment (often in government service).

A more wide-ranging policy rationale is given by the researchers on Kenya (see Chapter 3):

> 'The vision of the Kenya Government on education is to provide every Kenyan the right to primary education, no matter what his or her socio-economic status, through the provision of an all-inclusive quality education that is accessible and relevant. This vision is guided by the understanding that quality education contributes significantly to economic growth and the expansion of employment opportunities. [It] is in tandem with the Economic Recovery Strategy Paper (ERS), which provides the rationale for major reforms in the current education system, in order to enable all Kenyans to have access to quality lifelong education'.

They go on to comment:

> 'the realization that provision of education to all Kenyans is fundamental to overall development because education is the key to wealth creation and self-esteem; it through education that we learn to value ourselves and then to enhance and preserve and utilize the environment for productive gain and sustainable livelihoods. Having promised to eliminate poverty, disease and ignorance at independence in 1963 and subsequently through the Sessional Paper No 10 of 1965 on African Socialism and its application to planning in Kenya, the Government invested and continues to invest heavily in education ...'

There are several significant points in this statement. *First* is the decision to frame educational policy in the light of broad economic and social policy, relating education to wealth creation and livelihoods, and to the fight against poverty. *Secondly* is the shift from past discourse about employment to a discourse more realistic for most contemporary African economies about livelihoods. *Thirdly* are the non-economic elements included, such as self-esteem. *Fourthly,* educational quality is underlined. We have seen how in the last quarter-century, quality has often had to be sacrificed to quantity – now governments are encountering the issue of how to match quantity with quality. *Fifthly,* the expression 'life-long' is used; dealing with people past school age without ever having had meaningful access to schooling has led some countries, as we shall see, to move from the concept of UPE to UBE.

Policies were backed by legislation, with each country passing a series of education acts (or decrees). Ghana went further and enshrined 'free compulsory and universal educa-tion' in successive constitutions – 1969, 1979 and 1992. In Nigeria, the Federal Minister of Education in 2009 announced that the government was intending to revise the UBE Act to enforce compulsory enrolment and *retention.* He also promised legislation to estab-lish *quality assurance institutions.* These actions show an awareness of the same messages which we have derived from looking at past UPE experience and indicate that his govern-ment sees sustainability and quality as two current concerns.

Primary education in the five countries varied in the number of years offered, with lengths of time shifting when policy changed. The current primary cycles are:

Ghana	6 years followed by 3 years Junior Secondary
Kenya	8 years
Nigeria	9 years
Tanzania	7 years
Zambia	9 years (1–4 lower basic, 5–7 middle basic, 8 & 9 upper basic)

Zambia was only able to supply lower basic schools in some places, so that in principle pupils were expected to move on to another school to complete the rest of the cycle; in practice, many left the system at that point.

It will be seen that perceptions of primary education structures were quite diverse. In Ghana, Nigeria and Zambia a model of Basic Education is now being used. Ghana's pres-ent policy is Free Compulsory Universal Basic Education (FCUBE), with a component of two years pre-primary, 6 years primary and 3 years beyond; the institutions for the last three years are to be renamed junior high schools. In Zambia, the last two years are artic-ulated with the secondary system. Nigeria moved from UPE to UBE in 1999; this was a paradigm shift, since UBE embraces pre-primary, primary and junior secondary (as in Ghana), but also mass literacy and non-formal education. One of the objectives of UBE is to deal with drop-out from the formal system. The CEC researchers say: 'The major achievement of UBE is that it has remained in force; even in uneasy political terrain' and they note that in the four years after UBE's introduction both primary enrolments and completion rates went up. The Federal Minister's expressed intention to revise the legisla-tion implies that the concept has now taken root.

All the five countries experienced problems with planning. There were perennial problems of: lack of accurate data; pressures by politicians rushing to implementation before prop-er programmes could be worked out; lack of understanding of the true financial implications of embarking on (or re-launching) UPE; and occasional misunderstandings about responsibilities between different elements of government. In Zambia, there was, in addition, a lack of planning and implementation capacity. The World Bank and sometimes the UNDP intervened in many African countries to assist with planning, so there is a certain uniformity about strategies undertaken, even when there was no uniformity in the different countries' situations.

Often, even with the help of practiced national and international planners, it was not understood that introducing a new plan is not into a vacuum and there has to be allowance for 'lag-time' or left-over business from previous provision, such as teachers in the system with variant qualifications or pupils enrolled in earlier cycles and needing to take an obsolescent examination. It was also not always understood (particularly by politicians) that a plan does not come instantly into effect and there has to be preparation for change.

In the next sub-section, we move from planning to implementation. *Here, it must be re-emphasised that adequate planning, based on adequate data is critical to the guidance and maintenance of UPE and that each country needs its own high-grade planning capacity.*

Perils and difficulties

Effective planning depends on the availability of good data. Unexciting as it may sound, greater attention is needed than in the past to improving statistical information. This is necessary both at national and at local level and may have many applications. For instance, it is needed for school mapping and location, that is the distribution of schools in relation to population distribution. At the present day, with continuing large migration into towns and cities, there will be constant need for more school places in those urban areas. Planners should be able to help to assess the additional numbers.

The perils of 'planning without facts', to quote a famous book about planning in Nigeria[1], lead to such mistakes as those of the Ghana government in the time of Nkrumah, about the size of likely school populations. It has already been noted that many planners were caught unawares by the upward trend of populations, so that the size of additional provision, such as number of schools, number of classrooms, number of teachers, was not fully allowed for.

Perhaps no one could have forecast the economic decline of the 1980s, in which many African peoples suffered hardship and hunger, but governments had in any case not appreciated the *full financial implications of universalising primary education.* As already said, additional expenditure was (and is) needed year-on-year until populations stabilise; and there were extra costs, often entirely unforeseen, such as the appearance of many over-age children in the classroom when UPE schemes were launched or re-launched. The subsequent financial consequences of major capital expenditure in school building programmes were not always foreseen in the general eagerness to accommodate all pupils. After all, you cannot compel children to go to a non-existent school, nor to one falling down from lack of maintenance.

Dr Pius Okigbo, commenting on Nigeria's first development plan, said:

> 'The Nigerian planners did not fully take into account the recurrent burden associated with capital projects. In planning a capital programme, it is necessary to provide for the recurrent cost of running the facility when it is commissioned. The resources for this expense cannot be left to be found when the project is completed; it must be part of the planning. The lure of foreign financing blinded the Nigerian officials to the consequences of seemingly costless projects, whose running and maintenance costs must be borne fully by the recipient government in the fullness of time'[2].

With hindsight, some of these mistakes seem obvious, but they were factors in the difficulties experienced by African governments when UPE seemed to fall away from their grasp owing to its cost. Even at the present day, there are local and foreign donors, large and small, who prefer to provide buildings and plant (often with their name on!) and leave the recipients to pay for repairs and maintenance.

Effective planning requires *continuity* of policy and strategy. Constant lurching from one new initiative to another is not helpful. It reduces the value of planning, makes financial forecasting almost impossible and detracts from the stability of institutions. Both foreign donors and newly-elected politicians are prone to novel initiatives, but the message is that continuity is best. If UPE is to be attained and then to be sustained, only continuity will make it possible. This doesn't mean that mistakes noticed along the way should not be rectified and revisions made, but that any well-thought-out long-term plan should be used as a guide-post as long as possible. One of the misfortunes of the countries studied has at times been the rapid turn-over of personnel, both ministers and civil servants, so there is no institutional memory and no long-term familiarity and experience with plans drawn up, however carefully, by predecessors. Not surprisingly, this leads to inconsistency both in planning and implementation.

Crash programmes, driven by political urgency, carried their own problems. In 1974, Kenya hired large numbers of untrained teachers to cater for the increased enrolment which followed the introduction of Free Primary Education (FPE – see below). The cost per pupil rose by 500 per cent and later the government felt compelled to reduce teacher recruitment and raise Pupil-Teacher Ratios, with, arguably, a reduction in educational quality.

Several of the authors of our case-studies expressed doubt over the quality of education at times of major expansion. A balance was not kept in among others, Ghana and Zambia, between quantity and quality; and it bears repeating that in the long term UPE will only be sustainable if it delivers acceptable quality. Peter Williams has, however, argued in the past that rapid 'jumps' in numbers are important in creating political commitment and public enthusiasm (Williams, 1979) and are maybe justifiable in terms of overall political impact; but once UPE is neared or reached, it has to be associated with appropriate learning outcomes and a useful experience for the children.

A very different kind of difficulty, partly associated with haste in implementation, emerged in the sometimes fraught relationships between different parts of government

Lessons for the future

and sometimes between governments and other agencies, whether religious or for profit. In most countries, the chief actor has been the Ministry of Education, with greater or lesser degrees of decentralisation. In Kenya, for instance, the responsibility is divided between central and local government, and a similar system exists in Zambia. While Kenya has arrived at a very thoroughly accountable system, in Zambia there has been concern about the accountability of local authorities.

In the more complex federal system of Nigeria, the division of responsibilities has varied over time. Initially, the centre was weak and major educational responsibilities rested with the Regions; but the arrival of military rule shifted the balance to a very strong central government, with various coordinating mechanisms. The States have the main control over the primary system, including over the deployment of teachers; but there are cross-cutting federal quangos, such as the National Commission for UBE and lines of authority can be very unclear, leading to distractions and inefficiencies. The Commissioner for Education in each State (responsible to the elected State government) has charge over the whole education sector, but alongside him/her is a State Primary Education Board, headed by an executive chairman, who reports directly to the Governor – although elected, a Federal officer. Greater clarity is now emerging, as a result of judicial decisions when cases of jurisdiction have been referred to the courts.

In précis, problems encountered along the road to UPE have been: demographic (population increases); political side-lining of professional planning or planning which is faulty in itself; connected to timing (eagerness for short-term implementation); and issues in intra-governmental relationships.

Plans and strategies for maintaining UPE

Major lessons from the recent past

Facing and understanding the various issues we have so far discussed, what lessons from experience can be carried to the future by Commonwealth Africa?

Summing up so far, we can deduce the following principles:

a Political will twinned with public support enabled countries to move nearer to UPE and they are still crucial in a context in which post-independence euphoria is a distant memory and in which economic concerns may dominate voters' interests – more effort will now be demanded to ensure community and grassroots commitment;

b It is a good expedient to enshrine free UPE in the constitution;

c Education must be framed against economic and social policy, (e.g. NEEDS in Kenya) – this is both rational and may help education to maintain its place against other budgets;

d Good educational planning depends on having competent national planners and good data for them to work on (including demographic data);

e In planning and monitoring primary education, providing more school places doesn't necessarily mean reaching or holding onto UPE; provision has to keep pace with population increase;

f Further thought is often required into the place of primary education within the overall education architecture. How many years constitute a sufficient basis for it and how does it articulate with other parts of the system?

g Universal primary education may be supported within a framework of UBE;

h Governments need to face squarely the financial implications of continuing expansions of the education system until populations stabilise;

i Expansion and crash programmes pose the danger of concentrating on quantity at the expense of quality. At some stages, this may have been inevitable, but in the present, stabilising the system will depend on a quality education acceptable to the public. Quality assurance mechanisms will be called for;

j A clear definition and understanding of the roles and jurisdictional responsibilities in education of different government agencies will avoid time-wasting and misunderstanding.

Demand and supply in UPE: Fees, advocacy and finance

It has been recognised how positively the publics in the five countries have responded to UPE programmes, but if UPE is to be sustained, public enthusiasm cannot be taken for granted without other action. The most successful action in pushing up demand has been *making primary education free*. In Tanzania, enrolments in primary schools tripled between 1973 and 1981 after the decision to abolish fees. In Kenya, they went up by one-third when fees were no longer levied and by almost another quarter when the building fund was stopped (this had been introduced as an alternative to communal labour on school buildings). Free education has without doubt been the strongest motivating measure and keeping it free will sustain motivation, especially in the present times of recession and aggravated poverty. Free education, of course, means more than the abolition of tuition fees. Other charges, such as building funds, sports funds and uniforms also have a negative affect on enrolment and dampen public interest. The difficulty is that once fees are remitted, to bring them back, as several countries did, results in the immediate alienation of poorer people.

Sustaining public interest will also depend on *continuing political advocacy* – the enlistment of the media, the educated classes, NGOs and local communities – and regular consultation with the various people concerned with education: parents, guardians, teachers, local opinion-formers and others. Sometimes lip-service has been paid to advocacy and consultation and ministries may have public relations units, but the two activities have to be taken very seriously indeed if public interest in and support for UPE are to be kept alive. This may be better understood now, when countries have democratic regimes and elected members and ministers, who depend on votes.

It goes without saying that, in the light of what has been observed earlier, that the quality of education has to be sufficient to convince parents and guardians that children will benefit from it.

Turning from demand to supply, in any discussion about achieving and sustaining UPE, starts from *appropriate finance*. First, since schooling costs money and expanding school provision costs ever more money, there is a danger that ambitions for UPE will stagnate when the economy stagnates. This research was done at a time when economic conditions in Africa were improving, but the whole economic climate has now changed. We have already said how particularly important it will be to hold the international community to their pledges in support of EFA, but within a nation there will be tough decisions to be taken about budget priorities and education may have a hard fight to lay hold on the resources it needs. Tanzania showed what can be done in education in hard times, maintaining it 'on the cheap', but its achievement was due to special circumstances and does not provide an easily followed example.

Education, as noted, may survive better, in budgetary terms, if accepted as an essential part of development, through being embedded in wider social and economic planning. Recently, education in Commonwealth Africa has enjoyed a good slice of national cakes. In the countries studied, educational expenditure has taken from 14 per cent to 20 per cent and even up to 30 per cent of national budgets. Recently also, primary education has been allocated a good proportion of the general education sector finance (up to 60 per cent, reported from Kenya) – in contrast to its Cinderella status in the past. The important budget decisions will not now be between different educational sectors, but between education and other sectors of the economy. National priorities might shift away from education towards, for example, military spending. There will have to be hard bargaining and hard choices to be made, but at least, with civilian governments, military demands should not be as out of proportion as they have sometimes been.

Advocacy, mentioned above, may be of great importance in helping education authorities retain a reasonable budgetary share, even in these straitened times. At the same time, ingenuity in finding other sources of funding will be needed. The question of other sources will come up later.

Favouring and negative conditions for sustaining UPE

Educational policy-makers intent on strategies for successful UPE provision cannot ignore the fact that sustainability depends on *several non-educational factors* entirely outside their control. The state of the economy, already referred to, is one. Besides the effects on the budget itself, there are many other ways in which an enfeebled economy has an impact on education, including more particularly primary education:

- When an economy is weakened by a natural disaster such as drought, there will be other calls on the national budget, e.g. dealing with refugees in Tanzania;
- Disasters cause hunger among both the rural families and the urban poor. Hunger will keep many children from school and those who do attend will have a lowered capacity to learn;
- When there is inflation and salaries are low, teachers will be deflected from their responsibilities in school and may take on outside activities to support their households;
- Parents and guardians and civil society organisations will have less capacity to take an interest in school affairs;
- For poor people, there are always opportunity costs in sending children to school and when poverty is extreme, they may need their children's contribution to the family

economy, either through their labour or through their earnings, however small, in any kind of employment.

Other conditions with an obvious impact on education are *political.* If there is over-centralisation of authority, with little accountability, the UPE project may be endangered. At present, fortunately, most Commonwealth African countries, including all those studied here, have stable civilian administrations and basically democratic governments, in which people are participants. Democracy, however, does not necessarily imply that there are always strong accountable local community organisations ready to take on the tasks of advocacy and decentralised responsibility; their lack of capacity in the recent past was observed in Zambia. All the same, in the same country the phenomenon of community schools has emerged, and in some others there are beginning to be quite powerful local advocacy organisations, such as CSACEFA in Nigeria.

Allied to political conditions are *legal and constitutional* ones. Ghana's example in establishing a constitutional mandate for UPE is a reminder that such a commitment may make for an enabling political climate and is useful in reminding both governments and governed of their obligations (e.g. maybe even when it comes to the hard budget decisions mentioned earlier); but clearly it doesn't of itself bring about an any improvement in educational provision. Other elements of a legal framework may have an effect, such as laws making attendance compulsory (the newly proposed Nigerian legislation attempting to compel retention in schools is a new development). But laws which can't be enforced may simply bring the UPE project into disrepute.

Social factors will have an impact on the development of primary education and have to be taken into account in educational strategies. There are, for instance, a number of reasons why children may be absent from school. These include:

* Geographical distance and lack of transport;
* Family instability, owing to HIV/AIDS or migration – orphans having to find means of survival cannot easily go to school (and certainly can't find school fees);
* Gender-assigned responsibilities – at certain seasons, boys may be required to work in cattle-herding, farming, fishing or marketing, while girls may participate in farming and may also at any time be needed in the household for cleaning, food preparation, child-minding or looking after sick relatives; there are nowadays more of the latter, because of HIV/AIDS;
* Traditional ceremonies, such as initiation rites or village or family festivals;
* Sometimes there are cultural impediments to sending girls to school, including early marriage;
* Where parents have little or no education, the home environment may not be supportive of children's schooling;
* In some societies, children with a physical impairment, such as blindness, are left out of the school system.

All these are non-educational phenomena, but affect education. Policy-makers, in understanding such factors in the context of education, face challenges in mitigating their effects, such as conscious efforts to enlist civil society support for various programmes or devising stratagems to provide incentives to the poor (see below).

Strategies for success

A variety of measures and suggestions for upholding UPE have already emerged in this chapter. In this sub-section, some workable strategies employed by one or more of the nations studied are put forward for consideration and are supplemented by suggestions which were developed in the research team's discussions and consultations with a number of experts.

a The broad education agenda

A major issue is curriculum. This clearly works best if it is relevant to pupils' social and cultural background and takes account of some of the social factors listed above. At the same time, it seems that there is a deeply-rooted desire among parents to see teaching of a traditional 'academic' kind and this prompts a need for serious engagement with these opinions.

If the UPE programme is to reach the 'last 10 per cent', curricula will have to adapted to new categories of learner (cultural and linguistic minorities, children with special needs, less able and under-nourished children).

Large classes seem to be a persisting feature of the primary education scene. Different delivery mechanisms will have to be devised; those already used include double- and even triple-shift systems and open access programmes, such as Zambia's radio centres. Perhaps for technical difficulties, African countries seem to have done less in recent years to experiment with less orthodox means of educational provision, making use of modern technology, though there are successful programmes supported by the Africa Education Trust, in Uganda. Such programmes may be helped by current campaigns spearheaded by Ghana and India for Free Open Software.

b Partnership in provision

Partnership in the educational endeavour increases in importance in times of stringency. Such partnerships may be with international agencies (UN and similar bodies, national governments, international NGOs), civil society organisations and the private sector.

International donors, as already emphasised, may be very important to the survival of UPE. National governments are now used to negotiating with them and Kenya has found it fruitful to hold regular coordination meetings with them as a group. There are, of course, cautions in working with agencies which, quite naturally, have their own agendas and conditionalities. It may be counter-productive to accept an international partner's intervention, however well-meant, in matters of curriculum. We have a cautionary tale from Zambia, where FINNIDA provided everything for a Practical Studies course in the primary schools, but it was virtually ignored on the ground.

Major civil society organisations include religious agencies, which manage, or have in the past managed schools on behalf of the state. Each country already has mechanisms in place to ensure benefit from these organisations, which have often had a reputation for quality education (see for example the experience of Dr Wangari Maathai of Kenya, recounted in her book, *Unbowed,* 2007, London, Heinemann); but they too will have their own agendas. It may be useful for policy-makers to take a fresh look at the relationship.

Local communities have in the past made many sacrifices in support of primary education. In Tanzania in the 1970s, the ethos of self-reliance led to huge community involvement, with volunteer teachers and community construction of classrooms and teachers' houses. In future the role of communities could be that of active partners in a different way. However willing and concerned a community is, they ultimately become resistant to demands on their labour and to educational levies under the guise of 'cost-sharing', while they have no part in the decisions about their schools. A chance to play a part in the disposition of funds is provided in Kenya through its Constituency Development Fund.

The private sector may be involved in financial support, general or specific, e.g. the large American Foundations or a local company. At the same time private individuals or groups run schools as a business. Donations from companies or rich individuals tend to go more to higher education, by way of scholarships. Both Ghana and Nigeria already make a levy on business for educational purposes. In addition, it might be worth appealing to wealthy people to take more interest in primary education. Nationals abroad (the Diaspora) send generous moneys home to families and communities; they too would have an interest in primary schools if approached the right way. One cannot be too hopeful because the squeeze on business and employment may reduce what is available from both these kinds of private source.

Private schools, including many pre-schools, are now increasing in numbers and can be seen as taking some of the pressure off the state schools. At the same time, they benefit from such state provision as the training of teachers. Some countries already monitor their contribution and are working on regulatory systems to ensure integrity and quality.

c Appropriate teaching and learning environments
School buildings
For reasons of lack of maintenance, many school buildings are not very congenial places and there is also a constant need for new classrooms/schools, as there are still shortfalls. Where there is a substantial need for new build, the example of Zambia could be worth following, where the Ministry of Education set up its own building unit. Both for new build and renovations, there are minimal desiderata for a school for comfortable learning. The traditional rectangle of classrooms and dusty playground is not enough. A healthy school should have a source of clean water within easy distance and should have sanitation (separate for males and females). In areas where security is a problem, fencing for a safer environment will reassure parents, teachers and children. Although it is not the reason for providing such facilities, knowing they are there would be a factor motivating parents to send their children to school.

Besides school buildings, the old tradition of providing teachers with good low-rent housing in remote areas might act as an inducement for them to work for a stint in these less popular places.

There are of course situations in which the learning environment doesn't include a permanent building. Children of nomadic communities are served by mobile schools or 'flying teachers'. Incidentally, the Commonwealth Nomadic Education Forum, which met in Garissa, Kenya, in 2006, canvassed useful ideas.

Furniture and learning materials

In past times of stringency and economic stagnation, children have been asked to bring their own stools or chairs; but suitable furniture should be part of a school's normal accessories. So too should be simple materials to support learning, such as posters and pictures. These can brighten up even an old school building; though they need changing regularly, otherwise they become torn and dusty and merely add to the air of dilapidation.

Incentives to the poor

Although we have seen that many families are ready to make sacrifices to send children to school, all the cases showed a large rise in enrolment when fees were dropped and a further rise when other hidden levies were also stopped. Free education should be without hidden costs to the poor, who are the majority in all the countries studied. If it is truly free and if there are other motivating factors like the kind of learning environments just described, families may be more ready to forego the opportunity costs in losing child-labour for farming and housework.

Other valuable incentives are school milk and school meals. Kenya received assistance from the UN Food and Agriculture Organisation (FAO) to make school milk available to primary children. Ghana attempts to provide lunches and our researchers noted this with approval. It is a moot point whether breakfast would be better, for youngsters who arrive at school in the morning without having eaten anything.

There is a long tradition of boarding schools in all the countries studied, but usually it is regarded as better for children of primary age to stay with their families and go to school nearby. Sometimes the schools are not so close and Ghana has provided some transport, to help enrolment. Also, because of the large numbers of poor orphans, some governments have begun to think again about residential schooling, but this is an expensive option.

e Quality learning

To repeat, ultimately UPE programmes will be sustained and supported if they are of acceptable quality. It is encouraging to learn of new research into what is needed for quality in schools sponsored by the Hewlett Foundation in collaboration with the Gates Foundation; they have established an African Quality Education Forum. Meanwhile we are well aware that quality depends on a number of factors. We have suggested that teachers are central.

Teachers

A trained, high-morale and reasonably rewarded teaching force: this is the aim. At present only Kenya has an adequate supply of teachers and elsewhere teacher supply is not sufficient and classes are very large. Policy-makers and planners have an important challenge in reducing the pupil-teacher ratios. The Kenya study has a poignant quotation from a teacher in a school where there were five teachers for 500 pupils: 'You mark 500 books through the night – you have to relax and prepare for the following day's work. Even personal attention to weak pupils is impossible'. This is the fearful reality behind the neutral sounding statistic of a ratio of 100 to 1! Among targets for planners, reduction of such ratios must rank high.

Other tasks for planners and policy-makers are to:

- Regularly review the teacher education curriculum and consider the inclusion in it of ancillary skills, such as adult literacy (a long-standing component of teacher training in Tanzania). Obviously this would be unrealistic unless the teachers' work-loads were reduced;
- Provide up-grading opportunities for teachers brought in under emergency training schemes;
- Provide for regular teacher professional development;
- Work out programmes honouring and rewarding outstanding teachers, to help restore their status in their own and the public's eyes.

School inspection

Most countries have a system of school inspection, but reports are that it has often atro-phied. Plans for UPE could profitably include plans for a revitalisation of the inspection system. Effective and honest inspectors could be the front-line in any quality assurance system.

Support and reinforcement

Reinforcement of the work of primary schools by other institutions has been shown to be effective in maintaining UPE and maximising its benefits. First, *early childhood education* is recommended by many experts and the 2007 Global Monitoring Report, *Strong Foundations*, reminds us that 'Learning begins before a child walks through the classroom door' and advocates the value of ECC especially for 'the most vulnerable and disadvan-taged'. Our cases report quite significant numbers of children participating – over a mil-lion in Kenya – but it is likely that they are mainly from affluent and urban homes. Ghana has, however, long had experiments in pre-schools in the markets, for the children of mar-ket traders. The GMR has a package of useful suggestions to education authorities.

Secondly, *non-formal education* has fallen out of fashion, but adult literacy and various types of community education reinforce and supplement formal provision at very low cost, as demonstrated by the Tanzania literacy programmes in the 1960s and 70s. Adult literacy programmes are part of the Nigerian concept of Universal Basic Education. Provision for family members who have never been to school or who left school early both ensures equity and reinforces the learning of children who do go to school. The late Paul Bertelsen of UNESCO coined the saying: 'Every child deserves a literate mother'; this is a reminder of how to help girls stay in school.

Thirdly, while in relatively well-off capital cities access to computers has reduced the demand for books, *libraries* are still form an essential component in educational provision for most children and young people in Africa. They may be established in the school itself, in a community centre or even be mobile, such as the Camel Library in North Eastern Kenya. Responsibility for public libraries has often devolved to local authorities; if they are to live up to it, there is need for training in their value, and also some incentives for main-taining a good library service.

All these may appear obvious, but in practice few UPE programmes include this kind of activity – a pity, since it would give substantial help to sustaining UPE.

Stringency and emergency

Most of this chapter has been about positive prescriptions for strengthening UPE. As economies are now likely to turn down, governments may, as already hinted, be forced to adopt alternative ways of keeping UPE on track. The histories show that there is also likelihood of short-term emergencies, such as the refugee influx into Tanzania. It is always difficult for large institutions such as ministries to be flexible, but flexibility and inventiveness have saved UPE in the past. Among creative strategies (already mentioned above) are double- or multi-shift schools and use of volunteers to support trained teachers in the classroom. The example of Tanzania, entering onto UPE 'on the cheap' if not copiable in the present, at least provides an inspiration.

The main symptom of emergency in the march to UPE is a shortage of teachers, sometimes the result of political haste, sometimes owing to a miscalculation of numbers needed. Methods employed to meet this kind of emergency have been:

- drawing retired teachers back into service:
- shortening residential training and completing courses while student teachers are already in the classroom;
- part-time emergency training at evenings and weekends for apprentice teachers;
- training packages of face-to-face and distance instruction, as in Kenya.

After the emergency period is over and numbers settle down, there will be a surplus of teachers with very basic training. They can be given an opportunity to up-grade their skills; Nigeria is doing this on a very large scale through the Nigerian Teachers' Institute, which is offering 100,000 teachers a chance to upgrade themselves through distance learning.

Special categories of pupil

Some possible categories of left-out children have been hinted at and they should be mentioned before we end.

The most visible – because the largest number – would be *girls*. Gender parity in education by 2005 was one of the Millennium Development Goals and it has not yet been achieved, although the enrolment records in Commonwealth Africa show boys and girls not too far apart. Continuation and retention statistics, however, show more girls than boys dropping out. Methods to get to parity include:

- A public education campaign to emphasise the value to families and society if girls are educated, deploying, among other public figures, religious leaders, since their authority is respected;
- Reassuring parents that girls will be safe at school (e.g. by fencing round, as suggested earlier);
- Promoting literacy for mothers; once mothers become literate, research has shown that they then become keen for their daughters to go to school as well.

Another significant category is made up of *children in large scattered rural populations.* We have noted that there are new attempts to provide boarding schools, for orphans; but for the large number of rural children that would be a costly option. Small one- and two-teacher schools, with multi-grade teaching comprise an accepted answer at the present day and this solution clearly has to be recommended for the foreseeable future. Our CEC research has shown that some alternatives are being tried, such as mobile classrooms and rural transport. Now that the use of mobile phones is fairly widespread, in some countries it might be practicable to follow up the suggestion of the Commonwealth Telecommunications Organisation to provide distance education by that means.

Mobile classrooms have already been suggested for *children of nomadic populations*, another category calling for special attention. As said above, if full-scale mobile schools are not immediately feasible, at least a cadre of 'flying teachers' could be developed to bring some chance of education to nomadic children; it is understood that this expedient worked well in Somalia in the 1970s. Once again, new forms of distance education could be tried (including mobile phones).

There are other groups which may be left out and form part of 'the last 10 per cent'. Each country will be aware of their own circumstances, but everywhere there are 'handicapped' children, in some cases including, sadly, children mutilated in wars. Special schools in urban areas are feasible, with children attending by day. In rural areas, children may be welcomed into mainstream schools, but the Commonwealth is fortunate in having a number of specialist charities with long experience of special, often residential, provision for the blind, the deaf and young people with leprosy. Owing to the short time the CEC had to carry out the research, we were not able to follow up this issue.

Conclusion

All the issues around the sustainability of UPE, as well as the challenges to policy-makers and planners and the possible strategies they might use, were brought into focus by the case-studies which make up the bulk of this book. At the end of the day, the main lessons learnt take us back to the beginning: to the very great importance of committed political leadership and committed and informed policy-makers and planners. Much past achievement has been propelled by them, often against the odds. But more than adrenalin is needed for long-term success in maintaining UPE, with gender parity, few dropouts and of a quality to meet society's expectations. There is demand, but citizens are owed greater accountability and greater opportunity to share in decisions and to govern their own schools. Further, if public support is to be kept and cherished, there can be no going back now on the abolition of fees.

Above all, the first requirement for successful UPE is efficient, realistic planning, based on good data. Cautious planners may make politicians and the electorate impatient, but it is not caution but realism to understand that UPE will not be kept on a steady keel just from enthusiasm and hustle. It will take years and will only survive if that enthusiasm survives – but together with a realistic strategy and necessary funding.

To the trio of committed leaders, supportive communities and efficient planners, we must add fourthly all the teachers, who hold the key to school door. On their work depends the ultimate success or failure of Universal Primary and Basic Education.

The next few years are going to erode national economies while populations rise. We can only hope that their countries will once again beat the odds, with politicians, public, planners and teachers ensuring that UPE never drifts away again.

Notes

1   Wolfgang Stolper (1966) *Planning Without Facts*, Cambridge, Mass, Harvard UP
2   Pius Okigbo (1994) *National Development Planning in Nigeria, 1900–1992*, London, James Currey and others

Appendix

Growth in GER

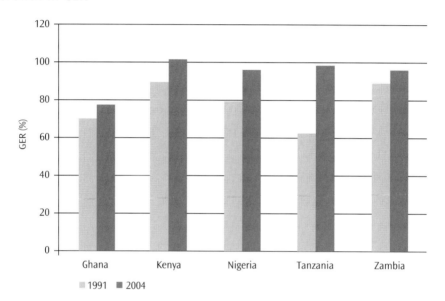

Gross enrolment rate between 1991and 2004

Sources and references

Abernethy, David B. (1969) *The Political Dilemma of Popular Education: An African Case.* California, Stanford University Press

Abu-Gyamfi, J. and M.W. Foster (eds) (2004) *Missing an Education.* Accra, Action Aid International Ghana

Acheampong, I.K. (1972) *National Redemption Council – Budget Statement for 1972–73. Accra,* Ministry of Finance

Agyeman, D.K. et al. (2000) *Review of Education Sector Analysis in Ghana1987– 1998.* Working Group on Education Sector Analysis. UNESCO

Anamuah-Mensah, J. et al. (2002) *Report of the President's Committee on Review* of *Education Reforms in Ghana.* Accra, Ministry of Education

Antwi, M.K. (1992) *Education, Society and Development in Ghana.* Accra, Unimax

Asare-Bediako, N. et al. (1995) *Quality Assurance and School Level Management System for Basic Education in Ghana.* Accra, MOE, Study Code 34

Avotri, R. et al. (2000) *Gender and Primary Schooling in Ghana.* Brighton, Institute of Development Studies

Baah-Nuakoh, A. (1997) *Studies on the Ghanaian Economy, Vol 1: The Pre-'Revolutionary' Years, 1957–1981.* Accra, Ghana Universities Press

BESIP (1997) *Report on the Mid-term Evaluation of the School Improvement Fund Pilot.* Accra, Ghana Education Service

Beveridge, M. et al. eds (2005) *Reintegrating Education, Skills, Life and Work in Africa.* Edinburgh, University Centre for African Studies

Binns, F. and T. Wrightson (2006) *Teacher Education at a Distance: Impact on Development in the Commonwealth.* London, DFID

Bray, Mark (1981) *Universal Primary Education in Nigeria: A Study of Kano State.* London, Routledge & Kegan Paul

Buchert, Lene (1994) *Education in the Development of Tanzania 1919–1990.* East African Studies Series London, James Currey

Burnett, Nicholas et al. (2005) *Literacy for Life: EFA Global Monitoring Report 2006.* Paris, UNESCO Publishing

CARE International (2003) *Reaching Under-served Populations with Basic Education in Deprived Areas of Ghana: Emerging Good Practices*. Accra, CARE International Ghana/Togo/Benin

Carmody, Brendan (2004) *The Evolution of Education in Zambia*. Ndola, Bookworld Publishers

Commonwealth Secretariat (2006) *The Commonwealth Yearbook, 2006*. Cambridge, Nexus Partnerships for Commonwealth Secretariat

Coombe, Trevor (1970) *The Proposal for Universal Ten-Year Schooling*. Planning Paper Number 3. Lusaka, Ministry of Education Development and Planning Unit

Coombe, Trevor and Per Lauvas (1984) *Facilitating Self-Renewal in Zambian Education*. Oslo, Norwegian Agency for International Development (NORAD)

Coombe, Trevor, James Banda, Patrick Haamujompa, Ezekiel Phiri, Ritva Reinikka-Soininen and Tuomas Takala (1990) *Supporting Zambia's Education Sector Under Structural Adjustment*, Report of the FINNIDA and Zambia Project Identification Mission, January–February 1990. Helsinki, Ministry of Foreign Affairs

Daily Graphic (June 6 2006) *The School Feeding Programme*. Accra

Daily Graphic (June 9, 2006) *Improvement in Enrolment in Basic Schools*. Accra

De Stefano, J., Hartwell, A and K. Tietjen (1995) *Basic Education in Africa: USAID's Approach to Sustainable Reform in the 1990s*. Technical Paper No 14. Washington, USAID

Education Sector Programme (2005) *National Work Plan and Budget (January – December 2005)*. Lusaka, Government of Zambia

Education Sector Programme (2005) *Draft National Work Plan and Budget (January – December 2006)*. Lusaka, Government of Zambia

Evans-Anfom, E. et al. (1986) *Report of the Education Commission on Basic Education*. Accra, Ministry of Education

Federal Republic of Nigeria/UNDP (2005) *Nigeria – MDG Report 2005*. Abuja, FRN/UNDP

Galabawa, J. (2001) *Developments and Issues Regarding Universal Primary Education (UPE) in Tanzania*. Paper prepared for ADEA Biennial Meeting (Arusha, October 7–11, 2001)

George, B.S. (1976) *Education in Ghana*. Washington DC, US Government Printing Office

Government of Ghana (1994) *Programme of Free Compulsory and Universal Basic Education by the Year 2005*. Accra, Government of Ghana

Government of Ghana Ministry of Information (n.d.) *Ghana's Education System*. http://www.ghana.gov.gh/studying/education/index.php. Accessed 08-09-06

Government of Kenya (1965) *Sessional Paper 10 on African Socialism*, Nairobi, Government Printer

Hoppers, Wim (1981) *Education in a Rural Society: Primary Pupils and School Leavers in Mwinilunga, Zambia.* The Hague, Centre for the Study of Education in Developing Countries (CESO)

IEG (2006) *From Schooling Access to Learning Outcomes: An Unfinished Agenda.* Washington DC, World Bank

Ismaila, U.Y., A.M. Mohammed, S. L. Durodola and E. N. Ekpunobi (2004) *Teacher Education at a Distance: Impact on Development in the Community: Country Report, Nigeria.* Cambridge, IEC

ISSER (2006) *The State of the Ghanaian Economy.* Accra

Kaonga, Martin (2001, July) *Cost-Sharing in Basic Education in Zambia: A community Analysis.* Study Sponsored by OXFAM-Zambia and Jesuit Centre for Theological Reflection. Lusaka, OXFAM & JCTR

Kaunda, Kenneth D. (1962) *Zambia Shall Be Free.* London, Heinemann

Kelly, Michael (1991) *Education in a Declining Economy: the Case of Zambia 1975–1985.* EDI Development Policy Case Series, Analytical Case Studies, Number 8. Washington DC, World Bank

Kelly, Michael (1998) *Primary Education in a Heavily Indebted Poor Country: the Case of Zambia in the 1990s.* A report for OXFAM and UNICEF, Zambia. Lusaka, OXFAM, UNICEF.

Kenya African National Union (1963) *What a KANU Government Offers You: Manifesto for the May General Elections.* Nairobi, Printing and Packaging Corporation

Kenya African National Union (1969) *KANU Manifesto for the October General Election.* Nairobi, The English Press Ltd

Lillis, Kevin (1986) *Community Financing of Education: Issues from Kenya.* Paper presented at an international conference on the Economics of Education, June 1986, Dijon, France

McWilliam. H.O.A. (1962) *The Development of Education in Ghana: an outline.* 2nd edition, Accra, Longmans

McWilliam, H.O.A. & M.A. Kwamena-Poh (1978) *Development of Education in Ghana.* London, Longmans

Mehra, A.N. (1979) *The Effect of Population Growth on the Development and Cost of First Level Education in Zambia.* Manpower Research Unit, Report Number 4. Lusaka, UNZA Institute of African Studies

Management Development Division, Cabinet Office (Zambia) (2001) *Report on the Restructuring of the Ministry of Education.* Lusaka, Cabinet Office

Ministry of Education (Ghana) (1994) *Towards Learning for All: Basic education in Ghana to the Year 2000.* Accra, Government of Ghana

Ministry of Education (Ghana) (1998) *Report on Government of Ghana Funding Agencies 3rd Consultative Panel on FCUBE.* Accra, Government of Ghana

Ministry of Education, Youth and Sport (Ghana) (2004) *Government White Paper on the Education Review Report.* Accra, MEYS

Ministry of Education (Kenya) (2006) *Delivering Quality Primary Education and Improving Access: An Impact Evaluation of the Instructional Materials and In-Service Teacher Training Programme.* Nairobi

Ministry of Education (Kenya) (2006) *Kenya Country Paper on Abolition of School Fees and Levies.* For a Workshop at the Hilton Hotel, Nairobi, 5–7 April, 2006

Ministry of Education (Kenya) (2006) *Building on What We Know and Defining Sustained Support,* Paper for Workshop held at the Hilton Hotel, Nairobi, 5–7 April, 2006. Nairobi

Ministry of Education and Culture (Tanzania) (2000) *Basic Statistics in Education, 1999 – Regional Data.* Dar es Salaam, MOEC

Ministry of Education and Culture (Tanzania) (2001) *Education Sector Country Status Report.* Dar es Salaam, MOEC

Ministry of Education (Zambia) (1977) *Educational Reform: Proposals and Recommendations.* Lusaka, MOE

Ministry of Education (Zambia) (1996) *Educating our Future: National Policy on Education.* Lusaka, MOE

Ministry of Education (Zambia) (2000) *The Basic School Curriculum Framework.* Lusaka, MOE Curriculum Development Centre

Ministry of Education (Zambia) (2000) *Basic Education Sub-Sector Investment Programme (BESSIP): 2000 Programme Performance Indicators.* Lusaka, MOE Planning Unit

Ministry of Education (Zambia) (2002) *Education in Zambia, Situational Analysis.* Lusaka, MOE

Ministry of Education (Zambia) (2003) *Zambia Strategic Plan 2003– 2006.* Lusaka, MOE

Ministry of Education (Zambia) (2004) *Educational Statistical Bulletin.* Lusaka, MOE Directorate of Planning and Information

Ministry of Sports, Youth and Child Development (Zambia) (2006) *National Child Policy.* Lusaka, MSYCD

Mushi, D.P. (2006) *Review of Experiences with Direct Support to Schools in Tanzania.* Draft report to CODESRIA. Dar es Salaam, University of Dar es Salaam Economic Research Bureau

Mutua, R.(1975) *Development of Education in Kenya: Some Administrative Aspects, 1846–1963.* Nairobi, East African Literature Bureau

Mwansa, Dickson (1998) *Community Schools: Strengths and Weaknesses; pupil and teacher profiles.* Lusaka, Zambia Community Schools Secretariat

Mwiria, K. *Harambee Schools and the Ideology of Educational Opportunity.* Discussion Paper No 4008. Nairobi, Kenyatta University Bureau of Educational Research

Ndiaye, B. (2002) *Securing Private Sector Participation in Basic Education at District and Community Levels in Ghana.* Accra UNICEF/Ghana Educational Programme

Obanya, Pai (1982, January) 'Colleagues' Perceptions of a New Breed of Professionals: the case of the UPE teacher in the Nigerian primary school.' *Benin Journal of Educational Studies 1/1*

Obanya, Pai (2005) *Sub-Saharan African Regional EFA Progress Overview: English-Speaking Countries.* UNESCO commissioned paper for the GMR 2006

Obanya, Pai (2006, February) *Sound Policy, Poor Implementation – a conceptual fallacy.* Keynote paper, NERDC Workshop on Strategic Planning for Educational Development

Okedara, J.T. (1979) *The Role of Social Sciences in Tackling Education Problems – the case of universal primary education in Nigeria* (cited in Soyibo, *The Power of Ideas and the Idea of Power,* Inaugural lecture series, University of Ibadan, Vol. I, pp. 206–625)

Omari, I.M., A.S. Mbise, S.T. Mahenge, G.A. Malekela and M.P. Besha (1983) *Universal primary education in Tanzania.* Ottawa, International Development Research Centre

Orbach, E. (2004) *The Capacity of the Nigerian Government to deliver Basic Education Services.* African Human Development Working Papers Vol. 61

Osaki, K.M. (1996) 'The changing forms and content of the 'primary' school curriculum, 1961–1994', in *Papers in Education and Development,* No. 17, University of Dar es Salaam

Osaki, K.M. and Agu (2005) 'Classroom interaction with gender and rights' in *Prospects,* Paris, UNESCO

Packer, Steve and Carlos Aggio (2006) *Achieving the Goals: The Performance of Commonwealth Countries in Achieving the Millennium Development Goals* in *Education and the Dakar Education for All Goals.* London, Commonwealth Secretariat

Republic of Ghana (1992) *Constitution of the Republic of Ghana.* Accra, Republic of Ghana

Republic of Kenya (1964) *Kenya Education Commission Report.* Nairobi, Government Printer

Republic of Kenya (1966) *Development Plan, 1966–70.* Nairobi, Government Printer

Sawyerr, Harry (1997) *Country-led Aid Coordination in Ghana.* Paris, ADEA

Somerset, Anthony (2007) *A Preliminary Note on Kenya Primary School Enrolment Trends Over Four Decades,* CREATE Research Monograph No 9. University of Sussex Centre for International Education

UNESCO (2008) *EFA Global Monitoring Report – Education for All by 2015: Will we make it?* Oxford University Press for UNESCO

UNESCO (2009) *EFA Global Monitoring Report 2009 – Overcoming Inequality: Why Governance Matters.* Oxford University Press for UNESCO

UNESCO Institute for Statistics (2005) *Measuring Exclusion from Primary Education.* Montreal, UNESCO Institute for Statistics

UNESCO Institute for Statistics (2006) *Global Education Digest 2006: comparing education statistics across the world.* Montreal, UNESCO-UIS

United Nations Development Programme (2007) *Human Development Report, 2007/2008.* Basingstoke and New York, Palgrave Macmillan for UNDP

United Republic of Tanzania (1969) *Second five-year plan for economic and social development,1st July 1969–30th June, 1974. Vol. 1 General Analysis.* Dar es Salaam

University of Dar es Salaam (1995) *Primary education issues in Tanzania.* Papers in Education and Development, No 16:
'Budgeting for basic education in Tanzania' (Andrew Lawson)
'The role of donors and non-governmental organisations in primary education' (Abuhashim Masudi)
'Primary education policies in Tanzania' (Herme J. Mosha)
'Enrolment trends in education in Tanzania' (Suleiman A. Sumra)

Wedgwood, Ruth (2005) *Post-basic education and poverty in Tanzania.* Working Paper No 1 in Post-basic Education and Training Working Paper Series, University of Edinburgh, Centre of African Studies

Williams, Peter (1979) 'Universal Primary Education and the Future' in Smith, R.L. (ed) *Universal Primary Education: A Report of a Workshop.* London, University of London Institute of Education

World Bank (1996) *Staff Appraisal Report, Republic of Ghana Basic Education Sector Improvement Program. Report No 15570-Gh.* Washington DC, World Bank

World Bank (2004) *Country Assistance Strategy – Zambia.* Lusaka, World Bank Office

World Bank (2004) *Strengthening the Foundation of Education and Training in Kenya: Opportunities and Challenges in Primary and General Secondary Education,* Washington DC

World Bank (2007, March) *Draft: Efficiency of Government Education Expenditures in Kenya.* Washington DC

Zambia Central Statistical Office (1990, 1995) *Zambia in Figures.* Lusaka

Zambia Ministry of Education (1975–81) *Annual reports.* Lusaka

Zambia Ministry of Education (1975) *Statistical Profile of Zambian Education, 1975, December.* Lusaka

Zambia Ministry of Education (October 1977) *Educational Reform: Proposals and Recommendations.* Lusaka

Zambia Ministry of General Education, Youth and Sport (1991) *Education Statistics, 1986.* Lusaka

Zambia Ministry of Education (2002) *Strategic Plan 2003–2007.* Lusaka

About the authors

Dr Francis K. Amedahe is an associate professor in educational measurement and evaluation at the University of Cape Coast, Ghana. He was a serving teacher before entering on university studies, first at Cape Coast and later at the University of Pittsburgh where he gained his doctorate. At Cape Coast, he has been head of the Department of Educational Foundations and Vice-Dean of the Faculty of Education and served as director of the Ghana Doctoral Initiative, a joint programme between Cape Coast and Florida A & M University, Tallahassee. He was recently a Fulbright Scholar at Elon University, North Carolina.

Dr Felicity Binns is Operations Manager for International Education in the consultancy company, Cambridge Education, Deputy Chair of UKFIET, and an Honorary Fellow of the Commonwealth of Learning. Her interest in education for development began twenty years ago with the International Extension College, which enhanced her skills in the management of a wide variety of education programmes and her knowledge of open and distance learning. She rose to be Executive Director of IEC, taking a particular interest in teacher and non-formal adult education. She is a Board member of CEC.

Lalage Bown is Professor Emeritus of Adult and Continuing Education, University of Glasgow. She ended thirty years of work in African universities as Dean of Education, University of Lagos, having served in all the five countries studied in this book. She is a past president of the Development Studies Association and of BAICE and is a former member of the CEC Board.

Dr Balasubramanyam Chandramohan is Senior Lecturer in Academic Development at Kingston University, London. His work includes teaching modules and supervising dissertations on the Ed.D. programme run jointly by Kingston and Roehampton Universities. He has previously taught at universities in the UK, continental Europe, Africa and Asia. He is co-editor of *Interdisciplinary Learning and Teaching in Higher Education: Theory and Practice* (Routledge, 2009). Dr Chandramohan is a member of the Governing Board (and Projects Secretary) of the Council for Education in the Commonwealth.

Dr Alba de Souza was born in Kenya and obtained her first degree at the University of Nairobi. She won a Commonwealth Scholarship and did her MA at the Institute of Education, University of London. Through a Fellowship at Stanford University, California and with research support from the Rockefeller Foundation, she obtained her PhD on reform in the financing of higher education in Africa. Dr de Souza began her career as an A-level teacher at Kenya High School, then became Deputy Head of the Planning and Development Department in the Kenya Ministry of Education. After working for 12 years as a consultant in education in international development, she is now the Programme Specialist in education at the UK National Commission for UNESCO. She is also a member of the Governing Board of the Council for Education in the Commonwealth.

Fidelis Haambote is a Zambian education consultant and a graduate of the University of Zambia.

Henry Kaluba taught at the University of Zambia before joining the Commonwealth Secretariat as Chief Programme Officer (Teaching Profession) in 1993. In 2003 he was promoted to become Adviser & Head, Education Department, Commonwealth Secretariat to oversee the achievement of the MDGs in education; and the Working Group on the Teaching Profession in Sub-Saharan Africa. His interests remain in the area of foreign aid to education and development and the cultural factors in national development.

Prof Pai Obanya, who describes himself as a die-hard academic, holds a PhD of the University of Ibadan, where he was Research Fellow and rose to become the Director of the Institute of Education in 1980. He followed this with almost twenty distinguished years in senior roles in UNESCO's Regional Office for Education in Africa and on return to Nigeria served as Coordinator for Universal Basic Education. The recipient of numerous honours, he now lives in active retirement in Ibadan and remains keenly interested in international and Nigerian education.

Dr John Oxenham is currently a joint Deputy Executive Chair of the CEC. The rural primary schools and out-stations of Eastern Zambia gave him his first experiences of the demand for education among the children and adults of a developing African country. They also underlined for him the difficulty of expanding the supply of education as well as sustaining demand in the form of regular attendance through to graduation. He continued his work on education at the Institute of Development Studies, Sussex and the World Bank.

Dr Gituro Wainaina graduated from the University of Nairobi with first a BA in Education and then an MBA. He received his doctorate in Agricultural Economics at Mississippi State University, USA. He joined the University of Nairobi in 1984 as a Lecturer in the Department of Economics, becoming a Senior Lecturer in Economic Statistics and Quantitative Methods in 1997. Having undertaken a number of consultancy assignments while still at the University, he worked for 6 years at the World Bank Regional Office, supporting World Bank projects in Kenya. He returned to the University of Nairobi in 2004 as the Business Development Manager of the Research, Teaching, Consultancy and Management Centre, where he is head of the consultancy unit.

Peter Williams, a joint Deputy Executive Chair of the CEC, has been Planning Adviser in the Ministries of Education in Kenya and Ghana and has served with education review bodies and processes in six African countries. He was Professor of Education in Developing Countries at the University of London Institute of Education from 1978 to 1984 and Director of Education at the Commonwealth Secretariat 1984 to 1994. Among his writings have been a number on UPE and in the last decade he has undertaken a series of consultancies in Mainland Tanzania and Zanzibar.